W9-CQI-638

COMMON CENTS

Product Order Form

ITEM	QUANTITY	PRICE	TOTAL
Common Cents™: The ABC Performance Breakthrough™ by Dr. Peter B.B. Turney Learn the fundamentals of ABC! *(Shipping & Handling $3.50 per book)*		$ 19.95	
EasyABC™ Software **EasyABC Plus™** Software **EasyABC™** Demo/Tutorial Software ☐ for DOS/Windows ☐ for Macintosh *(Shipping & Handling $10.00 per software package)*		$1,995.95 $2,495.95 $ 50.00	
Common Cents™ Posters Each 3' x 4' laminated poster highlights key elements of implementing and using your ABC system. Excellent for presentations or training. • *The Steps to Success* poster • *The Rules of Activity-Based Management* poster • *The Rules of Design* poster • *Three Poster Set* *(Shipping & Handling $3.50 per poster)*		$ 99.50 $ 99.50 $ 99.50 $ 249.50	
Sub-Total			
Plus Shipping and Handling*			
Total This Order			

*Include all applicable state and local taxes QUANTITY DISCOUNTS AVAILABLE ON ALL ITEMS.

Return to: **Cost Technology**
P.O. Box 25124
Portland, Oregon 97225-0124

VISA *and* MASTERCARD *users may order by calling Cost Technology at 1-800-368-COST.*

☐ Please send information on *Common Cents™* videos, training programs, audio cassettes, and EasyABC™ software.

Name_____ Title _____

Company_____

Street address_____

City_____ State_____ Zip Code_____ ☐ Check enclosed

☐ MasterCard ☐ VISA Acct. No._____

Exp. Date_____ Signature_____

[Please type or print clearly]

Peter B.B. Turney

The ABC
Performance
Breakthrough™

How to succeed with activity-based costing

Fold in half and seal with tape for mailing — do not staple

© Copyright 1991 Cost Technology. "Common Cents" and "The ABC Performance Breakthrough" are trademarks of Cost Technology. EasyABC is a trademark of ABC Technologies Inc.

• Shipping and handling charges to destinations outside North America vary by weight and destination — call Cost Technology at 503-628-3008 for more information

• All orders are shipped via UPS — other shipping options are available upon request and for an additional charge

• We accept VISA and MASTERCARD

Our Policy:

BUSINESS REPLY MAIL

FIRST CLASS MAIL   PERMIT NO. XXXXX   PORTLAND, OR

Postage will be paid by addressee

Cost Technology
P.O. Box 25124
Portland, OR 97225-0124

No Postage
Necessary
If Mailed
In The
United States

Comments on Common Cents

"The time is right for this book – the 80's was the time of world–class manufacturing (JIT, TQM etc)...*Now* we have a tool that allows us to measure and improve true business performance."

Gene Hendrickson, General Manager
Tektronix, Inc.

"What happened to our profits? *Common Cents* provides the answers...a must for the cost–conscious manager."

William C. Byham
Author of *Zapp! The Lightning of Empowerment*

"...an excellent book for ABC beginners and experts alike... could be the most insightful book on cost management since *Relevance Lost*."

Chris Pieper, CEO ·
ABC Technologies, Inc.

"*Common Cents* eliminates much of the confusion, mystery and misunderstanding surrounding ABC...must reading for everyone who is serious about improving their cost management system."

Michael W. Roberts
International Program Director, CAM-I

"...equally suitable for corporate executives and accountants– provides a comprehensive yet readable explanation of ABC, which is no small feat...well worth the read."

Barry J. Brinker, Executive Editor
Journal of Cost Management

"For the busy financial manager...a fast reading, easy–to– understand guide to ABC...allows you to implement its practical concepts on the job."

Patrick L. Romano, Director of Research
Institute of Management Accountants

COMMON CENTS™

The ABC Performance Breakthrough™

How to succeed with activity-based costing

Peter B.B. Turney

Cost Technology
Hillsboro, OR
1991

© 1992, 1991 by Peter B.B. Turney

All rights reserved. No part of this publication may be reproduced, stored in a retrieval system, or transmitted, in any form, or by any means, electronic, mechanical, photocopying, recording, or otherwise, without the prior written permission of the copyright holder. *Common Cents* and *The ABC Performance Breakthrough* are trademarks of Peter B.B. Turney.

Case material used in this book is included by permission of the company, or from published or other available sources. In some cases facts have been changed, or examples combined, to disguise strategic information.

This publication is designed to provide accurate and authoritative information in regard to the subject matter covered. It is sold with the understanding that the book does not represent a rendering of accounting or other professional service. If expert assistance is required, the services of a competent professional person should be sought.

Library of Congress Cataloging-in-Publication Data
Turney, Peter B.B.
    Common Cents: The ABC Performance Breakthrough (How to succeed
    with activity-based costing)
    Includes bibliographical references and index.
    ISBN 0-9629576-0-7
    Catalog Number: 91-075575
    1. Cost management. 2. Activity-based costing.
    3. Activity-based management. 4. Continuous improvement.

Printed in the United States of America

10 9 8 7 6 5 4 3 2

Table of Contents

Why You Should Read This Book

Activity-based costing (ABC) provides the performance breakthrough for the nineties. ABC empowers people with the information and tools to improve business performance. For everyone wanting to learn about this vital new topic, *Common Cents* is the place to look.

ABC reveals the problems you need to correct and the profitable opportunities that are available. Its ability to measure true business performance ensures that you improve where it counts the most—the bottom line.

Common Cents takes you through the world of ABC one step at a time. It explains the ABC fundamentals in no-nonsense terms. You don't need to be an accountant to take this tour (although financial managers will find it an invaluable information source). Industry standard terminology and concepts are defined with clear, useful, and understandable examples.

At the same time, *Common Cents* takes you to the leading edge of this new world. Much of the ABC conceptual framework outlined in this book has not been published before, and many case examples are found here for the first time.

You'll find the steps and guidelines to implement your own ABC system spelled out here. How do you convince management to adopt ABC? How do you get started? How do you collect the data? How do you design the model? How do you report useful information? The answers can all be found in *Common Cents*.

If you want to achieve a performance breakthrough, you'll find inspiration in the pages of *Common Cents*. Read about the rules of activity-based management. Learn about activity analysis, performance measurement, target costing, life-cycle costing, and other ways of putting ABC to work.

Who will benefit from *Common Cents*? Anyone who is interested in bringing the latest principles of activity management into their business. This includes managers and executives from many industries and walks of life. Whether you are in accounting, production, materials management, engineering, marketing, sales, human relations, or general management, this book will be *Common Cents* to you.

Acknowledgements

Terri Volpe of Cost Technology helped develop material for the book and provided important technical input. She also organized the first printing of the book. Terri deserves a special thanks.

Jim Reeve of the University of Tennessee reviewed the manuscript and provided moral support. Many ideas in the book originated in discussions and work with him.

Paul Collins of World Class International, Ltd., helped develop the link between activity-based costing and world-class manufacturing techniques.

Individuals who deserve special recognition are (in alphabetical order) Barry Brinker, Managing Editor of the Journal of Cost Management; Dave Cheesman, Consultant for World Class International; Adam Cywar, Senior Engineer of IBM; Gene Hendrickson, General Manager of the Printed Circuit Board Division of Tektronix; Scott Hildebrandt, Controller of the Oscilloscope Group of Tektronix; Mark Moelling, Manager of Activity-Based Cost Management Systems of Johnson and Johnson; Chris Pieper, Chief Executive Officer of ABC Technologies; Jan Rautio, Assistant Controller of Cellular One; Mike Roberts, CMS Program Manager of Computer Aided Manufacturing International (CAM-I); Stu Schaefer, Director of Operations Analysis of Dayton Extruded Plastics; Joe Short, Manager of Internal Audit of Stockham Valve and Fittings; and Alan Stratton, Plant Controller of National Semiconductor.

Bob Ramirez edited the book. His creativity and writing skills made an important contribution to the readability of the final document. Thomas J. Kitts did the page design. The typography was set by Anitra K. Rasmussen. Bill Cameron of Word Forms created the cover.

Finally, thanks are due to my family for their patience and support during the writing of this book. Without their support, this book would not have been possible.

Peter B.B. Turney
Portland, Oregon, October 1991

Part I

WHY YOU NEED TO CHANGE YOUR COST SYSTEM

Dealing with today's competition is challenge enough, even when you have all the right information. But, if you're responding to wrong information, you could well be in a losing battle.

In Chapter 1, you'll see how flawed cost information can sabotage your competitive position by encouraging you to set the wrong priorities and focus on the wrong problems. You'll see how it can lead you to:

- Sell the wrong products or services,
- Serve the wrong customers,
- Design costly products,
- Increase the cost of production,
- Incorrectly change the structure of your company,
- Institute cost cutting programs that fail, and
- Obtain the wrong parts from outside suppliers.

In Chapter 2, you'll learn why you need to scrap the outmoded cost systems that so mislead you. You'll see how changes in the world in which you compete have increased the value of good cost information while simultaneously reducing the cost of obtaining it. And you'll see why new approaches to manufacturing products (*or supplying services*) demand new types of cost information.

This is a new world in which conventional cost systems cannot compete because they:

- Don't communicate what matters to the customer,
- Don't report which products and customers are profitable or unprofitable,
- Are often costly to operate,
- Provide few insights about how to improve, and
- Encourage actions that damage competitiveness.

Chapter 1

THE MOUNTING COMPETITIVE CRISIS

Selling something for less than it costs can be common sense. Or it can be the wrong move.

There are all kinds of "common cents" reasons for selling a product or service at a loss. Retailers, for example, often under-price a selected product temporarily. They use this underpriced product as a "loss-leader" to boost customer traffic through the store. The basic premise is that increased traffic generates greater overall sales volume.

Companies* may also use a similar underpricing strategy on a broader basis to establish, protect, or regain market share. It's common sense when it's well-informed and intentional—and when it works.

Unintentional losses, however, are always the wrong move. Nobody stays in business long by selling products for less than they cost. Yet this is exactly what more and more manufacturers are doing with more and more of their products.

To put the problem into a dollar-and-cents perspective, consider this one simple example. It's one of many from companies that have implemented activity-based costing (ABC).

The company made a product at a cost of $2 per unit. Or, at least, that's the product cost the company's conventional costing system assigned. So management wisely priced the product for a nice "profit" at a competitive $4 per unit.

But guess what. There was no profit on the product. In fact, each sale resulted in a $498 loss! It was as if the company was

---

* *Common Cents* applies to any organization, whether manufacturing, service, or retail. The terms company, business, firm and organization are used interchangeably throughout this book.

wrapping dollar bills around the product each time it was shipped to a customer.

They had their priorities wrong. The company was devoting its energy to the wrong customer. The right customer was served by someone else.

The company was also devoting little effort to cutting the cost of this product. In reality, there were many opportunities to improve.

Now you are probably saying to yourself, "How could this be?"

Simple. At a $4 price, the low sales volumes of this product failed to cover its costs of production and distribution by a wide margin. A more appropriate ABC study revealed that the product actually cost $500—not $2—to make and distribute.

That's a 25,000% product costing error!

It would be nice if this example was an isolated product costing aberration. But it's not. Costing inaccuracies—and other strategic errors—are quite common when companies with a variety of products, or high overhead, use conventional cost systems. While these inaccuracies typically aren't as dramatic as 25,000%, they can still be quite significant.

The curve in *Figure 1-1* shows a profile common to many companies. Notice that the "true" cost of many products—primarily the low-volume, high-variety ones—is 1% to 600% greater than the conventional cost. High-volume, lower-variety ones error in the other direction. Their "true" cost drops by 10% to 80%, which is perhaps an even more significant correction for highly competitive products.[1]

Substantial costing inaccuracies in either direction lead to unintentional competitive mistakes. Pricing errors lead to economic losses. Producing and selling the wrong products (to the wrong customers) weakens the company in the marketplace. Focusing cost reduction efforts on the wrong products and the wrong costs makes it difficult to compete with low-cost offshore producers.

You can't afford competitive mistakes—especially in today's global economy. You need every advantage you can get to compete with Japanese, German, and other tough competitors, including U.S. companies. Cost systems that send you the wrong signals can put you on a crisis course from which recovery is difficult.

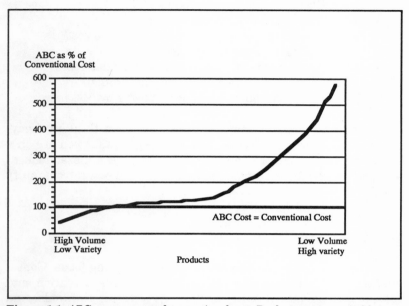

Figure 1-1. *ABC as a percent of conventional cost.* Product costs reported by conventional systems often differ substantially from the more accurate activity-based costing (ABC) results, as shown in this comparative example from a Northern Telecom assembly plant. Using the conventional costing data can result in severe errors in product strategies.

Are You on a Crisis Course?

Unreliable cost information is an open invitation to disaster. And unintentional mispricing is only one of many possible disasters. Cost information is used in making a wide range of strategic and operational decisions. So, with a flawed cost system, you are wide open for a variety of competitive problems.

The question is, how do you know if any of these problems are occurring in your company?

Well, you really can't know for sure without doing an activity-based costing study. Companies that have implemented ABC, however, have found a variety of problems. Based on their experience, consider the following questions:

- Are you selling the wrong products?
- Do you serve the wrong customers?
- Do your product designs unnecessarily raise cost?
- Do your process designs increase cost?
- Does the structure of your organization raise cost?
- Do costs go up despite cost cutting programs?
- Are decisions to source off-shore followed by cost increases?

If you find yourself answering "yes"—or even thinking "maybe"—to any of these questions, chances are good that you are on a crisis course. To explore this further, let's take a closer look at some of the possible strategic problems that can result from faulty cost information.

Focusing on the Wrong Markets

Cost is an important determinant of marketing focus. Consequently, it's only natural that managers devote attention and resources to the markets they perceive as the most profitable. And it's the cost system that reports the profitability of the products that are sold into these markets. Managers chase profits, but profits can be phantoms of the cost system.

The business of Mueller-Lehmkuhl, for example, was to combine two products—attaching machines and fasteners—and market them to customers as a package. The firm rented the machines to customers at a deliberately low price. This established a very competitive position. Then, to generate profits, the fasteners were priced to cover their cost and the remaining cost of the machines.

On the surface, everything seemed fine. Customers were happy and loyal.

However, Mueller-Lehmkuhl realized there was a problem with the cost system. It was tracing all costs to the fasteners and none to the machines. So the system was redesigned to separate fastener and machine costs. When this was done, it became clear that the previous perceptions of profitability were actually highly distorted.

Because some fasteners were labor intensive, and the old cost system was based on direct labor hours, they were assigned too much cost (including the cost of the attaching machines). This made those fasteners seem to be quite costly and unprofitable. So, over the years, Mueller-Lehmkuhl put little marketing effort into those "expensive" and "low-profit" fastener lines. Consequently, the company walked away from some attractive markets.[2]

Servicing the Wrong Customers

Have you ever checked to see how much profit is actually made from each customer? If you did this check with conventional cost information, everything would probably appear fine. However, if you were to do an ABC study of customer profitability, you might be shocked to see the differences. Some customers cost more than they are worth! Here's why.

It's common to find that different customers need different levels of support. Some customers buy standard products infrequently, but in high volumes. They rarely call your customer support department since their own engineers do all necessary training and solve most field problems.

Other customers, however, may buy nonstandard products. Moreover, their purchases are often frequent and in low volumes. They may constantly change their orders and expect a rapid response when they call. Plus, the complexity of the nonstandard products often requires a heavy engineering effort. As a result, these customers make frequent calls to the sales, order entry, and customer service departments.

Customers for nonstandard products demand a lot. But this is just the type of customer that marketing focuses most of its efforts on. This seems to make good sense because the cost system reports high profitability for these customers. They're the ones ordering the low-volume, specialty products that look really profitable. Plus, the additional cost incurred to service these customers is buried in departmental overhead accounts.

But are these customers really generating profits? To answer this question, let's take a look at a real-life example.

The case of the numerical control machine shop. A small machine shop ran three shifts a day, seven days a week. But it was making very little money.

The shop's major customer—a Fortune 100 company that the machine shop considered its bread and butter—provided 50% of the sales volume. But profitability was a different matter, as an ABC study revealed.

The major customer ordered high-precision machined parts in small lots. This required:

- Long setups,
- Intense engineering support,
- Heavy NC programming support,
- Substantial sales support,
- More order activity,
- More scrapped units,
- More inspection, and
- Higher inventory.

Unfortunately, the additional costs of these activities were not being assigned to the major customer that required them. The conventional cost system spread the costs across the machine shop's entire customer base. As a result, the major customer enjoyed subsidized pricing. More disastrously, though, the machine shop's number-one customer was actually its number-one loser.

Without this knowledge, the company missed some opportunities to better address this major customer. There were opportunities to reprice products to offset some of the additional costs. There were opportunities to redirect marketing effort towards profitable customers. There were opportunities to reduce the cost of serving the major customer through a program of continuous improvement.[3]

All these opportunities were lost because of an inappropriate cost system that focused management's attention elsewhere.

Costly Product Designs

Inappropriate cost systems can also thwart the benefits to be gained from *world-class* design.

We've learned a lot in the last ten years about designing world-class products. Today's products are designed faster and brought to market in a fraction of the time it used to take. Getting product part counts down seems to have reached the proportions of a national sport. And, thanks to world-class design, many companies have increased product quality while bringing costs down.

In fact, the opportunity for cost reduction via product design is enormous. For example, Ford Motor and others have estimated that as much as 60-80% of costs over a product's life cycle are already locked in by the time product design is completed. This rises to 90-95% by the time design of the production process is completed *(see Figure 1-2)*. So design alone offers tremendous cost reduction opportunities.

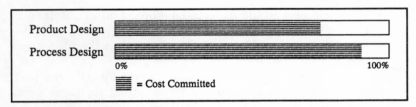

Figure 1-2. *The critical role of design.* Most product costs are locked in during design. Thus, the earlier you start thinking about cost reduction, the more leverage you'll have.

The question is, are you getting the leverage on cost that's possible with world-class design? More to the point, are your engineers able to apply the principles of world- class design? Or are they being frustrated by a cost system that tells them to do exactly the opposite?

This latter situation thwarted the efforts of an electrical accessories manufacturer. This company was on the path of world-class manufacturing. Lead times were down. Quality was up. Inventory levels were plummeting. The next step was to design products by world-class principles—low part counts, common parts, modular subassemblies, short time-to-market, and so on.

The design engineers understood the principles of world-class design. However, they were frustrated by a cost system that pushed them in exactly the opposite direction.

A case in point was a simple little brass strip. This strip was used to connect wires to a grounding circuit in several of the company's products. Connections were made via holes drilled in each strip (see *Figure 1-3*), and, depending on the product, this could require from one to three holes.[4]

It was possible to design a single strip with three holes (solution A in *Figure 1-3*). Such a strip could be used universally in all products. This approach made sense to the engineers because they would have only one part number, rather than three. Not only was this consistent with world-class goals of reducing parts inventory counts, but it seemed possible that one universal part would cost less than three variants.

Did their intuition make sense? Yes, if you look at the impact on activity of one versus three parts:

- Only one part would have to be ordered, not three;
- Just one part would have to be received, stored, and released to the shop floor;
- Only one part would have to be stored and maintained in the data base, not three;
- Just one part would need to be changed in the future, not three;
- It would be necessary to forecast volume for only one part;
- Forecasting was more likely to be wrong for three parts than for one, particularly if lead times were long;
- Less inventory would be carried with one part than with three; and
- Scheduling part production would be easier with one instead of three.

Unfortunately, the existing cost system torpedoed engineering's world-class intuition. The cost system said that a single strip was more expensive than three different strips (parts A, B, and C in *Figure 1-3*). After all, the three-hole strip required more material and direct labor than the one- or two-hole strips. And, to make things worse, the cost system assigned all overhead based on material and direct labor (which were a small portion of total cost).

It was difficult for engineering to fight this cost system. Its projection of product cost was considered to be an important performance measure for the company. In world-class design versus conventional costing, world-class design lost an uphill battle to convention. The company also lost an opportunity to cut costs on numerous activities associated with the connection strip. And that was for one simple part. How many other opportunities do you think were lost to conventional costing?

Costly Process Designs

Product design is certainly not the only place where opportunities can be lost to conventional costing. For example, take a look at how products are produced.

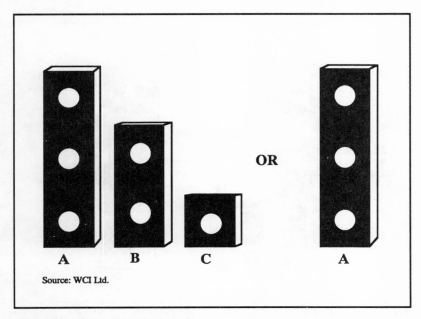

Figure 1-3. *Costing product design options.* How much can a simple wire-connection strip cost? Should you make individual strips for one-, two-, and three-wire applications, or a universal three-hole strip? Conventional costing says option C costs less for single-wire connections because it consumes less material and direct labor. Should you design to that or the world-class goals that point to reduced parts inventory?

Do your engineers buy big machines for your plant? Or do they favor small pieces of mobile equipment that can be moved into product cells?

Companies following the path to world-class manufacturing favor small, mobile pieces of equipment. In his book on world-class manufacturing, Dick Schonberger calls this "adding fixed capacity the way we add people: in small increments as demand grows."[5] People are flexible—they can learn new skills and move to new tasks as required. Similarly, small machines can also be tailored to specific types of products and moved to wherever they are most needed.

Chances are you have a "super" machine in your plant. It may be a wave-solder machine or a component inserter if you are an electronics company. It may be a paint shop or a chroming process if you make metal parts.

Figure 1-4. *Costing process design options.* Conventional cost systems often show that one large machine is less costly than several smaller ones. The reality may be that a single "super" machine not only increases cost, but reduces quality and flexibility, too.

How might your cost system bias you towards purchasing "super" machines? Let's say your choice was to buy one large machine or two small ones *(Figure 1-4)*. How did the decision look?

The direct labor required to run the large machine was less than for two separate machines. One large machine was also cheaper to purchase than two small machines, so the annual depreciation on one machine is less. And, with overhead loaded on direct labor, any calculation of relative cost shows a clear advantage for the single large machine.

But what really happens?

Let's look at the differences that weren't picked up by the labor-based cost system.

Scheduling. One large machine is difficult to schedule. Parts from all over the plant must be funneled into this one machine. This creates a potential bottleneck. However, if you have two machines, one can be dedicated to a high-volume product, while the other is used to produce low-volume specialty products. (To support specialty products, the second machine can be modified to facilitate fast changeovers.)

Inventory. Inventory levels will be greater with only one machine. Buffer stocks of parts are typically stacked in front of the machine to ensure that it's kept busy at all times. For the same reason, the machine's output will be greater than the rate of subsequent processes (creating buffers in front of these processes, too).

Quality. Inventory buffers, and production rates exceeding the immediate needs of downstream processes, inevitably reduce quality (because feedback is delayed until defects work their way through the buffers). This reduces customer satisfaction, lengthens lead times, and increases the costs of detecting and correcting defects.

Material handling. There is more material handling effort associated with one large machine. It must be placed in a single location, often inconvenient to points of supply and use. Parts have to be moved to the "super" machine, then moved back to product cells or downstream processes.

Maintenance. Big machines tend to break down more often than small ones. They take longer to set up. And big, complex machines often require specialists to perform maintenance. (You need to hire these specialists, send your own technicians to training classes, or sign an expensive maintenance contract with the manufacturer.)

In contrast, small machines can often be maintained by the machine operator. And, when a small machine does go down, only its product line is affected rather than the entire plant.

Supervision. Large machines are separate processes that need direct supervision. Small machines can be placed in product cells, which tend to be self-managing.

So, thanks to an inappropriate cost system, you can be led to a choice that actually increases your costs. It also reduces your flexibility, reduces quality, and leaves your customers short--changed.

Costly Organization Options

Some companies are always reorganizing.

Sometimes it's for strategic reasons. For example, "we can better focus on our traditional strengths in the market."

In other cases, it's to reduce cost.

A common cost reduction device is to centralize administrative services. This is particularly evident in the financial services industry for example. Those tall bank towers often house services, such as mortgage lending, that used to be provided in the branches *(Figure 1-5)*.

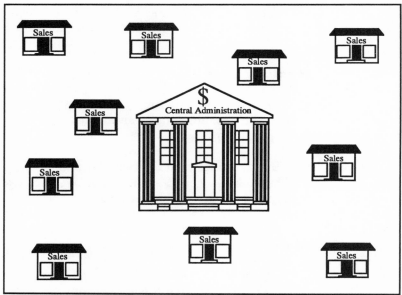

Figure 1-5. *Costing organization options.* Your cost system may show the centralized option as the most profitable. But be careful! There may be hidden costs, and service and quality may suffer.

What does a conventional cost system have to say about this?

It's likely to tell you that centralizing functions cuts cost. Branches can be closed. Depreciation comes down as buildings are closed. Salaries and benefits are reduced as staff are laid off or transferred to fill vacancies elsewhere.

There are also expectations that "skill group alignment" will increase efficiency. This should allow you to focus on the repetitive transactions in your function and search for productivity improvements.

But look at what really happens.

Communication, for example, becomes more difficult. This is because different parts of the transaction chain are located in different parts of the organization. Information processing costs go up as the bank tries to improve communication by electronically linking the separate functions.

Transactions are also batched to allow "mass production" and its associated "economies." However, lead times go up as transactions sit in queues or are in transit. Defects are common and require retransmittal and rework. And there is also a lot of effort (and cost) associated with these delays and defects.

Because of communication delays, decision lead times go up. Customers have to wait longer to get their mortgages processed. And, believe it or not, overall cost goes up.

Eventually, the bank recognizes the problem (but not necessarily the cause) and decides to reorganize again. Centralization didn't work. Perhaps decentralization will.

Increasing Costs Despite Cost Cutting Programs

When hard times hit, the gut reaction of many Western companies is to reach for the knife. We've all seen the headlines. *Company Lays Off 5,000. Company Cuts White Collars by 20%.*

Does this cost cutting really work? In the short run it does save money. But over time, people are rehired and costs creep back up. How can this be?

The typical cost report tells you *what* you are spending, but it doesn't tell you *why* you are spending it. So when you slash overhead costs, you're cutting the *result*, not the *cause*. Consequently, you're more likely to damage the quality of products and services than to reduce costs permanently.

It's the same with reducing costs. The way to reduce costs permanently is to change the way you perform the work. Unfortunately, conventional cost information *does not* tell you how to do this. Nor does it encourage you to do it. As a result, crash cost cutting efforts often fail to restore a company to lasting health.

Incorrect Sourcing Decisions

One source of competitive advantage in manufacturing is to focus on what you know best. For example, you can choose to manufacture those parts that are best suited to your equipment, technology, and skills. You can then obtain the other parts from outside suppliers. But, as indicated in *Figure 1-6*, there can be several sourcing options.

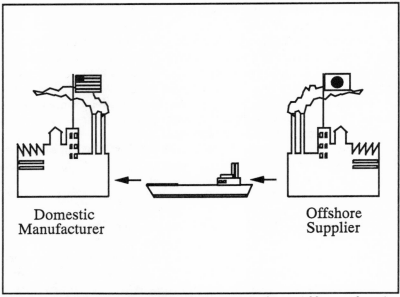

Domestic
Manufacturer

Offshore
Supplier

Figure 1-6. *Costing sourcing options.* Outsourcing is often a viable manufacturing strategy. Too often, however, the decision to source from outside is based on faulty or incomplete cost data. Contrary to expectations, costs go up while quality and service go down.

How does your company decide which parts to manufacture and which to source from outside? If you source from outside, is a local or offshore supplier best?

The biggest decision factor for some companies is the outside supplier's price. Quality and service may receive a sideways glance, but outside price versus the cost of manufacturing internally is often the final arbiter.

What does your cost system tell you about the cost of manufacturing a part in-house? It tells you what the material and direct labor costs are. But then does it load overhead onto the part based on the amount of direct labor? If it does, the in-house cost will inevitably be higher than the price charged by an off-shore supplier located in a country with low direct labor costs.

Experience tells us, however, that the price quoted by an outside supplier is a small fraction of the total cost of getting a part to its destination and getting there on time and in a condition fit to use. Even if we include the additional transportation costs, there are other "hidden" costs that are easily overlooked. They typically include ordering, expediting, handling, storage, and quality.

Let's take a closer look at these hidden costs in terms of acquiring a part from a supplier that's 5,000 miles away. Here's some of what you're up against:

Ordering. Distance increases the hidden costs of procurement and reduces supplier responsiveness. Order lead times are in weeks or even months. Requirements must be forecast well in advance of actual use, with the added risk that the forecast is wrong.

In contrast, a simple technique to trigger orders for parts can be used with local suppliers. This is the *Kanban*. It's a visible signal, such as the return of an empty container, to indicate that a new order should be filled. *Kanbans* are part of a "pull" system where the frequency and size of orders is determined by the demand of the next process (and ultimately the needs of customers).

A pull system simplifies the material procurement process. It eliminates activities such as inspection, receiving, and storing, and it reduces overall costs.

Expediting. Forecasting errors provide lots of work for expediters. In addition to the cost of the expediters themselves, there's the cost of airfreight and special handling.

Storage. Long lead times inevitably translate into more inventory with all the costs of storing and handling that inventory.

Quality. The best quality is achieved when customers and suppliers are closely linked. Close linkage is difficult, however, from a distance of 5,000 miles.

If the offshore supplier produces defective parts, it may be weeks before these parts make their way through the shipping and inventory pipeline. By this time, there may be thousands of defective parts in the warehouse or on the boat.

Sorting out such a mess isn't easy. It's not uncommon to put engineers and managers on planes to resolve the quality problems at the supplier's plant.

There are situations where the price quoted for offshore supply is so low that it more than offsets the hidden costs. But can you be sure that you've always made the right decision? To gain some insight, let's look at a real-life example of sourcing from Mexico.

The case of the Mexican subassembly. A Midwestern U.S. company was looking for ways to reduce cost. This company sold products into a marketplace recently invaded by foreign competition. Its customers lost 60% of their business to the Japanese and other off-shore manufacturers in just a few short months.

Losing the lion's share of its business so quickly was life--threatening. Survival required major surgery.

Transplanting assembly work to Mexico seemed to be an obvious way to reduce cost. Labor rates in Mexico were about 50¢ per hour at the time. By comparison, rates in the Midwest exceeded $8 per hour, even for fairly unskilled work.

So the company picked a subassembly requiring a lot of hand work and sent it to Mexico. The economics were compelling. Not only should labor costs come down over 90%, but overhead should plummet as well. (The "drop" in the subassembly's cost would occur because the cost system added manufacturing overhead as a percent of direct labor.)

The outsourcing was handled like this: parts were shipped by suppliers to the company's Midwestern location. The parts were "kitted" (parts were boxed, with each box containing the specific components for a single subassembly), and the kits were shipped to Mexico. After assembly in Mexico, the completed subassemblies were shipped back to the Midwest.

How did things work out? Did cost go down by 90%? Did the company become more competitive?

Well, there were some unanticipated problems.

For example, there was the extra work required by the company's procurement staff. Keeping track of all those parts arriving in the Midwest, in shipment to Mexico, in the Mexican plant, and in shipment back to the Midwest turned out to be a major headache. The company set up a special group in procurement just to keep track of all this movement.

Another problem was the quality of the subassemblies, which was poor. Many of the subassemblies required rework when they arrived in the Midwest. A special group of engineers was assigned to the problem, and a special rework group was established in the company's Midwestern plant to correct the problems.

What happened to cost? Well, procurement staff and engineers are quite costly. They require salaries, benefits, and resources to support them. Overall cost *went up*, not down.

A visible symptom of all the extra work was an additional seven weeks to complete a customer order. The company had lost one of the main advantages of domestic manufacture– avoiding the "slow boat from China," or Mexico in this case. The company's customers certainly weren't very happy about this either.

The irony was that the company's conventional cost system predicted that, overall, costs would go down and not up. If direct labor went down, overhead (according to the cost system) would go down, too. But the conventional labor-based cost system missed all the additional activity (and associated cost) required to service the Mexican plant.

Not all stories have a happy ending, but this one does. The company brought the subassembly operation back home to the Midwest. Costs went back down and both quality and customer service improved substantially. Along with this, the company built an ABC system to provide improved cost information for future decisions.

Summary

Incorrect cost information can put you on a crisis course from which you may never recover. It may lead to problems you can ill afford in today's competitive environment. You may focus on the wrong priorities and solve the wrong problems.

The ways you can be led astray are many, but include:

- Selling the wrong products or focusing on the wrong markets;
- Emphasizing the wrong customers and neglecting opportunities to improve the way you serve customers;

- Emphasizing the wrong customers and neglecting opportunities to improve the way you serve customers;
- Designing products that unnecessarily raise cost or missing opportunities to reduce part counts, use common components, or use low-cost processes;
- Acquiring the wrong type of equipment and designing processes in ways that increase cost;
- Centralizing functions in a vain attempt to reduce cost, but reduces service instead;
- Cost cutting programs that slash costs across the board without regard for the underlying work, the inevitable result being that cost creeps back up again; and
- Moving production off-shore, only to find that costs increase rather than decrease.

Even worse, your cost system may tell you not only to stay on one of these courses, but to increase your speed, too. The faster you go, the further behind you get.

Key Terms in Chapter 1

ABC–Acronym for activity-based cost or activity-based costing.
Activity-based costing (ABC)–A method of measuring the cost and performance of activities, products, and customers. In product costing applications, for example, ABC allows costs to be apportioned to products by the actual activities and resources consumed in producing, marketing, selling, delivering, and servicing the product.
Conventional cost system–Any of the older, traditional cost systems that use direct material and labor consumed as the primary means of apportioning overhead. This proved adequate when the overhead cost of indirect activities was a small percentage compared to direct labor consumed in actually making products. But today, automation has reduced direct labor substantially, leaving indirect activities as a far more significant cost factor. For this and other reasons, using direct labor as a primary apportioning device can cause significant costing distortions and poor strategic decisions.

References:

1. *Figure 1-1* is based on a chart prepared by Erik Horne of Northern Telecom Ltd.

2. Robin Cooper, "You Need a New Cost System When...," *Harvard Business Review*, (January-February 1989), pp. 77-82.

3. Peter B.B. Turney and James M. Reeve, "The Impact of Continuous Improvement on the Design of Activity-Based Cost Systems," *Journal of Cost Management*, (Summer 1990), pp. 43-50.

4. The source of Figure 1-3 and the example of the brass strip, was Paul Collins of World Class International, Ltd.

5. Richard J. Schonberger, *World Class Manufacturing: The Lessons of Simplicity Applied,* (New York: Free Press, 1986), p. 82.

Chapter 2

WHY CONVENTIONAL COST SYSTEMS FAIL

Cost systems are information systems—nothing more, nothing less. They require certain types of information such as direct labor hours and units produced. Then, from these data, product costs and other information are derived according to the cost system's defined methodology *(Figure 2-1)*.

If the costing results are suspect—and we saw examples in Chapter 1 where this may be the case—it stands to reason that either the input data or the methodology is wrong. Usually the data are blamed.

After all, the cost system is tried and true. It's been in place in its basic form for years. Sure, there have been some modifications. But the costing results have always been reasonably reliable. Why should that change now? It must be production; they're just not giving us accurate enough data.

Sound familiar?

So what happens next?

The usual, of course. Reporting procedures are tightened up. Material and hours are accounted for in greater detail and with unerring precision. And the cost system still produces suspect results.

Marketing pushes the wrong products. Engineering inadvertently designs unnecessarily costly products. Production incurs excessive cost (but thinks it's doing the opposite). Management initiates a campaign to cut costs, only to see costs creep back up again.

As a result, profits continue to decline, even though sales are increasing. You've seen the financial headlines—*XYZ Corp. Reports Record Sales, Posts Fourth-Quarter Loss*.

What is clear is that better cost information is needed. Record sales should mean record profits.

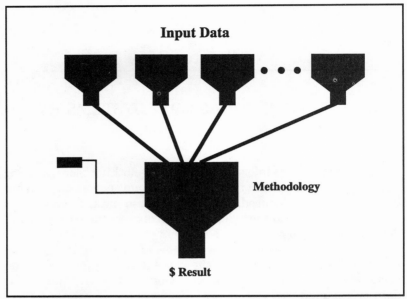

Figure 2-1. *Cost systems are information systems.* They process raw data according to a defined methodology and report product costs and other information.

The problem is that conventional cost systems are no longer in tune with the external and internal conditions affecting today's business environment. External conditions have changed because of global competition, technological advances, and access to low-cost information systems. There's a new competitive environment out there that we must learn to thrive in.

The New Competitive Environment

Global competition was not part of our lexicon before the 1980s. Now major sectors of the U.S. economy are dominated by foreign competitors.

The pace of technological change has accelerated rapidly. Products once took years to develop and stayed on the market for decades. Now products are routinely replaced every eighteen months.

The cost of computing power has plummeted, and its availability has increased dramatically. Today's computers are so small and cheap that most people can afford to have a powerful machine on their desktop. Computerized manufacturing control systems have facilitated deployment of new technology and reduced the cost of capturing operational data on a real-time basis.

Success—let alone survival—in this new competitive environment is no longer assured by "business as usual." Successful companies now have a new way of doing business: It's called *world class*.

The World-Class Company

Describing a company as *world class* means a number of things. It means the company has achieved high standards of business performance and has undergone fundamental changes in the way it's managed. But above all, it's profitably meeting the needs of customers while continuously improving its ability to do so.

Success in the world-class company is measured in the eyes of the customer. The goal is not simply to satisfy customers, but to positively delight them. The Japanese call it *miryokuteki hinshitsu*—designing products that are not only reliable and cheap to make, but also fascinating and delightful to the customer.

What delights a customer?

The specifics vary from industry to industry, and from product to product. But most customers want the same basic things:

- *Customers are interested in quality*—they want their purchase to work, to do the things they want it to, and to please them in the process.
- *They desire good service*—they want their products and services delivered on time.
- *They want flexibility*—they want the ability to obtain the specific product or service they want.
- *They covet value*—they don't want to pay a price that exceeds the value received from the product.

Delighting customers is not something you do once and then rest on your laurels. With hungry competitors breathing down its neck, the world-class company continuously improves its ability to delight customers.

Everyone is committed to improving continuously in a world-class company. Often the individual improvements are small. Japanese companies such as Toyota are famous for "improvement by inches." But small improvements, if done year after year, grow in measure to provide an insurmountable lead.

What do world-class companies improve?

They improve the things that matter to their customers—quality, service, flexibility, and cost. And they do it differently than other companies that haven't yet started on the path to world-class competitiveness. These differences permeate every function in the company.

For example, world-class companies design and build in quality the first time. They don't have teams of inspectors looking for defects. There aren't any rework departments fixing faulty products. Instead, everyone in a world-class company is responsible for the quality of their own work.

Moreover, world-class companies make only what the customer needs. And they do it in a continuous flow. Parts are purchased or built *just-in-time* for the next process. Gone are the large batches of yesteryear—the goal is a lot size of one. Gone are the large buffer stocks of parts piled next to every machine or assembly station. Gone is the end-of-month scramble to meet sales goals—a scramble that *increases cost* and *reduces quality*.

Products in a world-class company are designed by teams from engineering, production, marketing, and procurement. Gone are the days when designers "tossed a product design over the transom" and challenged manufacturing to produce it. Tools such as *quality function deployment* (QFD) ensure that customer desires are reflected in the product design.

It's people who make the biggest difference in world-class companies. Employee involvement—pushing decision making responsibility down to the lowest levels of the organization—energizes the talents of everyone.

The result is a flat organization structure that facilitates cross-functional communication. This eliminates layers of bureaucracy (or what some people call "hardening of the categories" or "functional silos").

The activities of the world-class company are linked to form what Dick Schonberger calls *a chain of customers*. Each activity in the company has a customer—the next activity in the process. Each activity is dedicated to serving its customer. This forms a chain that ends with the paying customer.[1]

Measuring Performance

The new competitive environment has increased the value of information about a company's performance. Competition and the pace of change have made it more important than ever to have information about how well you are achieving your goals. Changes in information systems technology have also reduced the cost of information. This makes it increasingly easier to obtain useful information.

New ways of doing business in a world-class company have also changed the *type* of information that's useful. This is inevitable—the goals are different, and the means of accomplishing them are different, too.

All these changes are reflected in the characteristics of a typical cost system in a world-class company. A cost system in a world-class company should:

- Report information about what matters to the customer,
- Measure the profitability of customers and the products they buy,
- Prove economical to implement and easy to use,
- Provide insights on how to improve profitable delivery of service to the customer, and
- Encourage actions that improve the company's ability to profitably service customers.

Let's take a closer look at these characteristics.

What Matters to the Customer

The first step in establishing world-class characteristics is to understand what matters to your customers. How important is the quality of the product or service, and what does quality mean to the customer? How important is the ability to obtain different products and services fast? Is price (and therefore cost) an important issue for your customers?

The second step is to find out how each part of your company contributes to what is important to your customers. Quality in the world-class company, for example, is not created in the inspection department. Rather, it's the combined work of many activities all over the company. As another example, order lead times (which govern flexibility) are determined by the elapsed time of all the activities involved in meeting the order.

Unfortunately, conventional cost systems provide little useful information about what matters to the customer. Factors such as quality and service are out of their domain. They report only financial information. Nonfinancial information, about defects and throughput rates in each activity for example, is outside the scope of the conventional system.

Even the financial information in conventional systems has limited utility because of the following factors:

- *Cost information is an indirect measure, at best,* **of quality and time.** Direct measures of defects and throughput time are easier to interpret than a maze of cost variances.

- *Cost information is not reported by activity.* As a result, it's not known how much it costs for each activity to service its customers. Instead, conventional cost systems report cost by "line item," such as salaries and depreciation, and by function, such as engineering or marketing. This information is too aggregated (related to several activities) to permit analyzing the value customers receive from any one activity.

- *Cost information is typically reported too late to support improvement efforts.* Cost system reports are prepared monthly. Distribution usually occurs a few days after the end of the month. A monthly report released in the middle of the following month contains information that is, on the average, 30-days old. By this time the trail has gone cold, reducing the likelihood that action will be taken.

Let's say, for example, you find an *unfavorable spending variance* in your department report. Investigation suggests that this additional spending results from quality problems in a prior process. You walk across the plant to find out what happened, only to discover that nobody can remember, and nobody cares.

Customer and Product Profitability

A world-class company not only delights its customers, it does so profitably. Low price may provide a short-run advantage to your customers. But as an unprofitable supplier, you become a weak link in the value chain and cannot sustain your customers in the long term.

How does conventional costing help you assess how profitably you are delivering value to your customers? The answer is poorly, and for several good reasons.

Stuck inside the plant (if there is one). Assessing customer profitability is hindered by the failure of conventional cost systems to step outside the plant. By design, they're stuck in the plant. That's because their main function is inventory valuation. As a result, they focus only on costs incurred in product manufacturing since those are the *only* costs that can be included in inventory valuation.

Once you step outside the factory door, you're outside the domain of conventional costing. Yet there is much activity— order entry, sales, marketing, engineering—relating to customers and the products and services they buy. What's more, in some companies, the cost of activities outside the plant *exceeds* the cost of manufacturing activities.

Service companies are an extreme example. Banks, hospitals, and insurance companies don't "manufacture" products. They don't maintain inventories of their services, so they don't need a product cost system for financial reporting purposes. As a result, service company cost systems are nonexistent or primitive at best.

Reported product costs that are way off the mark. An important factor that determines customer profitability is the type, number, and cost of the products or services purchased. Conventional cost systems do measure the manufacturing cost of each type of product. But how good is this measurement?

Unfortunately, conventional cost systems *often* report inaccurate product costs. Experience shows they often err by hundreds or even thousands of percent.

The problem is in the underlying methodology of conventional cost systems. They adhere to the assumption that *products cause cost*. Each time a unit of the product is manufactured, it's assumed that cost is incurred.

This assumption does make sense for certain types of cost. For example, the cost of activities performed directly on the product unit, such as direct labor, fits this assumption.

Direct labor activities are performed directly on a valve, housing, circuit board, or other product unit. If the number of units produced goes up, more units must be assembled, and the cost of direct labor will go up, too.

The assumption does not work, however, with activities that aren't performed directly on the product units. For example, some activities are performed on batches of products. When you set up a machine to produce a type of part, you produce a batch of the parts rather than an individual unit. Conventional cost systems deal with units, *not* batches.

Other activities are performed by product type. When you change engineering specifications on a product, for example, all future product units are affected, *not* just a single unit. Again, this doesn't fit into the unit methodologies and assumptions of conventional costing.

The correct assumption—one that fits what's really happening—is that activities cause costs, and products (and customers) create the need to perform activities. But this assumption requires a very different type of cost system, as the next Chapter shows.

For now, let's continue our investigation of why conventional cost systems report inaccurate product costs. Fundamentally, it's because they try to assign cost directly to product units rather than to activities first, then from activities to product units.

Figure 2-2 is a case in point. Products A and B are different. Product A is a mature product. Its technology is quite simple. As a result, it requires little inspection effort. But it does require quite a lot of direct labor for assembly.

In contrast, Product B is a new product. It's a complex product that requires a lot of inspection time, though the amount of labor required to assemble it is less.

The conventional cost system assigns overhead cost to Products A and B using direct labor hours. Direct labor hours is a measure of activity that is performed directly on each unit of A and B. It's also a commonly used costing measure in conventional cost systems.

Product A
100 units
1 inspection hr.
3 direct labor hrs.

Product A
Conventional:
3 x $120 = $360/100 = $3.60
ABC:
1 x $100 = $100/100 = $1

Product B
100 units
5 inspection hrs.
2 direct labor hrs.

Product B
Conventional:
2 x $120 = $240/100 = $2.40
ABC:
5 x $100 = $500/100 = $5

Inspection Overhead = $600
Cost per direct labor hour = $120
Cost per inspection hour = $100

Figure 2-2. *Conventional costing breaks down when products differ.* Direct labor hours, for example, *do not* accurately measure the cost of inspecting Products A and B.

The problem here is that inspection effort is determined by the relative complexity of the products, not by the amount of direct labor. In fact, direct labor is negatively correlated with complexity in this example.

Product A, the simpler product, requires less inspection effort than B, but more direct labor time. Product A is, therefore, overcosted in the conventional cost system. Product B, which requires more inspection effort but less direct labor time, is, therefore, undercosted.

What if we assign cost based on the number of inspection hours? Would that be a better measure?

The number of inspection hours required for each product measures the inspection effort directly. Thus, it provides a more accurate measure of how each product consumes the cost of this activity. (Inspection hours provides an example of the type of measure used in activity-based costing, or ABC, as the next Chapter explains.)

The extent of conventional costing inaccuracy can be demonstrated by calculating the inspection cost of each product. The results of this are shown in *Figure 2-2.* Notice that Product A's cost falls by 72%, and Product B's cost increases by 108%. The relative cost of the two products is the reverse of what it was before.

The example in *Figure 2-2* is typical of the inaccuracies reported by conventional cost systems. When inaccuracies are removed by introducing an ABC system, it's quite common to see shifts in cost ranging from drops of 10% to 30% to increases of several hundred (or even thousands) of percent. Not surprisingly, such large shifts in cost lead to drastic reappraisals of product mix and pricing strategy.

Is it better to be reasonably right, or precisely wrong? If you use a conventional cost system, it may be hard to believe that *your* product costs are inaccurate by such orders of magnitude. But it's probably true.

Conventional cost systems often report the cost of products to fractions of a penny. For example, the cost of a product may be reported as **$5.258637**. Carrying product costing to such precision is a tribute to the power of computers and the accountant's traditional desire for exactness.

It's a brave manager who challenges the accuracy of such a precise number. *But keep in mind that precision doesn't necessarily mean accuracy.* Computers always compute with great precision. But if you put in inaccurate numbers or use the wrong computational methodology, all you get is precision without accuracy.

So how much should you trust the $5.258637 that your conventional cost system gives you? Too often the first digit is wrong. Worse yet, the decimal point is often in the wrong place, too.

Which companies are most likely to have large inaccuracies in reported product costs? It's those with large amounts of overhead and high diversity.

In recent years, the importance of overhead has increased tremendously. Knowledge workers, particularly engineers and software specialists, have displaced much of the direct labor force in many plants. In some cases, overhead outside the plant—engineering, marketing, and distribution—has increased to where it exceeds direct labor. *Figure 2-3* illustrates this trend.

The more overhead there is, the greater the chance for distortion in reported costs. As a rule of thumb, overhead that exceeds 15% of total costs may cause inaccuracies in conventional systems.

But overhead is not the only factor. Diversity—products or services that differ from one to another—is another important factor. Diversity results from differences in design, maturity, volume, or scope of the service. Each difference makes a product unique and gives it a unique cost.

As an example of diversity, consider a valve manufacturer that makes different sizes of valves in iron or brass. This diversity exists to meet different customer needs. A hospital, as another example, has patient diversity. One patient may be in the hospital for a triple heart bypass, while another is in for gall bladder removal. Each product or service requires different activities or different amounts of the same activities and, therefore, incurs a different overall cost.

You can easily visualize the effects of diversity by looking at the opposite case. Think about the company that makes only *one* product and has only *one* product cost. All products are identical and, therefore, must cost the same.

For an example of this, let's go back to the 1920s, to the Ford Motor Company's Rouge River Plant. At that time, Ford made only one product—*the black Model T*. Ford's cost system was very simple, but quite effective in costing these automobiles. One person counted the cars coming out of the plant. This count was then divided into the total cost of running the plant over the period of the count.

A variation of Henry Ford's cost system is alive and well today. It's used in world-class plants with one product or a limited number of similar products, and it's called *backflush costing*.

But if you sell variety, you won't know what your products and services cost under a conventional costing system. To sort out the costs of different products, you need to use an ABC system. If you don't, you'll be operating based on inaccurate cost information.

Inaccurate product costs make it difficult to correctly chose which products to sell, how to properly price those products, and how to design them for low cost. Inaccurate costs can also send you chasing after the wrong customers and markets.

The price of using inaccurate information can be very high, even deadly in some cases. But, on the other hand, how much does it cost to get accurate information?

Happily, the answer is not much—*if you use the right system*.

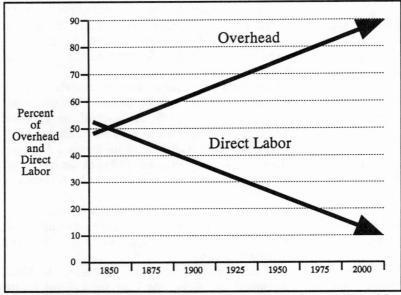

Figure 2-3. *The importance of overhead cost.* The relative importance of direct labor and overhead have changed over 150 years. Thus, the focus of yesterday's cost systems on direct labor must give way to cost systems that focus on overhead.

Economical to Implement, Easy to Use

A cost system should provide information to help eliminate waste, but it should not be wasteful itself. This means that the resources required to design, implement, and maintain a cost system should be reasonable.

It's in this area—cost of operation—that conventional cost systems have another significant failing. For example, the Tektronix Oscilloscope Group reported the actual direct labor used for each of forty to sixty operations on each production line. The cost of recording, processing, correcting, and analyzing the actual cost of labor per operation cost more than the value of the labor itself.

A complete redesign of the group's cost system substantially reduced the number of transactions processed in the division. On one major instrument line, for example, the volume of monthly labor measurements decreased from 30,000 to about fifty when

---

The Oscilloscope Group of Tektronix

Tektronix manufactures a wide range of electronic equipment and software systems. Its Oscilloscope Group manufactures its principle product, oscilloscopes, used to display graphically the magnitude and timing of electrical phenomena. This Group is a pioneer in the development of new cost systems.

---

labor tracking was abandoned. The elimination of an inventory tracking system reduced the transaction count by an additional 25,000 per month.[2]

It's possible to make cost measurements without adding waste. Experience with ABC systems shows that they can be both economical and unobtrusive. The next Chapter, for example, describes an ABC project that was completed at little cost in forty-eight hours. Nonetheless, it provided tangible and important benefits to the company.

Insights on How to Improve

An underlying ethos in world-class companies is the drive to improve continuously. It follows that, to be useful, information from a cost system should provide insights about how to improve.

Improvement focuses on the work—*the activities*—of the organization. But conventional costing doesn't report useful information about those activities that have the most potential for improvement. Thus, little insight on improvement is gained.

For example, conventional cost systems in manufacturing companies provide plenty of detail about direct labor. This owes much to the influence of Frederick Taylor and the scientific management movement at the turn of the century.

Taylor is the father of work study. This is where work on the product is divided into its component parts, studied, and timed. The goal is to discover ways to cut direct labor costs. The importance of this goal gave birth to a whole era of scientific management and industrial engineering.

Cost accountants built standard cost systems around the work of industrial engineers. The cost of each operation of direct labor was determined in advance and compared with the actual cost of doing the work. Variances—*the differences between standard and actual*—were computed. Then teams of industrial engineers returned to the plant to figure out how to minimize the variances.

Scientific management and standard costing were very successful. The productivity of direct labor has increased in most years of this century. This helped fuel Western prosperity.

The focus on reducing direct labor cost may have been sensible through the first part of the twentieth century. But in today's world, it's a focus on something that is falling in significance and is even disappearing in some companies.

One company, for example, measured direct labor cost for each of sixty operations in the assembly of its product. The problem is that these sixty operations took less than four minutes *total* and represented a mere fraction of the product's cost.

But, as direct labor cost has decreased, overhead cost has increased. Overhead is now the major source of cost in most manufacturing companies.

In contrast, overhead activities—the major source of cost in most manufacturing companies (and the *only* source of cost in service companies)—have been virtually ignored by scientific management and accounting. But they also represent fertile ground for improvement in an aspiring world-class company.

To reach world-class status, a company must focus on eliminating waste from overhead activities. Waste refers to the use of resources to perform nonessential or inefficient activities. It can be eliminated without diminishing the value received by the customer.

Setting up machines, moving parts, and inspecting parts are examples of overhead activities that contain waste. They are all prime candidates for improvement efforts.

Can conventional costing help in eliminating waste from overhead activities?

Probably not.

Conventional costing can give you information about salaries and depreciation at the department level. Such functional overhead reports tell you nothing about the work going on in your department. They don't tell you what work is done by the people earning the salaries. And they don't tell you what machine is represented by the depreciation or the activity the machine performs.

Also, functional overhead reports assume that organizations can be neatly compartmentalized into departments. Yet many processes have little respect for lines on an organization chart.

For example, look at the new product introduction process illustrated in *Figure 2-4*. This activity cuts across several departments. Department heads do see a line-item report about their department. But a department report contains no information about the activities in the department, and it provides only a fractional view of the entire process.

What it all boils down to is this: Good information about activities will not make you a world-class company. Activity information is just one of the improvement tools. However, activity information does help focus efforts to improve. It helps set improvement priorities, and it gives you feedback about progress.

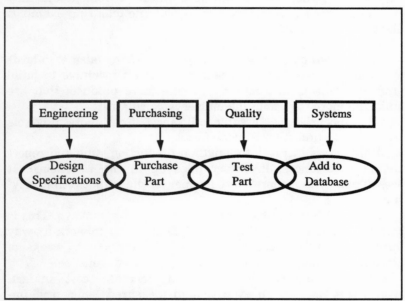

Figure 2-4. *Cross-functional processes.* The new product introduction process crosses organizational boundaries. While conventional cost systems do supply information about the cost of departments, they unfortunately do not report information about cross-functional processes.

Moreover, conventional cost systems do not report the activity information needed to gain insights about how to improve. It takes a radically different approach, such as ABC, to support any serious quest for improvement and world-class status.

Encourages Improvement

To get going in the right direction, you need a beacon— some kind of signal—to guide you. For example, cost measures are signals that stimulate action. People pay attention to cost signals, because they are often used to gauge and reward performance.

It's important, therefore, for a cost system to send the right signals. The wrong signals may misdirect improvement efforts, may encourage actions that interfere with improvement, and may even endanger the company's existence. The following examples illustrate this further.

Unwanted output and poor quality. Using labor standards to evaluate direct labor efficiency creates an incentive to build products. This is understandable. The more products that are built, the more favorable the efficiency calculation.

The incentive of "greater efficiency" from more products creates some unfortunate side-effects.

Batch sizes increase to lengthen production runs and report favorable variances. Inventory piles up in the warehouse. It doesn't matter that there's no customer for the output. "Efficiency" is up.

Along with unwanted output, quality also goes down. This is because it takes a long time for a defective part to work its way through the warehouse to detection. By that time, weeks of defective production can be stacked up in the warehouse.

Excess inventory and poor quality increases cost. In fact, overall cost may go up even though measured "efficiency" improves.

Functional myopia. Conventional cost systems are dominated by functional classifications. These functional classifications are accompanied by use of cost variances as performance measures. These measures often cause behavior that improves functional performance at the expense of overall performance.

For example, you could use purchase-price variance to evaluate the purchasing department. This will encourage changing suppliers to reduce purchase costs. Purchasing's performance goes up.

But, unfortunately, the penny saved on a part may be at the price of lower part quality or supplier reliability. The result can be reduced product quality and disrupted production—*penny wise, pound foolish.*

That kind of scenario occurred at the Tektronix Oscilloscope Group. Purchasing reduced the purchase price of a part by changing suppliers. The cost "saving" was significant for purchasing—it represented about half of their target favorable purchase price variance for the year.

But the quality of parts from the new supplier was poor. The parts did not fit. Considerable time was spent reworking the parts to make them fit, and production was disrupted. The purchasing department looked good, but the division as a whole (and its customers) suffered.

Misdirected cost reduction. Loading overhead cost via direct labor sends a clear signal that direct labor is a costly resource. This is because small amounts of direct labor are magnified by overhead rates that can reach several hundred percent.

Such exaggeration of direct labor cost encourages production and engineering to take steps to reduce direct labor. While this is done in the sincere belief that overall cost will go down, the reality may be quite different.

For example, engineering may modify the design of an existing product to reduce its labor content and associated reported overhead. In the case of an electronics plant, this could be accomplished by replacing high-volume, hand-inserted parts with new machine-inserted parts.

The activities to support hand-inserted parts are already in place, and no additional resources are required. The new machine--inserted parts, however, require additional effort that includes new part number support, vendor relations, and purchasing. Thus, it's possible for the reported cost of the re-engineered product to go down while overall overhead and cost go up.

The death spiral. Conventional costing adheres to the requirement that all manufacturing costs be attached to the products produced. This *full absorption* of cost can be dangerous to a company's health.

Full absorption creates an incentive to produce even when customers are not in sight. Production triggers the *attachment* of cost to units. If these units disappear into a warehouse, the cost disappears with them. But are your customers happy and are you making money?

Sounds similar to the problem of unwanted output and poor quality resulting from direct labor efficiency, doesn't it?

But things can get much worse with full absorption.

What happens if you don't have enough products to absorb the cost? Let's say you dropped some products or outsourced parts to the Far East. What happens if you have no other products or parts to take up the slack?

In these circumstances, full absorption can lead to a "death spiral." It works like this.

An uncompetitive product is dropped, but not all of its costs "go away." You can't close part of the plant, turn off half the boiler, or saw machines in half. Also, it may take months to reduce engineering and other staff.

Now, what happens to that left over *unabsorbed* cost?

Simple. It gets dumped into the unfortunate remaining products. So now their reported costs go up.

Up pops another "uncompetitive" product—the next candidate for outsourcing. This product is dropped. But some of its costs remain and are reassigned to other products. So the cycle repeats itself, taking profits and competitiveness into a downward spiral as products are plucked away.

It doesn't take many cycles of the "death spiral" before there's nothing to do but close the plant. Even if the plant doesn't close, it may be badly wounded. Plus many jobs are lost and sent unnecessarily overseas. (It doesn't have to happen this way. Chapter 3 will show how the unabsorbed costs can be identified as *idle-capacity costs* and isolated from product costs.)

When seen in its entirety, the death spiral seems to be too obvious a trap for anyone to fall into. But don't bet on it. It happens more often than you'd like to think. Take a look at what happened in the following case.

The Case of the Electronics Plant

It's quite sobering to walk into this plant. It's one of the plants where a large company manufactures electronic products. It's a huge plant, occupying over 750,000 square feet. But a lot of the space is currently unused.

Gone is most of the workforce. Some jobs and products that once flowed off the assembly lines have been taken over by some far-off "Asian tiger." Other jobs are victims of new technology—some new electronics products require half the labor of the products they replaced.

This is an all too familiar story in U.S. electronics plants. What happened? And what was the role of cost information?

It started back when the plant employed about 5,000 people. This was a time of turmoil for the parent company. It was coping with the aftershocks of rapid technological change and global competition.

As a result of these new forces, the plant saw a drop in market share for its products. This forced a layoff of over 2,500 employees in just one year.

A key problem for the plant was that the overhead cost was difficult to eliminate as volume went down. The direct work force was the easiest to reduce in step with volume. Laying off management and technical ranks, however, took more time. And other overhead costs—such as space, heating, and maintenance—just didn't go away.

The result was that volume decreased by half, but overhead went down only by a third. This dramatically increased overhead cost per unit of production—by 25% over the previous year.

This led to a dramatic cost increase for some products. The unit cost of one product, for example, went up by 25%, another by 40%.

This created a further problem for the plant. Since it was one of several plants located around the world, the parent company was constantly evaluating the issue of sourcing. Where in its manufacturing network should any given product be produced?

Answering sourcing questions was a complex issue that required consideration of product design, manufacturing technology, quality, and strategy in addition to cost. Cost was a key issue, however, because the plant went head to head with low-cost plants located in Asia. It was also key because of the drop in the plant's market share resulting from increased competition.

The company had a staff group that made recommendations for sourcing. This group required that every plant make calculations on a full-cost, *fully absorbed* basis.

This put the plant at a significant disadvantage because it had to include the costs of all excess capacity in fewer remaining products. In other words, the costs of manufacturing associated with activities and assets *not used* by the current products were included in their calculated product costs.

As a result, the plant lost its highest volume product in one year. This product was considered too costly to manufacture after its overhead rate increased by 65%.

The plant's response? It launched its *Excellence* program to introduce *world-class manufacturing* into the plant. Using just-in-time, focused factory, and other world-class concepts, the aim was to make the plant *world class* within a year. To do this, the program focused on cutting throughput times, improving quality, reducing cost, and focusing totally on the needs of its customers.

The Excellence program had immediate success. Throughput time on one product, for example, was reduced from 3-4 weeks under the old functional approach to 1 hour and 50 minutes on the first day of the new Excellence program. Asset turnover doubled as work-in-process inventories fell. Quality improved dramatically—about 99% of the products met customer quality standards by the following year.

These dramatic improvements were recognized when the plant received a national productivity award. The plant was also featured in business publications as one of the top plants in the United States and one of the best hopes that U.S. manufacturing could become competitive with the rest of the world.

Unfortunately, volume fell another 30% in year two. As a result, overhead cost per unit increased 36% over the previous year. This was despite the dramatic improvements in the plant's manufacturing capabilities and efficiencies *(Figure 2-5)*.

Year four saw the plant in a holding pattern. Market share increased in some key products. The additional volume—and continued improvements in efficiency—caused the overhead cost per unit to fall. Optimism increased.

However, the plant was actually just fighting a rearguard action. It was now below 50% capacity, and overhead cost per unit was still increasing despite continued improvements in quality and productivity. This cost increase was enough to push several products into the loss-making column. Another major product was pulled from the plant and moved offshore.

Much energy was expended to keep all remaining products by demonstrating the plant's ability to produce them efficiently. Emphasis was placed on strategic advantages in quality and service, particularly the ability to manufacture and ship product to customers on a timely basis. (After all, products manufactured at this plant for the U.S. market didn't have to spend six weeks on a boat from the Far East.)

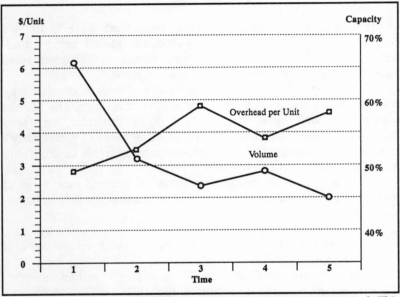

Figure 2-5. *The Death Spiral.* "Doing it right" doesn't guarantee survival. This electronics plant struggled to stay in business despite winning awards for quality, productivity, and service. The culprit?–a cost system that unfairly penalized products for excess plant capacity.

Would year five be the last flutter in the death spiral, or would the plant manage to survive for another year?

The bad news is that the plant has continued to lose products to offshore plants.

The good news is that the plant was able to continue operating. Some new products were introduced to replace current products. The plant introduced some innovative ways of distributing its products which reduced cost and improved customer service. Low-technology work (not suited to the plant's manufacturing capability) was moved to a new satellite plant in Mexico.

It looks like this plant will survive and prosper. What's frightening about this story, however, is that one of the best plants in the United States had to fight for survival. It's a story of a world-class plant in a losing battle with improper cost information.

Summary

It's clear that yesterday's cost systems don't work in today's competitive environment. This is because global competition, technological change, and information system development have radically changed the rules of the marketplace.

There have been equally dramatic changes in the way companies are coping with the competitive challenge. The phrase *world class* defines a new way of doing business, one that embraces continuous improvement in all aspects of a company's business. And the goal of the world-class company is to profitably meet the needs of its customers.

But, new ways of conducting business demand new ways of measuring performance. The world-class company needs information that:

- Shows what matters to its customers (such as quality and service),
- Reveals how profitable its customers and products are,
- Costs a reasonable amount to report,
- Identifies opportunities for improvement, and
- Encourages actions that enhance meeting customer needs profitably.

Conventional cost systems fail to do any of these things well. Such systems may have worked well in an earlier era, but the world-class company of the 1990s needs a different approach.

Criteria of world-class cost information.	Why conventional cost systems fail.
1. Customer focused	Indirect. No information about activities. Too late.
2. Reveals sources of profit	Plant activities only. Inaccurate product costs. No customer costs.
3. Economical	Intrusive. Many unnecessary transactions.
4. Identifies opportunities	Direct labor focus. Little information about activities. Functional silos.
5. Encourages improvement	Promotes excessive output and poor quality. Functional myopia. Misdirected effort. The death spiral.

Key Terms in Chapter 2

Continuous improvement–The relentless and on-going search for ways to improve business performance.

Death spiral–The sequential outsourcing or dropping of products in response to inaccurate cost information.

Flexibility–The ability to respond to changing customer needs quickly.

Focused factory–The organization of production around a narrow range of products to provide low cost and high throughput.

Full absorption–A requirement that all overhead costs, even those associated with unused capacity, be assigned to existing products.

Functional silos–Vertical dimensions of an organizational hierarchy where functional considerations override organizational considerations.

Just-in-time (JIT)– 1.) the determination of work load based on the use of output by the next activity; 2.) Continuous improvement.

Quality function deployment (QFD)–The design of products and processes based on customer requirements.

Real-time–Rapid reporting of data from an activity or process. Provides the ability to change the performance of the activity while the work continues.

World class–An organization that has achieved high standards of business performance and is continuously improving its ability to profitably meet its customers' needs.

References:

1. Richard J. Schonberger, *Building a Chain of Customers*, (New York: The Free Press, 1990).

2. Peter B.B. Turney and Bruce Anderson, "Accounting for Continuous Improvement," *Sloan Management Review*, (Winter 1989), pp. 37-48.

Part II

WHY ACTIVITY-BASED COSTING IS THE SOLUTION

OK, you're convinced.

Conventional costing not only *does not* work well, it's positively dangerous. The consequences of conventional costing—such as selling the wrong products, mispricing products, or improving the wrong things—are not acceptable in today's competitive world.

So what's the solution?

It's something called activity-based costing—or simply ABC for short.

ABC is not an upgrade of conventional approaches. It's too late for upgrades; the problem is too serious for "business as usual" solutions. What's needed is a radically different approach to costing—the ABC approach.

ABC is a methodology for providing information to help companies improve. In Part IV of this book you'll see how ABC is used in an activity-based improvement program.

For now, let's focus on the methodology itself. To do this, Part II shows you:

- What ABC is,
- Why ABC corrects the deficiencies of conventional cost systems,
- What ABC reveals about the problems you need to correct and the opportunities you should take advantage of, and
- Why ABC fits like a glove with the *world-class* approach to managing a company.

Chapter 3

THE ABC INNOVATIONS

Cost information should reveal problems to tackle and opportunities to exploit. But, as previous chapters show, that's not always the case. Conventional cost systems *actually* hide problems and fail to identify opportunities.

Relying on conventional cost information is quite similar to the situation of *Figure 3-1*. Conventional cost information is like the sea that hides dangerous rocks. On the surface, all appears calm and smooth; there's no inkling of unprofitable products and customers, and there's no hint of waste in the operations. And, like the unwary mariner, the good ship *World Class* sails on, oblivious to the dangers lurking below.

What the ship's officers need is a look below the surface of misinformation. This would reveal the rocks and shoals of poor quality, high cost, lack of responsiveness, improperly designed products, overpriced products, and neglected customers. These are the very things that sink the ships of enterprise in today's competitive world.

And nearby, lurk sharks of all kinds. Some may be hungry competitors looking for the opportunity to bite off parts of your business. Others may be hostile asset-strippers or hungry conglomerates. Trouble is the smell of blood to these sharks. Overpriced products, neglected markets, and underperforming assets are their feeding grounds.

Can the aspiring world-class company be saved from these perils?

Yes. It can.

Part of the solution is to lower the sea of inventory to reveal the rocks. This involves eliminating inventory buffers and long lead times that mask problems. As those problems become visible, they can be tackled. Set up times can be reduced, sources of poor quality can be eliminated, people can be trained and empowered and machines can be properly maintained so they don't break down.

A second part of the solution is to provide activity-based information about the rocks lurking below the surface. This information complements visual inspection of the rocks. It identifies what each one is, describes its importance (some rocks are more costly than others), and shows how successful you are in eliminating its threat.

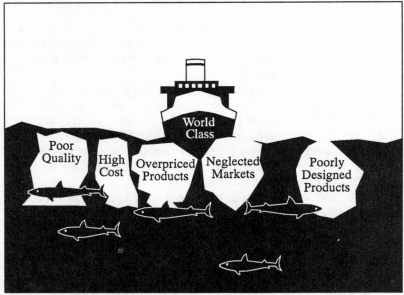

Figure 3-1. *Rocks and sharks.* Like submerged rocks, problems and opportunities are hidden from view. ABC information helps reveal and identify the problem rocks, improve competitive position, and avoid getting eaten by sharks.

Activity-based information also reveals those tasty morsels so prized by the sharks of competition. Which products and customers are unprofitable? Which products are improperly priced? Which profitable products and customers are being neglected? What opportunities are there for reducing the cost of products?

To answer such questions—to avoid the rocks and sharks—today's corporate ship needs a world-class navigation system. Activity-based costing (ABC) is just such an information system. ABC allows you to identify problems and plot safe courses to solutions and opportunities. It does this by providing cost and nonfinancial information about activities and cost objects.

Activities are descriptions of work that goes on in a company. Entering the details of a customer order at a computer terminal, setting up a machine, inspecting a part, and shipping a product are examples of activities.

Cost objects are the reasons for performing activities. They include products, services, and customers. Entering the details of a customer order at a computer terminal (*the activity*), for example, is performed because a customer (*the cost object*) wishes to place an order.

Activities and cost objects are basic to the ABC concept. This chapter shows you how ABC uses them to:

- Report more accurate cost information, and
- Provide useful information about activities.

You'll also find out:

- What ABC reveals about the rocks and sharks that lie in wait for the unwary, and
- How well ABC fits the information needs of aspiring world-class companies.

It's also important to realize that navigation by ABC information is imperative whether times are good or bad. The tide is in during boom times, covering up the rocks and sharks. Don't wait until the recession hits and the tide is out. You may already be on the rocks, with the sharks tearing you to pieces.

How ABC Gives You Accurate Cost Information

The underlying assumption of ABC is quite different from that of conventional costing. Conventional costing assumes that products cause cost. ABC is more realistic. As shown in *Figure 3-2*, ABC assumes that activities cause cost and that cost objects create the demand for activities.

As an example of how activities and cost objects work, let's say you're involved in auditing the quality of printed circuit boards. Auditing is an activity. It involves checking the thickness of the circuits, the placement and sizes of holes and pads, and the flatness of the board.

Performing the audit activity requires various resources. These include the salaries of individuals doing the work, equipment and software to measure and record the checks made on the boards, and floorspace for the work.

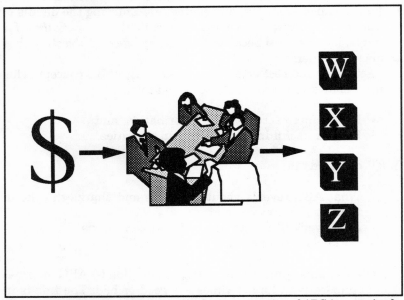

Figure 3-2. *The ABC assumption.* The basic assumption of ABC is very simple. Work is performed to create products and satisfy customers, and work requires incurring cost. This may be a simple concept, but it's exactly the way your company and every other company functions.

The auditing activity is performed on boards received from the finishing department. Receiving a batch of boards from finishing is the trigger that initiates the work associated with the activity. The boards themselves are the cost objects that demand activity (more boards means that the auditing activity must be performed more frequently).

ABC's underlying assumption makes intuitive sense when applied to an activity such as quality auditing. But why does it make a difference to the accuracy of reported cost information? To understand this, let's take a closer look at how ABC helps in costing the quality auditing activity.

The 1st Innovation—
Assigning Costs to Activities

The first innovation of ABC is assignment of costs to the auditing activity. This assignment is based on measurements of resources used.

Salary costs, for example, are assigned based on determinations of who is doing the work and how much of their time is spent on auditing boards. *Figure 3-3* shows the costs assigned to the auditing activity.

Test equipment depreciation	$58,000
Salaries and benefits	88,000
Space	61,000
Supplies	6,500
Fixtures	120,000
Total activity cost	$333,500
Number of boards tested	667,000
Cost per board	$0.50

Figure 3-3. *The cost of a quality auditing activity.* Cost information directs attention to high-cost activities and confirms that savings have been achieved subsequent to improvement.

Knowing what activities cost helps in identifying important activities—those with the greatest potential for cost reduction. Knowledge of activity cost also allows you to model the impact of cost reduction actions and to subsequently confirm that savings were achieved.

By and large, however, activities *are not defined* in conventional cost systems. You can learn about the cost of the quality control department, but you'll rarely find any information about the cost of the auditing activity within the departmental accounts.[1] This is unfortunate because activity cost knowledge is important.

In contrast, cost assignment in a conventional cost system is to departments or cost centers. The auditing activity, for example, could be a cost center in a conventional cost system. In some cases, cost centers are defined so narrowly that they are equivalent to activities.

The 2nd Innovation—
Cost Assignment to Cost Objects

ABC's second innovation is the way in which costs are assigned to cost objects. *ABC assigns activity costs to cost objects based on activity drivers that accurately measure consumption of the activity.*

The ABC Methodology

ABC is a method for assigning cost and measuring performance. It uses technical terms—such as *activity driver*—to describe how the assignment and measurement works.

This chapter avoids the use of technical terms wherever possible. A complete description of the ABC conceptual model is found in Chapter 4. Definitions of all the terms in this model are included in Chapters 4 and 5.

An activity driver is a measure of the consumption of an activity by a cost object (such as a product). The number of hours devoted by engineers to each product, for example, measures each product's consumption of engineering activity.

In the case of the auditing activity, for example, *number of batches* best measures the consumption of the activity by each type of board. This is because the quality audit is only performed on one board in each batch received.

Figure 3-4 shows how this works for two different types of printed circuit boards. The activity driver *number of batches* assigns two times more ABC cost to Board B than it assigns to A. This is correct, because Board B is audited twice, whereas Board A is audited only once.

The audit cost per batch in *Figure 3-4* is the same for both products ($50). This assumption is correct if the quality audit of each board takes roughly the same length of time and uses the same resources regardless of the product checked.

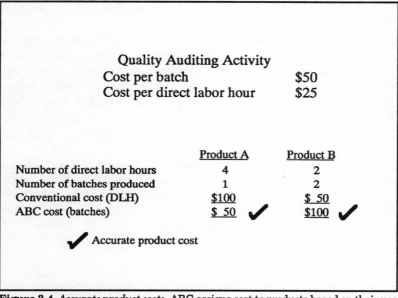

Figure 3-4. *Accurate product costs*. ABC assigns cost to products based on their use of activities, which is cost per batch in this example. The result is accurate product costs.

If this were not true (if, for example, Board A requires significantly more checking time because it has more holes), then a different activity driver would be used. *Number of holes checked*, for example, might then be a better activity driver, because it would capture variations in effort from one board type to another.

Now, let's take a moment to look at how conventional costing treats the same auditing example.

Conventional costing uses direct labor hours as the activity driver. Direct labor hours is a measurement of the "touch labor" needed to produce a unit of the product.

In *Figure 3-4*, the cost assigned to B by direct labor hours is half that assigned to A. This is because B uses half the labor hours of A.

This would only be correct, however, if the amount of direct labor correlated well with the number of batches. In this case, it doesn't, so the two products are miscosted by substantial margins. Product A is overcosted by 100%, and Product B is undercosted by 50%.

The inaccuracy in conventional costing for this example is no accident. It results from limitations in the activity driver used to assign cost; direct labor hours *does not* accurately measure the use of the auditing activity by the products.

ABC corrects for this inaccuracy by choosing an activity driver that does accurately measure cost consumption by each product. In this case, the driver is the number of batches. However, it could have been the number of holes checked, the number of checking hours, or the number of direct labor hours if the facts had been different.

In short, ABC is generally superior to conventional costing because it reports more accurate product costs. This occurs because ABC uses *more* activity drivers and more *types* of activity drivers than conventional costing. Like a toolkit that contains a wide range of tools, ABC uses different activity drivers to fit different circumstances.

The number of activity drivers. It's common to find ten to thirty activity drivers in the typical ABC system. However, some ABC systems have as few as two activity drivers and some have as many as a hundred. Conventional systems, on the other hand, usually have one activity driver; occasionally they have as many as three.

More activity drivers allow ABC to "do it more ways" than conventional cost systems. Most companies have many activities that are consumed in different ways. It's unlikely that one activity driver (such as direct labor hours) can capture this diversity even in a small company.

Types of activity drivers. Another fundamental innovation of ABC is the recognition that there are different levels of activity in most organizations. Different activity levels require different types of activity drivers *(Figure 3-5).*[2]

Let's start by looking at three levels of activities that exist in many manufacturing companies:

- *Unit* activities are performed on units of the product. Tapping threads in a metal elbow is an example of a unit activity.

Activity	Activity driver
Unit	
Assembly	Direct labor hours
Stamping	Machine hours
Batch	
Moving material	Number of movements
Inspecting first piece	Number of runs
Product	
Modifying product design	Engineering change notices
Maintaining routings	Number of part numbers
Customer	
Processing customer orders	Number of customer orders
Sustaining	
Managing the plant	(No good activity driver available)

Figure 3-5. *Activity and driver levels.* ABC recognizes that activities relate to cost objects at different levels, and different levels require different activity drivers. In the case of sustaining activities, it is not possible to meaningfully assign the cost to products or customers.

- *Batch* activities are performed on batches of products rather than individual product units. Setting up a machine to produce a batch of products or inspecting the first piece of the batch are examples of batch activities.
- *Product* activities benefit all units of a particular product. An example is preparing a numerical control (NC) program for a product.

Accurate assignment of the cost of unit activities is accomplished by using measures of the product unit. The number of direct labor hours needed to tap threads in a metal elbow, for example, accurately measures operator effort.

Unit activity drivers are the *only* activity drivers found in conventional cost systems. Direct labor hours, machine hours, material cost, and product units are all used as unit activity drivers.

The problem is that unit activity drivers do not accurately cost non-unit activities. You need batch activity drivers for batch activities, and product activity drivers for product activities.

Let's see why this is the case.

In *Figure 3-6*, making tools and dies is a product activity; it benefits all the units produced of each product type. The cost of this activity ($1,000) is assigned to the two products using a *unit activity driver* (the number of units) and a *product activity driver* (the number of products).

Under ABC in *Figure 3-6*, the product activity driver assigns an equal amount of cost ($500) to each product. This assumes that each product requires the same amount of effort to manufacture tools and dies.

Product B, however, is a low-volume product, so its cost per unit ($10) is much higher than that of Product A ($2.50). This makes sense, because Product A is able to share its activity cost over a larger number of units ($500/200).

Under conventional cost in *Figure 3-6*, the unit activity driver assigns cost directly to the product units. This has two results. First, each unit receives an identical amount of cost ($4). Second, Product A has more product units than B, so in total, A receives the lion's share of the cost ($4 x 200).

Both of these conventional costing results are wrong. *It's the products that benefit equally, not the units*. The high-volume product shouldn't pick up more cost simply because it's successful.

ABC avoids these conventional costing errors by picking activity drivers that match the type of activity. Setting up a machine to produce a batch of parts is costed using the number of set up hours or the number of production runs. Changing the engineering specifications of a product is costed using the number of engineering change notices or the number of engineering change hours.

Assignment to Customers. ABC's activity cost assignment innovation works just as well for customers as it does for products. The difference is that the cost of customer activities is assigned to customers rather than products.

Examples of customer activities are processing customer orders and providing engineering and logistics support. Activity costs are assigned to customers using activity drivers such as the number of customer orders and the number of customers.

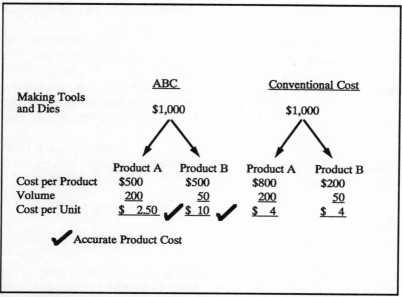

Figure 3-6. *Accurate cost assignment.* ABC traces the cost of sustaining products to each product type. As a result, high-volume products correctly receive less cost per unit than low-volume products.

ABC also makes customer profitability analysis possible. It provides new perspectives about service to customers and opens up opportunities that don't exist in conventional cost systems.

The Reporting Limitations of ABC. There are limits to ABC's ability to report accurate product costs. This is because there are always some activities not directly associated with products or customers. Activities that sustain a plant, for example, are very difficult to assign to products. Such activities include cleaning, securing, and landscaping the plant.

It's fairly easy, however, to assign cost to these sustaining activities. The cost of an alarm monitoring service, for example, can be assigned directly to the plant security activity. The cost of a landscaping service can be assigned to the landscaping activity.

But you can't assign the cost of these activities to products directly. You don't landscape products (or customers), and it's not possible to obtain information about the landscaping cost of each product.

There *are* two possible solutions. The first is *not to assign* the cost of sustaining activities to products. This recognizes the difficulty of assigning these costs to products in any meaningful way.

The second solution is to assign the cost of sustaining activities using nonmatching activity drivers. For example, the cost of landscaping can be assigned to products based on direct labor hours (a unit activity driver). Alternatively, the cost can be distributed evenly to each product. This ensures that the cost reaches the products, but it's not clear that the result has any economic meaning.

The lesson is this: ABC reports more accurate costs than conventional costing, but it isn't perfect. Use ABC information with confidence *and* with care.

The 3rd Innovation— Information About Activities

The third innovation of ABC is the improved quality of information about activities. In addition to cost information, you find nonfinancial information about the work that is done.

For example, there's a lot of useful nonfinancial information you should know about the quality auditing activity *(Figure 3-7)*. The number of holes in the circuit boards and the density of the circuitry determine how much effort is required to perform the activity. (More holes and greater density require more work). These determining factors are called *cost drivers*.

It's also important to know how well the activity is carried out. Indicators of the results achieved in an activity are called *performance measures*.

The primary performance measure for quality auditing is the frequency of warranty returns. This measure should be zero if the audit is done right every time. A second measure is how often the checker's inspection mark is missing from a board. A batch that isn't stamped as checked will be returned by the customer.

The ABC analysis in *Figure 3-7* shows that the auditing activity is a *non-value-added* activity. A non-value-added activity is one that *does not* contribute to the value received by the customer.

Quality Auditing Activity

Type of activity:
- Non-value-added

Cost drivers:
- Number of holes
- Density of circuitry

Performance measures:
- % of boards returned
- % of boards not marked

Figure 3-7. *Information about performance.* In addition to the costing benefits of ABC, nonfinancial information, such as shown here, permits judgements about performance.

The purpose of the auditing activity is to catch defects in the printed circuit boards. The defects can then be corrected prior to shipment to the customer.

This is a valuable contribution as long as the quality of prior processes is suspect. But the customer does not value the auditing per se. Instead, the customer values the quality of the boards.

A better cost solution is to improve the quality of prior processes so much that the auditing activity is no longer necessary to ensure that the customer receives a quality product. At that point, the auditing activity can be discontinued without any negative impact, and cost is reduced.

Providing nonfinancial information such as this may be the most important contribution of ABC. Its purpose is to help improve the activity. It is, after all, better to improve or eliminate work than to more accurately assign the cost of unnecessary work to products or customers.

ABC supplies a powerful combination of nonfinancial and cost information. These two types of information work together to help manage and improve the performance of the company.

The Drama of ABC

Introducing ABC into a company has a dramatic impact. Perceptions about profitability–about which products and customers are profitable and which are unprofitable–completely change. The understanding of where and why cost is incurred changes, too.

You may suspect that many of your products are unprofitable. You may have seen case studies that show the extent to which ABC reveals miscosted and unprofitable products. But there is nothing that really prepares you for the truth about your own company.

Once you're over the shock, what do you do with this radically new picture of your company?

The first step is to grasp the implications of the ABC information. Which products and customers are unprofitable? Does your product mix need changing? Is your market focus wrong? Should you redesign your products? Is overhead cost too high? What opportunities are there for cost reduction?

The second step is to create an action plan for improvement. This plan lays out the specific actions needed to improve your competitive position.

As an example, let's look at the impact of ABC at one company. It's a dramatic story, but one that has been repeated at plant after plant.

The Case of the Printed Circuit Board Plant

> At the time we moved into the marketplace we had none of the skills and experience of our competitors. Our performance was poor and we were losing money. Fifty percent of our products were generating less than three percent of our revenues. However, we didn't have accurate cost information, so we didn't know how unprofitable these products were.
>
> *—General Manager of the Plant*

The story began when the Printed Circuit Board Plant (PCB) received permission to sell to outside customers in 1986. Previously, PCB sold only to other parts of its parent company.

Venturing into the marketplace created major challenges for PCB. How do you set prices for the printed circuit boards? (Products were previously priced according to parent company transfer price rules.) Which products would provide the most profit potential? Which customers should be the target of sales efforts?

PCB was certainly not short of choices. It manufactured over 4,000 different types of printed circuit boards. These boards varied in number of layers, density and placement of circuitry, fineness of the metal lines, and size and placement of the holes.

PCB produced boards that covered all segments of the printed circuit board market. These segments covered a wide range of products from simple low-technology boards, to complex high-technology boards.

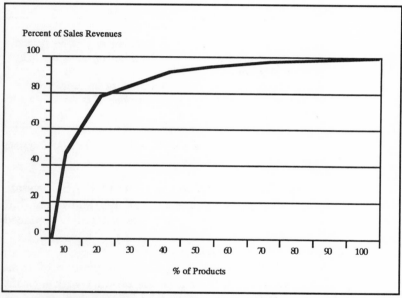

Figure 3-8. *The Pareto effect.* Pareto's rule (20% of what you do accounts for 80% of what you care about) is alive and well in this company. The large numbers of products with low sales value owes a lot to inaccurate cost information.

The conventional cost system. PCB's cost system in 1986 reported two types of cost. Material cost consisted of sheets of copper, fiberglass laminate, and metals (such as gold and nickel) used in plating. Material costs were traced to boards via the bill of materials. All other manufacturing costs (overhead plus direct labor) were assigned to boards using machine hours. Non-manufacturing costs were expensed.

Few at PCB would have staked their reputation on the accuracy of product costs reported by this system. It was felt that a single activity driver (machine hours) *could not cope* with the complexity and range of activities in the production process. Also, excluding nonmanufacturing costs—about 40% of total cost—was believed to be a critical omission.

A review of the relationship between products and sales revenues provided a startling premonition of what would be learned from ABC *(Figure 3-8)*: 60% of the products accounted for only 6% of the plant's revenues. It seemed likely that the effort required to sustain these low-value products greatly exceeded the revenues earned.

• Number of work orders	• Number of times pressed
• Number of customer orders	• Number of holes drilled
• Number of part numbers	• Number of sides
• Square feet per circuit board	• Image perimeter
• Number of layers	• Number of tests
• Number of sheets	

Figure 3-9. *Activity drivers.* Examples of activity drivers used by the ABC system employed at the Printed Circuit Board Plant.

ABC's Impact. The decision to implement an ABC system was made in 1987. It took two years to complete the system, but the design was radically different from the system it replaced *(Figure 3-9)*.

The results were quite startling, too.

Products—The old cost system painted a picture of comfortable profitability. There wasn't a single product with a profit margin of less than 26%.

The picture portrayed by ABC couldn't have been more different. Fifty percent of the products were unprofitable when only manufacturing costs were included. Over 75% of the products were unprofitable when all costs, including the nonmanufacturing costs, were included. *Figure 3-10* shows what this picture looks like for a representative product line.

How could such a radical shift in cost and profitability occur?

Let's examine one of the products that looked quite different under the two systems *(Figure 3-11)*.

The ABC manufacturing cost of board XYZ is 542% higher than the old standard cost ($4.30 versus $0.67). The total cost is a whopping 2,930% more than the old cost.

Why such big increases in cost?

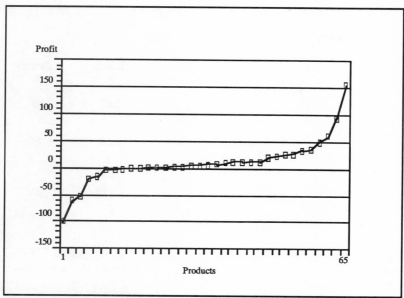

Figure 3-10. *New perceptions of product profitability.* The PCB plant thought that all products were profitable by a comfortable margin. But a close look at this product line, using ABC as the navigational aid, showed that over a quarter of the products were unprofitable (based on manufacturing costs), and over a half of them were no better than breakeven.

The old cost system used machine hours to assign cost to the boards. This resulted in a "peanut butter" spread of overhead across different products regardless of variations in volume and use of nonmachine activities.

The fact was, board XYZ required extra nonmachine activities and special handling. For example, the board required hand taping and untaping of the gold borders, hand pinning and unpinning of each image during routing, extra baking of the edges, and hand sanding of the edges. All this special handling required additional support overhead. None of these "extras" were picked up by machine hours.

On the nonmanufacturing side, the cost of accepting and launching an order of board XYZ was estimated by ABC to be $800. With only 50 units manufactured, the ordering cost per unit was $16.

Printed Circuit Board #XYX

	Price $	Cost $	Margin $	Margin %
Conventional standard cost	1.00	0.67	0.33	33
ABC Manufacturing cost	1.00	4.30	(3.30)	(330)
ABC total product cost	1.00	20.30	(19.30)	(1,930)

Figure 3-11. *The cost of low-volume, specialty products increases by orders of magnitude.* ABC radically changes perceptions of cost and profitability for low-volume, specialty products such as this one.

None of the real costs of the board were known under the old cost system. So, at a selling price of $1 per board, PCB was happy with the profit margin of 33% reported by the old cost system. In reality, the margin was about a negative 2,000%—not a cause for happiness, but rather a cause for action.

Customers—An ABC analysis of customer profitability was a real shocker.

Several key customers were found to be extremely unprofitable. These were customers that had previously appeared profitable under the old cost system. As a result, they had been targeted with additional sales effort.

Let's look at a typical customer. This customer bought 22 different boards from PCB, all of them reported as profitable by the old system. Six of these products were also reported as profitable by the ABC, but the remaining 16 were losing money.

Figure 3-12 shows the bottom line. Although the first few products are profitable, the addition of losing products brings down the cumulative profit earned from the customer. By the time all the money losers are included, PCB lost nearly $45,000. This represented 30% of the revenues earned from the customer.

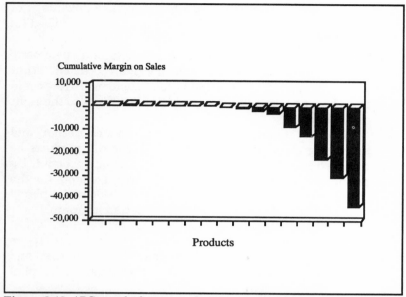

Figure 3-12. *ABC reveals the true profitability of customers.* ABC shows a loss of about $45,000 on this customer. This stunning revelation contrasts with a previous picture of solid profitability. The question: Why was marketing spending so much time with this customer?

Management buy-in—How did management respond to such shocking information?

Production, engineering and general management bought in readily. But marketing initially rejected the results.

A profitability analysis of key customers was presented to a meeting that included representatives of marketing. The marketing staff rejected the ABC costs and walked out of the meeting.

Such resistance was not surprising. Marketing had put a lot of effort into those customers, and it was natural that they felt let down. The ABC information was correct, but it showed that their efforts were misdirected.

Further discussions turned the situation around. Marketing eventually accepted the validity of the ABC methodology and the ABC information. From that point, the marketing department was in the vanguard of the changes that ensued.

Plan for change–PCB moved rapidly to take advantage of the knowledge gained from ABC. In particular, ABC was used to:

- Develop a strategy for targeting products and customers. (Which market segments should the plant focus on? What was the profile of the desired type of customer? How could sales be guided to sell the right kind of products to the right customers?)
- Develop a strategy for improving product design and improving the production process. (How could products be designed to reduce cost? Which cost reduction opportunities promised the greatest payoff? What arrangements for the supply of raw materials best served the needs of the plant? What performance measures were most appropriate?)

The lessons? Be prepared for dramatic results. Take active steps to ensure that everyone in the company buys into ABC and the actions that are implied. And, finally, prepare an action plan that ensures positive change.

How PCB used ABC information to guide these decisions is an important part of the story. We'll return to PCB in Chapter 9 to see how the plant was transformed into a world-class competitor.

Supplying Information for the World-Class Company

In Chapter 2, we saw how conventional cost systems fail to report useful information for the aspiring world-class company. In this chapter we've looked at ABC, a radical replacement for conventional costing. How does ABC stack up?

What matters to the customer. ABC reports information about what matters to the customer–how well each activity contributes to the needs of customers. Measures of performance in quality, time, and cost, for example, are reported for each activity.

ABC reports this information when you need it. The PCB plant, for example, reports the cost of poor quality in each process on a shift-by-shift basis (three times per day). This information is used daily to set priorities for efforts to eliminate quality-related problems.

Customer and product profitability. ABC reports *accurate* customer and product costs. It does so by using more and more types of activity drivers to assign cost to customers and products. It also assigns nonmanufacturing cost in addition to manufacturing cost. The result is that ABC costs often differ substantially from conventional costs.

Economical to implement, easy to use. Experience with companies that have implemented ABC suggests that ABC can be modest in cost. In particular, ABC doesn't require the heavy volume of otherwise unnecessary measurements common in conventional systems.

The DeVilbiss Company Limited

The DeVilbiss Company Limited manufactures spray gun products in the United Kingdom. A proponent of world-class manufacturing techniques, DeVilbiss saw ABC as a more accurate and relevant costing method in this new environment.

Depending on the circumstances, ABC can be extremely low cost. The DeVilbiss Company Limited, for example, completed an ABC study in forty-eight hours using a small spreadsheet on a desktop computer. While the study was limited to just four major product lines and relied on management's rough estimates of cost consumption, the information was used to win a major export order.[3]

Insights on how to improve. ABC supplies cost and nonfinancial information about the company's activities. This information directs improvement efforts and provides feedback on what the improvement has accomplished.

For example, The Oregon Cutting Systems Division of Blount was surprised by the extent of waste associated with a batch processing activity. This waste was revealed by their ABC system. The batch processing activity was a large process that required lengthy setup, and parts movement to and from the process. This centralized approach was inconsistent with Oregon Cutting

Oregon Cutting Systems Division

The Oregon Cutting Systems Division of Blount, Inc., is the world's leading manufacturer of cutting chain for chainsaws and chainsaw accessories. It sells its products to professional loggers, chainsaw manufacturers, and consumers in 112 countries on six continents. Formerly Omark Industries, Oregon Cutting Systems was a U.S. pioneer in applying world-class manufacturing techniques.

Criteria of world-class cost information	Why ABC works
1. Is customer focused	Information about what matters to the customer, when you want it.
2. Reveals profit sources	Accurate product and customer costs. Includes nonmanufacturing and manufacturing costs.
3. Economical	Does not require unnecessary measurements. Can be as simple or as complex as necessary.
4. Identifies opportunities	Cost and nonfinancial information about activities, helps direct and reinforce improvement efforts.
5. Encourages improvement	Direct measures of activity performance. Activity drivers help identify improvement opportunities. The problem of excess capacity is confronted head on.

Systems' cellular manufacturing; the cost and time associated with the extra activities were excessive.

Encourages improvement. ABC sends the right signals, signals that encourage continued improvement. Direct measurements of activity performance—quality, time, and cost—focus the activity on what is important to customers.

Carefully chosen activity drivers correctly signal cost-reduction opportunities. For example, the activity driver *number of different part types* shows that products with many low-volume parts are costly. It also shows that redesigning products with high-volume common components reduces cost.

Additionally, ABC does not require the full absorption of cost. The cost associated with the unused capacity of a plant is not attached to products or customers in ABC. Rather, it is correctly separated as a cost of excess capacity. The death spiral, an inadvertent consequence of the full absorption of cost is, therefore, not associated with or promoted by ABC.

Summary

Even the best run company has problems and opportunities—rocks and clear channels—that are hidden from view. And there are always hungry competitors—the sharks— waiting to take advantage of those who run aground on the rocks.

ABC provides important information about problems and opportunities. It reports accurate cost information that leads to a better understanding of product and customer profitability. It also provides information about activities that is useful in directing and accelerating improvement efforts.

And, unlike conventional costing, ABC fits the information needs of the aspiring world-class company. It helps keep you off the rocks and out of the jaws of hungry sharks.

Key Terms in Chapter 3

Activity–A description of the work that goes on in the organization and consumes resources. Testing materials is an example of an activity.

Activity-based costing (ABC)–A method of measuring the cost and performance of activities and cost objects. Assigns cost to activities based on their use of resources, and assigns cost to cost objects based on their use of activities. ABC recognizes the causal relationship of cost drivers to activities.

Activity driver–A factor that measures activity consumption by a cost object. If drilling holes is an activity performed on a board, the number of holes drilled could be an activity driver.

Batch activity–An activity that is performed on a batch of a product. Inspecting the first piece of each batch is a batch activity.

Cost driver–An event or causal factor that influences the level and performance of activities and the resulting consumption of resources. The percent of parts received that are defective is an example of a cost driver.

Cost object–The reason for performing an activity. Products and customers are reasons for performing activities.

Non-value-added activity–An activity that is judged *not to* contribute to customer value. Also, an activity that can be eliminated without reducing the quantity or quality of output. An example is the activity of moving parts back and forth.

Performance measure–An indicator of the work performed and the results achieved in an activity. An example is the average elapsed time to perform an activity.

Product activity–An activity that benefits all units of a type of product. Changing engineering specifications on a product is a product activity.

Sustaining activity–An activity that benefits a part of the organization rather than a product or customer. Landscaping the plant is an example.

Unit activity–An activity that is performed on a unit of a product. Inserting a resistor into a printed circuit board is an example of a unit activity.

References:

1.   German cost systems have been documented that have as many as a thousand cost centers. There are so many cost centers that each one may represent an activity. See, for example, Robert S. Kaplan, "Metabo GmbH & Co. KG," Case 9-189-146 (Boston: Harvard Business School), 1989.

2.   The idea that there are different types of activities is not new. Authors that have discussed these concepts include Dunne, P.M. and Wolk, H.I., "Marketing Cost Analysis: A Modularized Contribution Approach," *Journal of Marketing*, (July 1977), pp. 83-94; Crissy, W.J.E. and Mossman, F.H., "Matrix Models for Marketing Planning: An Update and Expansion," MSU Business Topics, (Autumn 1977), pp. 17-26; and "Report on the Committee on Cost and Profitability Analyses for Marketing," *The Accounting Review Supplement*, (1972), pp. 575-615. R. Cooper was the first to identify unit, batch, product, and process activities as characteristics of activity-based cost systems in "Cost Classification in Unit-Based and Activity-Based Manufacturing Cost Systems," *Journal of Cost Management*, (Fall 1990), pp. 4-14. P.B.B. Turney and J. Reeve extended this analysis and included customer activities in "The Impact of Continuous Improvement on the Design of Activity-Based Cost Systems", (Summer 1990), pp. 43-50.

3.   The DeVilbiss example was provided by World Class International, Ltd.

Part III

WHAT ABC LOOKS LIKE

This section answers the question: What does an ABC system look like? A detailed answer is provided for both the user and the designer. It describes how ABC systems are organized to supply information about a company's activities, products, and customers.

If you're interested in improving your company's ability to profitably meet customers' needs, this section tells you:

- *What* information is available in an ABC system,
- *How* information can be pulled from the system in a useful form, and
- *Why* that information is useful.

And, if you're interested in designing an ABC system, this section also describes:

- The *architecture* of the system,
- The *types* of information you must create within the system, and
- The *attributes* you must add to the system to make it easy to extract useful information.

Chapter 4 uses the ABC model to show you what modern activity-based costing looks like. This provides an introduction to the *cost* and *process* dimensions of ABC— what they are and why they are important.

Chapter 5 takes you a step further by laying out the building blocks of an ABC system. This is a decidedly nontechnical tour of the mechanics of activity-based costing. You'll find out what each building block is and how each one yields valuable strategic and operational information.

Chapter 6 shows you how to make important ABC information "jump out at you." A wealth of tips are provided for enhancing the meaning of information in the data base. You'll also see how information and activities can be organized for improved decision support.

The ABC concepts described in these chapters parallel the Computer Aided Manufacturing International (CAM-I) *Glossary of Activity-Based Management*. The ABC model, the building blocks, and all terminology follow the industry standards adopted in this CAM-I document.[1]

---

1.   Peter B.B. Turney and Norm Raffish, *A Glossary of Activity-Based Management*, (Dallas: Computer Aided Manufacturing International), 1991.

Chapter 4

THE ABC MODEL

The power of activity-based costing is in its ability to clearly portray cost and nonfinancial information. This includes portrayal of the relationships between the two as well.

These capabilities are best described through an overall, two-dimensional model. This is a model that's significantly different from those used in guiding earlier ABC applications. Those earlier models were essentially one-dimensional and limited in their abilities to provide cost and process information about activities.

Even with their limitations, the earlier one-dimensional models were still far more enlightening than other tools in use at that time. Indeed, those first successes formed a solid foundation for the evolution of ABC. Thus, it's certainly worthwhile to begin any introduction from those earlier applications.

With an understanding of the one-dimensional foundation, discussion can then proceed to the current two-dimensional model. This second-generation model contains both cost and nonfinancial information about activities and provides a more powerful management tool.

Early Activity-Based Costing

Early ABC systems were designed for strategic purposes. Specifically, they were designed and viewed as tools for improving the accuracy of reported product costs. They proved themselves in helping to determine better product mixes and to set prices based on both actual cost and customer willingness to pay.

You've read of some early ABC successes in previous chapters. For example, you saw how small, yet significant, strategic gains could come quickly in one back-of-the-envelope study. You also saw how strategic insights from other, more in-depth, ABC studies could be so significant as to suggest changes in business direction.

These and other successes set the course for early ABC systems. The primary objectives of these systems were:

- To improve the accuracy of product costs by carefully changing the type and number of factors used to assign cost; and
- To use this information to improve product mix and pricing decisions.

The Use of Early Systems

The initial objective of ABC in most plants in the late 1980s was strategic product costing. But that's *not* how most plants ended up using ABC information.

In plant after plant—at Honeywell, Northern Telecom, General Motors, and others—ABC systems were designed for strategic product costing. In plant after plant, the systems were eventually put to other uses. These included:

- *Additional strategic uses,* such as profitability analyses of customers, markets, and distribution channels; and
- *Internal improvement uses,* such as activity management, waste identification, prioritizing cost reduction opportunities, and simulating costs of alternative product designs.

This broadened usage was a direct result of the wealth of information that companies found in their ABC data bases. In addition to more accurate product costs, there was information about the work going on, the resources required to perform this work, and reasons why the work was being performed.

In plant after plant, managers scoured their ABC data bases for insights into how to improve their production processes. Where was the greatest opportunity to eliminate waste? What specific changes in product design would lead to the greatest improvement in competitiveness for that product?

This search yielded useful information to support improvement efforts. But it also supplied an equal amount of frustration and confusion. It was difficult to use an ABC system for one purpose—

internal improvement–when it was designed for a different purpose–*product costing.*

The Limitations of Early Systems

The primary limitation of early systems was the absence of direct information about activities. This basically was a result of how overhead cost was dealt with.

Overhead cost was divided into broad cost pools. Each cost pool corresponded to a group of activities that were consumed by products in approximately the same way. The activities themselves, however, were not defined individually. As a result, cost *was not* traced to each activity. It was also impossible for the system to include operational data about the performance of activities.

This situation can be explored further with the aid of *Figure 4-1*. This figure illustrates an early system used at the John Deere Component Works (JDCW) to cost screw-machine parts.

The system in *Figure 4-1* divides overhead cost into seven broad cost pools. Each cost pool contains the cost of activities consumed by products in roughly the same way. Also, each cost pool is assigned to products using a unique factor that approximates the consumption of cost.

For example, look at the overhead cost pool for activities associated with production orders. Overhead consumption is assigned to the screw-machine parts using *the number of production orders*. Each individual screw machine part consumes cost from the pool based on the *cost per production order* multiplied by *the number of times the part was ordered.*

For John Deere, this ABC system met the strategic goal of significantly improving the accuracy of reported costs. Products that were heavy consumers of activities were assigned more cost than products that were light consumers. For example, a frequently scheduled part received more cost than one scheduled once per year.

More accurate product costs provided a *definite strategic advantage* for John Deere. At the time, JDCW was emerging from a sheltered role as a captive division to become a competitive entity that sold products to other companies. To do this successfully, JDCW needed accurate cost information to guide the choice of products to sell externally and to help set prices. ABC filled this need.[1]

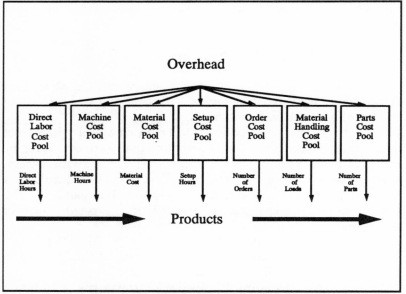

Figure 4-1. *An early ABC system.* Early ABC systems, like this one at John Deere, broke overhead cost into multiple cost pools and used innovative ways of assigning cost to products. The result was a significant increase in the accuracy of reported product costs and important strategic insights.

Despite its clear advantages in supporting strategic decisions about product mix and price, the JDCW system was of limited help in supporting internal improvement. The system did not reveal the cost of individual activities, nor did it provide operational data about the performance of those activities.

Early ABC systems such as the one at John Deere could not be used to answer key operational questions. For example, how long did it take to perform the key activities? What was the quality associated with these activities? What factors increased the time and effort required to perform the key activities? The activity information required to answer these questions existed *outside* those early ABC systems.

Two-Dimensional Activity-Based Costing

The desire for operational information about activities led to the appearance of second-generation ABC. This second-generation was specifically designed to supply information for internal as well as external improvement purposes.

Second-generation ABC has two main views. The first is the *cost assignment view*. This is the vertical part of the model shown in *Figure 4-2*.[2] It reflects the need for organizations to assign costs to activities and cost objects (including customers as well as products) in order to analyze critical decisions. These decisions include pricing, product mix, sourcing, product design decisions, and setting priorities for improvement efforts.

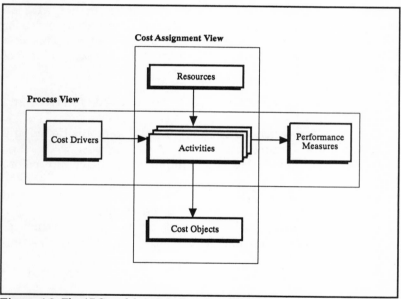

Figure 4-2. *The ABC model.* Activity-based costing has come a long way in a short period of time. Once thought of as just a better way of costing products, ABC now has more points of focus and additional uses. Cost and nonfinancial information work together to yield strategic and operational insights.

The second part of the ABC model is the *process view*. This is the horizontal part of the model in *Figure 4-2*.

The process view reflects the need of organizations for a *new* category of information. This is information about events that influence the performance of activities and activity performance—that is, what causes work and how well is it done. Organizations can use this type of information to help improve performance and the value received by customers.

Let's take a closer look at the cost assignment and process views, beginning with the cost assignment view.

The ABC Cost Assignment View

The cost assignment view provides information about resources, activities, and cost objects. The underlying assumption is that cost objects create the need for activities, and activities create the need for resources.

Let's examine this underlying assumption further with an example. Assume that a valve manufacturer receives an order for a specific type of valve. The order is the cost object. This cost object—filling the order—might require the following kinds of activities:

- Required materials are identified, ordered, received, and stocked;
- Production is scheduled, and material is requisitioned and moved to the production area;
- Tapping and machining equipment are set up before production;
- The materials are melted in a foundry, molds are made, and the molten metal is poured into the molds;
- When the metal cools, the molds are broken and removed, and the parts are machined, tapped, finished, and assembled;
- The first piece of each production run is inspected for defects;
- Parts are moved from one process to another upon completion of each process step;
- The completed valves are inspected, packed, and shipped to the customer; and
- The customer is invoiced, and payment is received and processed.

The cost object—the order for valves—creates a demand for activities. The activities, in turn, create a demand for resources. The *flow of cost*, however, is in the opposite direction. This is shown by the arrows in *Figure 4-2*. Notice that the flow of cost is from the resources to the activities and then from the activities to the cost objects.

To explore this flow further, consider salaries and other costs for the valve inspection activity. The amount of salaries assigned is determined by the number of people performing this activity, the proportion of their time spent on the activity, and their salary level. Other costs are assigned in some logical way reflecting their use by the activity. The total cost of the inspection activity is then assigned to the valves based on the frequency of inspection and the effort expended to complete inspection of each type of valve.

This cost information, provided by a second-generation ABC system, is quite different from that of early ABC systems. You still get markedly more accurate product costs. But you also get high-quality information about activities and cost objects.

Information about activities. Unlike earlier systems, second-generation systems identify the significant activities and attach cost to them. Knowing the cost of activities makes it easier to understand why resources are used. Moreover, the information provided makes it much easier to address such questions as:

- Which activities require the most resources?
- What types of resources are required by these activities? and
- Where are the opportunities for cost reduction?

It was difficult to answer such questions with early ABC systems because they focused on accurate product costs rather than on improved information about activities.

Information about customers. Second-generation ABC systems have more points of focus. For example, they've added the customer as a cost object. This makes sense, since customers often vary in their needs for support. Also, customer-support activities *are costly* in many companies.

Careful study in one plant, for example, revealed that several key customers were actually unprofitable customers. This certainly came as a shock to marketing. Key customers are supposed to be profitable; that's why they're *key*.

But in this case, the fact was that marketing had been misled. The conventional cost system had shown that the key customers were profitable. Consequently, marketing had put a lot of effort into building up these customers.

What's Wrong with Overhead?

Traditional accounting descriptions of indirect cost have negative connotations. The term *overhead* implies disconnection from the real work of the organization. The term *burden* suggests a handicap for those unfortunate enough to bear it.

A distinction between *overhead* and *direct cost* is meaningless in today's company. For one thing, ABC has taught us that much of the overhead is direct to activities, and via the activities, direct to products and customers.

For another, overhead is the only significant nonmaterial cost in many companies. Direct labor is in danger of being relegated to the history books in some manufacturing companies. In most service organizations, overhead is the only important cost category.

By contrast, the term *resources* covers all types of cost, regardless of traditional distinctions or type of organization. The concept of a resource also evokes an image of opportunity. After all, resources represent people, computers, technology, equipment and other factors that allow productive activity to take place and the customer to be served.

Without ABC, marketing wouldn't have discovered the high cost of supporting their key customers. They would also have been blissfully unaware of the strategic implications of this knowledge—the need to redirect marketing resources to develop a profitable customer base.

Information about nonmanufacturing activities. The addition of customer focus takes costing into new parts of the organization. Customer-support activities, for example, invariably take place outside the manufacturing plant—in marketing, order entry, and customer service. In contrast, early ABC systems resided exclusively within the walls of the plant. Their focus was exclusively on manufacturing activities.

It makes better business sense to focus just as carefully on nonmanufacturing activities as manufacturing activities. To verify this, look at the income statement for your company. Add up the nonmanufacturing costs. Then compute them as a percent of total manufacturing and nonmanufacturing costs.

You may be shocked at the significance of these costs. Nonmanufacturing costs representing 50% or more of the cost of running a company are not uncommon. But these are the very costs that are completely ignored by cost systems that focus exclusively on the plant.

The extension to service organizations. Examples of first--generation ABC systems were almost exclusively from manufacturing companies. Second-generation ABC systems, however, are found increasingly in service organizations such as financial and health-care institutions.

Figure 4-3 shows examples of activities in a bank such as processing a deposit and making a commercial loan. These activities relate to cost objects such as bank customers, accounts, and loans.

Such examples reinforce the value of second-generation ABC systems. These systems provide detailed *economic intelligence* about the work going on in the company and the reasons for performing that work. This intelligence facilitates calculation of the cost impact of various strategic and operational decisions. These include decisions about the strategic direction of the company, the design of products and services, and the simulation of cost reduction opportunities.

In summary, the cost assignment view allows management to obtain answers to the following kinds of questions:

- What are the high-cost activities?
- What are the opportunities for improving product and service design to reduce cost? and
- What are the opportunities for profitably shifting the focus toward more profitable products, services, or customers?

The Process View of ABC

The horizontal part of the ABC model contains the process view (see *Figure 4-2*). It provides information about the work done in an activity and the relationship of this work to other activities.

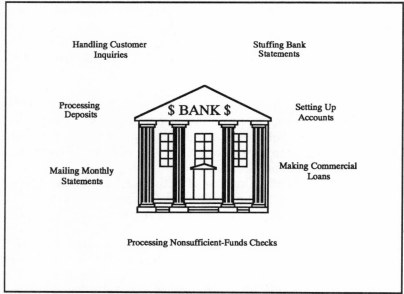

Figure 4-3. *Bank activities.* Banks have activities just like manufacturing companies. They look different, but these activities perform work, consume resources, and serve cost objects (such as accounts or loans) just as manufacturing activities do.

To expand on this, a process is a series of activities that are linked to perform a specific goal. Each activity is a customer of another activity and, in turn, has its own customers. In short, activities are all part of a *customer chain*, all working together to provide value to the outside customer *(Figure 4-4).*[3]

At the valve manufacturer, for example, metal is melted in the foundry. Then it's forwarded to molding. Molding pours the molten metal into the molds, allows them to cool, and passes them on to an activity that breaks and removes the molds to release the parts. All these activities—and many more—work together to provide finished valves to the company's customers.

On a more detailed level, the process view of ABC includes information about cost drivers and performance measures for each activity or process in the customer chain. These cost drivers and performance measures are primarily *nonfinancial*. They are useful in helping to interpret and improve activity—and process—performance.

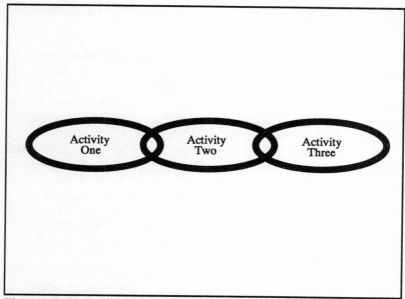

Figure 4-4. *The linked chain of activities.* Each activity is a customer of another activity and in turn has its own customers. Together, activities form a *chain of customers* all working together to provide *value* to the outside customer.

Cost drivers are factors that determine the work load and effort required to perform an activity. They include factors relating to the performance of prior activities in the chain as well as factors internal to the activity.

Cost drivers tell you *why* an activity (or chain of activities) is performed. Specifically, activities are performed in response to prior events. Scheduling a batch of parts, for example, is a response to a customer order or the scrapping of inventory—*the why*. In turn, scheduling the parts requires setting up equipment—*the effort*.

Cost drivers also tell *how much effort* must be expended to carry out the work. A defect in the part or data received from a prior activity, for example, can increase the effort required. A requisition containing the wrong part number requires correction prior to completing a purchase order. An engineering drawing that doesn't reflect the current process causes additional effort during machine setup.

Cost drivers are useful because they reveal opportunities for improvement. A reduction in the defect rate for incoming requisitions, for example, allows wasted effort and resources to be eliminated in the purchasing activity.

Performance measures describe the work done and the results achieved in an activity. They tell *how well* an activity is performed. They communicate how the activity is meeting the needs of its internal or external customers. They include measurements of the *efficiency* of the activity, the *time* required to complete the activity, and the *quality* of the work done.

The efficiency aspect is judged by first determining the activity's output volume. This is then compared to the resources needed to sustain that activity and its output level. For example, the number of molds processed in a month is computed for a molding activity. This measure of output is then divided into the resources required by that activity during the month. The result is a cost per mold, say $20, which may be compared with internal or external standards of efficiency.

Still another dimension of performance is the time required to complete the activity. For example, assembling Norstar telephone terminal systems in one Northern Telecom plant takes about two hours from the time when parts arrive in production to the time when assembly is complete.

Such measures of elapsed time are indirect measures of cost, quality, and customer service. The longer it takes to perform an activity, the greater the resources required. These additional resources include the salaries of staff required to do the work and the cost of equipment used to carry out the work. Also, the longer it takes, the more likely it is that work has to be redone to correct mistakes or defects. Conversely, the shorter the elapsed time, the quicker the activity's response to changes in customer demand.

The short elapsed production time in Northern Telecom's telephone terminal plant is indicative of low-cost and *world-class* quality. Additionally, customer service from the plant is excellent. This is because the production mix can be shifted from one variation to another at short notice in response to a changing customer order mix.

A third aspect of performance is quality. For example, what percent of the molded parts need to be reworked, and what percent are scrapped? The higher these percentages, the lower the quality of the activity, the higher its overall cost, and the greater the detrimental influence on the next activity in the process. The value received by the customer may eventually be diminished as well.

Performance measures focus attention on the important aspects of activity performance and stimulate efforts to improve.

To recap, the ABC process view provides *operational intelligence* about the work going on in a company. This includes information about the external factors determining how often the activity is performed and the effort required to carry it out. Operational intelligence also includes information about the performance of an activity, such as its efficiency, the time it takes to perform the activity, and the quality with which it's carried out.

This operational information allows management to obtain answers to questions such as:

- What events trigger the performance of the activity?
- What factors negatively affect the performance of the activity? and
- How efficiently, how fast, and with what quality is the work carried out?

Moreover, the ABC process view brings the world of operations directly into the heart of the cost system. Cost and nonfinancial information join forces to provide a *total view* of the work done, thus facilitating management of activities and improvement of performance.

The power of combined cost and nonfinancial information can be illustrated in the process of selecting areas for improvement based on potential returns. For example, at the printed circuit board plant (PCB), the number of defects in each activity was computed daily for each of the three shifts. This provided important information about the quality of each activity to the operators of the activity. The ABC system, however, allowed the plant to go one step further—*to compute the cost of the defects*. This additional step riveted attention on the highest cost defects, allowing operators to focus their attention on the corrective actions with the greatest payoff.

The importance of this benefit cannot be emphasized enough. While there were many quality improvement opportunities in the plant, there weren't the resources to tackle them all at once. ABC information allowed PCB to set priorities and focus on the important opportunities first.

A Linked-Chain Example

A process is a chain of activities that work together to perform a specific objective. Activities in a process share common cost drivers and performance measures *(Figure 4-5)*.

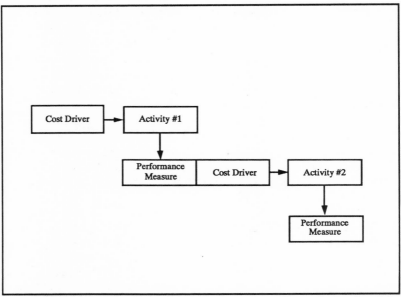

Figure 4-5. *The interdependency of activities in a process.* The work of each activity affects the performance of the next activity in the process. Performance measures for one activity, therefore, become cost drivers for the next activity.

This is true of the product and tooling development process of Dayton Extruded Plastics. There are three activities in this process: designing new products, designing new tools, and manufacturing new tools *(Figure 4-6)*.

As shown in *Figure 4-6*, designing new products has two cost drivers. The *number of new customer specifications* determines the volume of work. The *classification of products* (more complex products are difficult to design) determines the effort required to complete the designs. This second cost driver is common to all three activities in the process.

Designing new products
Cost drivers
- number of customer specifications
- classification of products

Performance measures
- number of tangible shapes
- number of changes in shapes
- average design time

Designing new tools
Cost drivers
- number of new shapes
- number of changes in shapes
- classification of products
- volume of production

Performance measures
- number of changes in specifications
- number of new drawings
- average design time

Manufacturing new tools
Cost drivers
- number of new drawings
- classification of products
- number of changes in specifications

Performance measures
- number of tools
- number of changes in tools
- elapsed tooling manufacturing time

Figure 4-6. *A product development process at Dayton Extruded Plastics.* These three activities work together to develop products and related tooling to meet customer specifications. The performance of each activity is linked by common cost drivers and performance measures.

There are three performance measures for the activity of *designing new products*. The number of tangible shapes is a measure of activity output. The number of changes in shapes (a quality measure) and the average design time measure how well the work is done.

Designing new tools has four cost drivers: the number of new shapes, the number of changes in shapes, the number of product classifications, and the anticipated volume of production (volume influences the engineered life of the tooling). Note that the first two cost drivers are performance measures from the prior activity (its performance affects the downstream activity).

Performance measures for *designing new tools* include the number of changes in specifications, the number of new drawings, and the average design time. These performance measures are cost drivers for the next activity in the chain—manufacturing the tools.

This example shows how each activity depends on the performance of its suppliers and the impact it has on its customers. Cost drivers and performance measures help you understand —and manage—these interdependencies.

Dayton Extruded Plastics

Dayton Extruded Plastics, a division of Stolle Corporation, manufactures vinyl parts for windows in their plant in Ohio. It specializes in the design and manufacture of custom window systems. Its ABC model provides many examples of second generation design for this and subsequent chapters.

Summary

There are two dimensions to modern activity-based costing. The cost assignment view provides information about the work going on in a company as well as information about the products and customers benefitting from the work. The process view provides information about *why* work is performed, what factors determine *the effort* required to perform it, and *how well* the work is carried out. All of this facilitates management of activities as a *chain of customers* collectively dedicated to meeting the needs of the external customer.

The real power of two-dimensional ABC is that judgments can be based on the combination of cost and nonfinancial information. It directs product and customer strategy towards profitable opportunities. And it guides the improvement of a company's ability to design and build products and serve customers in its chosen markets.

Key Terms in Chapter 4

Activity—A unit of work performed within an organization.

Cost assignment view—The part of ABC where cost is assigned to activities and the cost of activities is assigned to cost objects.

Cost object—The reason for performing an activity. Cost objects include products, services, customers, projects, and contracts.

Cost driver—A factor that determines the work load and effort required of an activity and the resources needed. An activity may have multiple cost drivers associated with it.

Performance measure—An indicator of the work performed and the results achieved in an activity. A measure of how well an activity meets the needs of its customers. Performance measures may be financial or nonfinancial.

Process—A series of activities that are linked to perform a specific objective.

Process view—The part of ABC that provides operational information about activities.

Resources—Economic elements applied or used in the performance of activities.

References:

1. R.S. Kaplan, "John Deere Component Works," 9-187-107/8 (Boston: Harvard Business School), 1986.

2. Figure 4-2, and later developments of this figure, are based on joint work with Norm Raffish of Ernst and Young.

3. Richard J. Schonberger, *Building a Chain of Customers: Linking Business Functions to Create the World Class Company*, (Free Press: New York), 1990.

Chapter 5

THE ABC BUILDING BLOCKS

This chapter takes you on a tour of the mechanics of activity-based costing. You'll learn all about the different types of activity-based information. You'll learn about the wealth of useful information residing in an ABC data base. And, if you plan to design an ABC system, you'll learn what information to include in your system.

In this tour, you'll follow the flow of information through the activity. You'll discover that the activity exists at the intersection of the cost and process views of ABC. You'll also discover that much of the information in ABC either resides in, or flows through, the activity *(Figure 5-1)*.

To help you grasp the key concepts as quickly as possible, the tour is presented in two parts. The first part follows the vertical flow of cost information through the activity. The second part follows the horizontal flow of nonfinancial information through the activity.

The Cost Assignment View

The cost assignment view is where an *economic picture* of the organization is created. Here you apply the improved methods of ABC to yield accurate and useful information for key business decisions.

The following items are the basic building blocks of the *ABC cost assignment view*:

- Resource,
- Activity,
- Activity center,

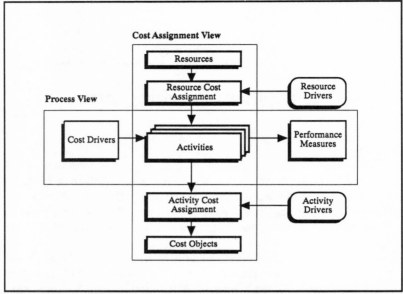

Figure 5-1. *ABC building blocks.* Activity-based costing comprises several building blocks. The building blocks in the vertical dimension work together to assign cost from resources to activities and from the resources to the cost objects. The building blocks in the horizontal dimension supply information about the performance of activities.

- Resource driver,
- Activity cost pool,
- Cost element,
- Activity driver, and
- Cost object.

Let's first take a quick look at these building blocks and their general relationships. Then with that overview in mind, we can take a more detailed look at these various building blocks. *Figure 5-2* shows how these building blocks fit together.

Resources are economic elements directed to the performance of activities. They are the sources of cost.

Resources in a manufacturing company include direct labor and material, production support (such as the salary cost of material procurement staff), indirect costs of production (such as the power cost of heating the plant), and costs outside of production (such as advertising). Resources found in both manufacturing and service companies include the salaries of professionals and office support staff, office space, and costs of information systems.

Resources flow to *activities*, which are processes or procedures that cause work. In a customer service department, for example, activities can include processing customer orders, solving product problems, and processing customer returns (see *Figure 5-3*).

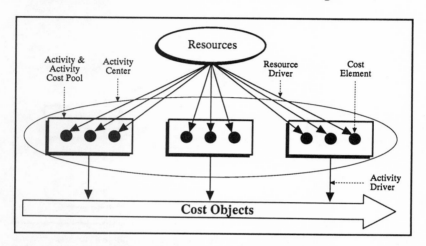

Figure 5-2. *The building blocks of the cost assignment view.* ABC uses several technical terms to describe the process of cost assignment. This diagram shows the relationship of each of these terms to the cost assignment process.

Typically, related activities are enclosed in an *activity center*. The activity center is a cluster of activities (usually clustered by function or process). In *Figure 5-3*, for example, the activity center contains all customer-support activities.

Various factors, referred to as *resource drivers*, are used to assign cost to activities. These factors are chosen to approximate the use of resources by the activities. In *Figure 5-3* customer service cost is traced to three activities.* The percentages shown (60%, 20%, and 20%) are based on estimates of the effort expended on each activity. An example of this would be ten people in the department with six solving customer problems full time, while

---

* It's assumed that the cost of resources used in the customer service department has already been determined.

the other four split their time between processing and testing returns.

Each type of resource traced to an activity (e.g., the salary cost of processing returns) becomes a *cost element* in an *activity cost pool*. The activity cost pool is the total cost associated with an activity.

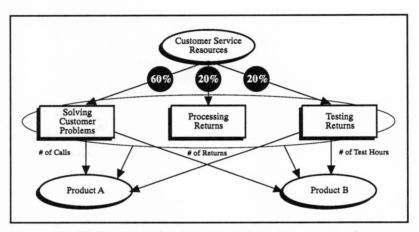

Figure 5-3. *The building blocks for the cost of a customer service department.* Resources are assigned to three activities based on estimates of effort. Cost is assigned to the products using three *activity drivers*.

Each activity cost pool is traced to the cost objects via an *activity driver*. The activity driver is a measure of the use of the activity by the cost objects. It is used to assign resources from the activities to the cost objects.

To relate this back to *Figure 5-3*, each activity has a unique activity driver to trace its cost to the products. Solving customer problems, for example, is traced to products based on the number of phone calls. This makes sense because the product that creates the most customer problems is likely to generate the most phone calls.

The *cost object* is the final point to which cost is traced. A cost object is the reason why work is performed in the company. It may be a product or a customer. Engineering, producing, marketing, selling, and distributing a product requires a number of activities. Supporting a customer also comprises a number of activities. The cost traced to each product or customer reflects the cost of the activities used by that cost object.

This vertical flow of information in ABC defines the economics of the company and the organization of work within it. It also provides the basic building blocks for creating accurate and useful cost information about the strategy and operations of the company.

Resources

ABC operates with measurements of the cost of resources. For example, how much have we paid in salaries so far this year? How much depreciation did we have? How much did we accrue in taxes? How did it all compare with the budget (what we should have spent)?

A primary source of cost information is the general ledger. The key is to assign the costs in the general ledger accounts to activities in a way that reflects how the resources are used to perform the work. If a piece of equipment is used in a machining activity, for example, its cost should be assigned to this activity.

Activities

Activities are units of work. As such, they are part of the real organization of the company—not abstractions of an accounting system. Activities include processing a deposit to an account, drilling holes in a circuit board, issuing invoices, and maintaining employee data. They are the centerpiece of ABC and must be defined before the assignment of cost.

Activities differ in type and location from one company to another. These differences exist because of variations in each company's technology, size, and approach.

Look at technology for example. A valve manufacturer has machinery for tapping and grinding metal parts. An electronics manufacturer, by contrast, has machinery for inserting parts into circuit boards and soldering those parts to the boards.

Another difference is that large companies often group activities into functions, whereas small companies typically disperse activities around the organization. For example, companies the size of AT&T or General Electric have corporate quality departments. These departments perform many activities, including quality training and vendor management. In contrast, companies with fewer than 100 employees often assign quality activities to engineering and manufacturing.

The number and type of activities also differ according to its business approach. For example, a manufacturing company that is doing "business as usual" has an "inspect the quality in" approach to quality control. Designated staff specialists are responsible for quality control activities such as those listed in *Figure 5-4*.

- Developing quality specifications
- Inspecting incoming materials
- Inspecting in-process parts
- Inspecting finished products
- Controlling tools and gauges
- Maintaining and operating inspection equipment
- Certifying vendor quality

Figure 5-4. *Activities in a quality-control department.* If your approach to quality is traditional, you may have a similar list of activities in your quality-control department. If you have moved to a world-class approach to quality, you will have dispersed or eliminated some of these activities.

However, a company that is world class may have abolished its quality-control department. In these companies, the responsibility for quality belongs to every employee, not just to a select group of specialists. Ask an employee in such a company, "whose job is quality?" The response will be, "it's mine." That's because world-class quality involves doing it right the first time, not "inspecting it in" after the fact.

Quality activities in world-class companies either disappear or are disbursed to all employees. Checking process specifications is the responsibility of the equipment operator, not a staff person. As a result, inspecting incoming components, for example, may become unnecessary because of improved part quality.

The list of activities in the world-class plant is therefore a lot shorter than that in a "business as usual" plant. This is because many activities have either been eliminated or reduced to insignificance. Also, those that remain with line employees become tasks associated with the primary work and are not identified as separate activities.

Despite these differences, there are common activities across functions and across industries. A divisionalized company, for example, has material acquisition functions in each of its divisions. Each function includes qualifying vendors, purchasing parts and receiving parts among others.

Plants in the same industry often have common activities. Plants that manufacture printed circuit boards, for example, have photoimaging, hole punching, plating, and other common activities.

Resource Drivers

Resource drivers are the links between the resources and the activities. They take a cost from the general ledger and assign it to the activities.

Let's say we have two significant resources associated with the inspection department—$100,000 in salaries and benefits and $20,000 for supplies. Salaries and benefits are assigned to each activity based on estimates of the effort devoted to each activity. This estimate of effort is the *resource driver* for salaries and benefits.

For example, the estimate of effort may be determined by a count of the people assigned to an activity and by estimates of the time each person spends on that activity. If two out of ten people in the department are found to spend 50% of their time on inspection of customer complaints, then 10% (i.e. 2/10 multiplied by 50%) of salary and benefit cost (i.e. 10% of $100,000 = $10,000) is traced to this activity.

These estimates (which are usually quite reliable) are ordinarily obtained during interviews with the managers of the departments. (Interviewing and other data gathering tools are described in Chapter 12).

In the case of supplies, departmental records may show that $15,000 in supplies are used in first-piece inspection and $5,000 to handle customer complaints. The resource driver in this case is the direct measurement of the use of supplies by the activities.

The part of each resource assigned to an activity becomes a *cost element* of that activity. In this example, $10,000 of salary cost and $5,000 of supplies (as determined above) are cost elements of responding to customer complaints.

Cost elements are important if you wish to know which specific resources are consumed by an activity. To gain this knowledge, you need to create a list of an activity's cost elements. Such a list is shown in *Figure 5-5* and is called a *bill of costs*.

Knowledge of cost elements helps in managing resources. Improving the efficiency of an activity does not, in most cases, translate into automatic cost reduction. The resources may be idle, but they remain committed to the activity unless steps are taken to remove them. The value of cost elements is that they clearly indicate which resources need to be removed or redeployed.

The total of all cost elements for an activity is the *cost pool*. The overall total in the cost pool is a guide to the significance of an activity as a resource user. This allows cost pools to guide setting of priorities in improvement programs. Not all cost reduction opportunities are equal. The activities with the largest cost pools provide the greatest potential for cost reduction.

Activity: Placing nonproduction purchase orders

Bill of Costs:

GL Account		Year-to-Date Resources	Actual%
6311	Salaries	$4,000	44
6312	Benefits	1,200	13
7566	Postage	775	9
7642	Telephone	1,600	18
7756	Miscellaneous	1,500	16
	Total cost pool	$9,075	100%

Figure 5-5. *The bill of costs.* The bill of costs reveals the resources used by an activity. This is useful information for managing activities, because any changes in activity performance should be reflected by changes in resource requirements.

Activity Centers

Just as your company has an organization chart to show its structure, so too must ABC organize activities in a meaningful way. There may be literally hundreds of activities in the data base, and you can easily become lost without some method of organization.

The most common approach is to group activities into activity centers. An activity center is a collection of related activities, such as those in a particular department. A credit department activity center in a cellular telephone company, for example, includes the activities of checking credit and collecting overdue accounts.

Figure 5-6 shows activities in an inspection activity center. This center directly parallels the inspection department in scope, but contains information about the activities that would not be found in any conventional departmental report.

Inspection Department

Inspecting Incoming Material
Inspecting Incoming Components
Inspecting the First Piece of Each Batch
Inspecting Customer Complaints

Figure 5-6. *The Activity Center.* Activities are grouped in activity centers. Illustrated here are four activities in the inspection department. An activity-center report to the manager of this department contains a wealth of information about the work done.

This information includes the cost of each activity, the resources used by each activity, and operational information about activity performance. It may also show the flow of work from one activity to another.

The purpose of the activity center is to facilitate management of functions or processes. It does this by supplying pertinent information about all the activities in a particular function or process. It contains in one place strategic and operational information relating to the center's activities. This information is used to help answer the following types of questions about the work of the center:

- What work is performed in the activity center?
- Which activities consume most of the resources of this department?
- Which activities contain *waste* and are candidates for improvement?
- How does each activity meet the needs of its customer (i.e. the next activity in the process)? and

- What is the overall performance of the department or the process?

It's common—*but not necessary*—for activity centers to parallel the company organization chart. In the next chapter you'll learn how to use activity centers to obtain useful information about processes—the chain of linked activities.

Cost Objects

The cost object resides at the bottom of the cost assignment view of ABC. But *it is* the starting point from which the work required by the company is defined—the activities required to produce the products and support the customers targeted by the company.

The value of cost objects. Tracing costs to cost objects provides several important items of strategic information:

- It helps *define* how valuable cost objects are to the company that provides them, where value is computed as:
  profit = revenue - activity-based cost.

- It helps *measure* the value received by the customer, where value is computed as:
  customer realization - customer sacrifice.
  In this equation, customer realization is the sum of the product features, quality, and service received by the customer. Customer sacrifice is the ABC associated with this realization plus additional costs incurred by the customer (such as the time spent learning how to use the product).

- It *yields insights* about how cost object value might be increased by reducing the cost of cost objects. These insights come from information about the cost of each activity used by a cost object.

The hierarchy of cost objects. Most companies have hierarchies of cost objects, one for products, and one for customers (see *Figure 5-7*). Each hierarchy represents opportunities to review

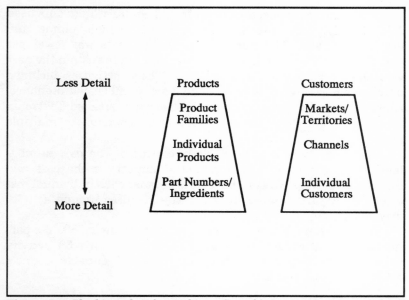

Figure 5-7. *The hierarchy of cost objects.* Cost objects vary in type and detail depending on the purpose of activity-based costing. For example, if you are interested in broad strategic issues, estimates of market profitability will be important. If you wish to determine the sourcing for a part, you need costs at the part number level.

value at differing levels of detail (where the bottom represents the greatest amount of detail).

Part number costing. The most detailed cost object in the product hierarchy is the part number or ingredient. Tracing cost to this level of detail reveals varying patterns of cost if parts differ in design or volume.

Part number costing provides economic intelligence to guide various decisions. These include choices about the manufacture of parts internally or by an outside supplier and choices between product and process design alternatives.

One plant, for example, put in an ABC system to improve its ability to make sourcing decisions. When it compared the new costs with its standard costs it found that only 15% of its parts were sufficiently well costed under the old cost system to make meaningful sourcing decisions. And this plant was struggling to stay in business as products were incorrectly moved to outside suppliers.

In another example, the Oscilloscopes Group of Tektronix used ABC to highlight cost differences between high-volume and low-volume parts. The cost of high-volume parts was lower per part used because the cost of activities required to sustain the part was shared across a larger volume. These activities included purchasing, receiving, storing, and part number maintenance. Knowing that high-volume parts cost less encouraged Tektronix product designers to use parts that were common to multiple products.[1]

However, there is a downside to costing at the part number level. That downside is the potential impact on the cost and complexity of the ABC system. This is because each individual cost object—each part number in this case— requires unique activity driver data that reflects its use of activities.

At Stockham Valve and Fittings, for example, 80,000 part numbers were costed using an ABC system with 58 activity drivers. This required millions of pieces of data to connect activities to cost objects.

Stockham Valve and Fittings

Stockham is one of the largest full-line producers of bronze and iron valves and fittings in the United States. Stockham's vertically integrated production process extends from foundries where the metal is melted to final finishing. Their ABC system provides numerous examples for this and later Chapters.

This was not an insurmountable problem for Stockham Valve. The data for all but one of the activity drivers resided on its mainframe computer and were downloaded to the ABC system. The major cost was an information systems specialist who planned and facilitated the download.

But it may not be so easy in your company. Check the data requirements before you attempt costing at the part number level. The cost could be prohibitive.

Product costing. Part numbers and ingredients make up products, and this is the next level up the product hierarchy. Products are the individual items that are sold to customers.

Product families are groups of products that are related by design, process, or market.

You saw in earlier chapters how conventional cost systems often significantly *miscost* products. Focusing the ABC system at the product level corrects these gross inaccuracies. It provides strategic intelligence about your ability to manufacture products or deliver services and to sell them at profit-generating prices.

Customer costing. Customer costing makes it possible to assess the profitability of individual customers or groups of customers. It often reveals levels of profitability that vary significantly from customer to customer.

Customer costing is the calculation of the total cost of serving customers. This cost includes two components. One is the cost of the products purchased by the customer; the other is the cost of support activities received by the customer.

Figure 5-8 shows a profitability report for a customer for one month. The customer bought three products for a total cost of $4,850. The customer placed ten orders during the month, received customer support over the phone, and had one visit from a field engineer for a total support cost of $850. Unfortunately the customer was not profitable because revenues earned were insufficient to cover the total cost of products and support.

The ability to assess customer profitability has proved valuable to a number of companies. This was the case at the Kanthal division of Kanthal-Hoganas, a Swedish manufacturer of electrical resistance heating elements.

Kanthal's study of its customers revealed that, while 30% of the customers were very profitable, 70% of customers were unprofitable or breakeven. The least profitable 10% of the customers collectively lost an amount equal to the entire reported profits of the company.

Armed with this knowledge, Kanthal shifted marketing resources from unprofitable to profitable customers. Over the year following their ABC study, sales increased by 20% while employment decreased by 1%. Profits increased by 45%.[2]

Groups of customers can also be combined to provide pictures of profitability for distribution channels. This analysis is useful where resource requirements and profitability vary from one customer group to another.

For example, one company completed an activity-based analysis of the cost of distributing products through six different channels. This study revealed that the cost and profitability varied significantly from one channel to another. Marketing and administrative expenses varied from a high of 23% of sales to a low of 10% of sales. Profit margins varied from a high of 22% to a low of -19%.

The knowledge of channel profitability prompted a series of competitive actions. Marketing efforts were transferred to the more profitable channels, prices were adjusted, and discount structures changed.[3]

Customer: Bryant Manufacturing, Inc.

Product	Sales	Cost	Profit
A	$2,500	$2,160	$340
B	1,750	1,575	175
C	1,300	1,115	185
Total	$5,550	$4,850	$700

Customer Activity	Quantity	Cost per unit of driver	Cost	Profit
Ordering	10	$50	$500	
Customer support	2	75	150	
Field engineering	4	50	200	$850
Customer profit				($150)

Figure 5-8. *Activity-based customer profitability report.* Think what you can do with information about customer profitability. It can help you pick and choose which customers you prefer to serve and the level of support that is necessary. It may show that adjustments to price are appropriate. And it may show opportunities to improve the value you provide your customers.

Activity Drivers

Activity drivers are methods for assigning the cost of activities to cost objects. They measure how often activities are performed on each type of product or customer and the effort involved in carrying them out.

An example of an *activity driver* is the number of production runs by part number. This *cost assignment measure* reflects the use of batch-level activities, such as production scheduling or setting up a machine, by each batch of parts.

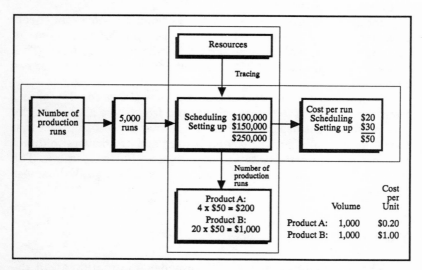

Figure 5-9. *How ABC costs products accurately.* ABC recognizes that different products use different amounts and types of activities. In this example, a batch of Product B is run five times as often as product A, so it is scheduled and set up five times as often. The activity driver, *number of production runs*, correctly assigns five times more scheduling and setup cost to Product B than to Product A.

Cost objects *are costed accurately* when activity drivers measure the use of activities directly or correlate closely with their use. The amount of time spent scheduling or setting up for a product directly measures the use of these activities. The number of production runs assigns the cost of scheduling or setup reasonably well, however, because each production run corresponds to a change in the schedule and a machine setup (see *Figure 5-9*).

The objective is to pick the right number and type of activity drivers. Enough of the right type are needed to report accurate costs—though too many may be costly and may create a system that's too complex to understand.

Activity drivers are a far cry from the arcane allocation procedures of conventional cost accounting systems. They are linkages between the products and the activities that represent opportunities for improvement in product or process design.

A design engineer at Hewlett-Packard's Roseville Network Division, for example, is likely to design a circuit board with fewer manual part insertions and more machine insertions. This occurs because ABC shows that the cost of a machine insertion is less than the cost of a manual insertion.[4]

John Deere Component Works decided to move the heat-treating facility in-line with the screw-machine process to eliminate the cost of moving parts one mile back and forth. This move was prompted by ABC data that revealed the high cost per move.[5]

To summarize, the cost assignment view shows the flow of cost from the resources to the activities, and from the activities to the cost objects. Cost assignment uses resource drivers to direct cost to the appropriate activities, and it uses activity drivers to direct the cost of each activity to the cost objects that consume it. The result is useful and accurate cost information to guide business improvement.

The Process View

The second dimension of ABC provides information about the work done in the activity. Much of this information is nonfinancial. It encompasses information about factors affecting the work load of activities and information about how well the activity is executed.

The key terms in the process view are:

- Cost driver and
- Performance measure

Cost driver is a causal factor that helps determine the work load of an activity. The number of active parts, for example, is a cost driver of the vendor management activity. The more different parts there are to procure, the more vendors there will be and the greater the work required to establish and maintain relations with these vendors.

Working to reduce the negative effects of cost drivers can yield important gains in efficiency. Reducing the number of different parts, for example, reduces the demand for part-related activities. Costs come down as resources are freed up, so production becomes easier and faster.

Performance measures define how well an activity meets the needs of its internal or external customers. Internal customers receive the output of an activity. Typically, an internal customer is the next activity in the manufacturing or business process. External customers are the individuals or companies who purchase the company's goods and services.

Performance measures differ from one activity to another and from one company to another. These differences reflect different customers and requirements.

The number of customer complaints, for example, is an appropriate performance measure for customer service activities. This number should be small if customer service is an important goal.

The number of modifications to products after the commencement of production is a measure of the success of engineering activities. This number should also be small if "getting it right the first time" is an important goal of design engineering.

Performance measures can be monitored over time, compared with performance goals, or compared with the performance of comparable activities inside or outside the company. This latter comparison is called *benchmarking*. Such comparisons are used to gauge how well the activity is performed and to identify areas where improvement is needed.

For example, *first-pass yield* is a measure of quality performance. Let's say last month's performance is calculated as 92%. This is an improvement over the same period last year when first-pass yield was 85%. However, a similar activity in a sister plant is achieving 95%, and a benchmark plant with a competitor is achieving 98%. Clearly the activity has a long way to go before it is matching the "best practices" in the industry.

As we saw in Chapter 4, performance measures for one activity can become cost drivers for the next activity in the process. The frequency of "out-of-specification" machining, for example, is a measure of the quality of work in the machining activity. It's a cost driver for *finishing*, which is the next activity to work on the parts.

A Manufacturing Illustration

Figure 5-10 illustrates how two-dimensional ABC works. The total resource pool of $6,000,000 is the total budget for the procurement department. Of this cost, $450,000 is traced directly to the purchasing activity. (The resource drivers include estimates of effort expended on the activity, and a specific measurement of the use of supplies.) The cost of the purchasing activity is traced to part numbers via the number of purchase orders per part number (the activity driver).

The number of purchase orders measures the output of the activity (the number of times the activity was performed). Other performance measures include the number of errors made, the number expedited, and the elapsed time required to complete a purchase order. A volume of 6,000 purchase orders and an activity cost of $450,000 yields a cost per purchase order of $75.

In this example, the activity driver and the performance measure of output are the one and the same. This matching of activity driver and performance measure is common in ABC, but there are exceptions.

For example, if the number of purchase orders per part number is not captured by the company's information system, an alternative activity driver (such as the number of different parts) is required. Alternatively, if the effort required to complete a purchase order varies systematically from one type of part to another, a different activity driver (such as a direct measurement of the effort involved) may be necessary.

On the input side, the activity must cope with a volume of incoming requisitions of 8,000. A requisition *is not* a cost driver of the purchasing activity. Rather it is the paperwork, or "trigger," that initiates the work.

The volume of requisitions is determined by two cost drivers—the number of customer orders and the number of scrap tickets. Customer orders and scrap tickets are factors that trigger preparation of a purchase requisition (and the need to complete a purchase order).

Figure 5-10 shows the demand for the purchasing activity coming from purchases of parts. The level of work, however, is determined by the cost drivers—end product demand (number of customer orders) and the quality of the parts and their processing (the number of scrap tickets). An improvement in the quality of a machining activity, for example, reduces the number of scrap tickets and, in turn, reduces the number of requisitions and the demand for purchasing replacement parts.

Performance is monitored by several measures. The cost per purchase order averages $75. The frequency of errors is one in four (1,500 out of 6,000 per year). Over half the purchase orders were expedited rather than completed in the normal processing cycle. It took an average of twelve days to complete the processing of a purchase order.

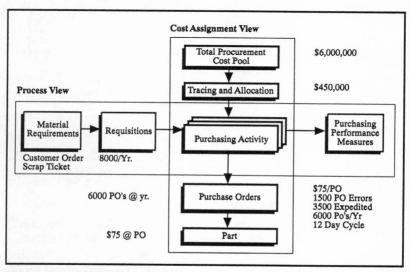

Figure 5-10. *An illustration of two-dimensional activity-based costing.* Preparing purchase orders occurs in both manufacturing and service organizations. ABC provides information for *managing* the activity's performance, *understanding* what it costs, and *quantifying* its impact on the cost of obtaining parts.

Performance is judged by comparison with past performance and comparison with similar activities elsewhere. The graph in *Figure 5-11* reveals a pattern of improvement. But it also reveals a large performance gap that needs to be closed before "best practice" is equalled.

A Service Illustration

Two-dimensional ABC also applies to service organizations. Consider the example of a cellular telephone company that performs credit checks on new customers.

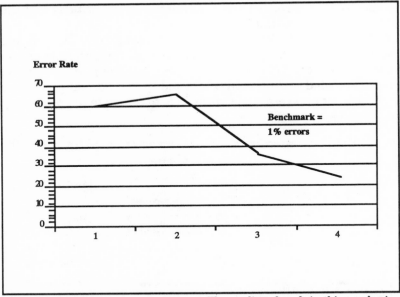

Figure 5-11. *Performance measurement.* The quality of work in this purchasing activity has improved. But it's still a long way from matching the benchmark activity.

Credit checking is one of several activities in the credit department. The cost of department resources is divided between these activities based on headcount and percent of effort devoted to each activity (this is the resource driver). The cost of the credit checking activity is assigned to new customers (the cost object) using *the number of new account activations* as the activity driver.

The two primary cost drivers are *the number of sales prequalifications* and the *percent of prequalifications performed outside of office hours*. The first cost driver recognizes that sales activity creates the need to complete credit checks.

The second cost driver reflects a policy that credit checks outside of regular office hours be performed by a service bureau. This affects cost because a service bureau credit check is more costly than one done in the credit department.

Two performance measures are tracked for this activity. The *number of new account activations* keeps track of the volume of work done. The *percent of new accounts that suffer credit problems* monitors the quality of the work done.

Summary

The building blocks of ABC provide cost and operational information about the work going on in the company. They provide answers to questions about this work and reveal opportunities for improvement. Here's a summary of these building blocks and their uses:

	Building Blocks	Purpose
1.	Resources	Resource management
2.	Activities	Activity management
3.	Activity Center	Process management
4.	Resource driver	Resource management
5.	Activity cost pool	Cost reduction
6.	Activity cost element	Resource management
7.	Activity driver	Activity management
8.	Cost object	Strategic management
9.	Cost driver	Cost reduction
10.	Performance measures	Performance assessment

Key Terms in Chapter 5

Activity–A unit of work performed within an organization.

Activity center–A report of pertinent information about the activities in a function or process.

Activity cost pool–Total cost assigned to an activity. The sum of all the cost elements assigned to an activity.

Activity driver–A factor used to assign cost from an activity to a cost object. A measure of the frequency and intensity of use of an activity by a cost object.

Cost driver–A factor that determines the work load and effort required of an activity and the resources needed. An activity may have multiple cost drivers associated with it.

Cost element–The amount paid for a resource and assigned to an activity. Part of an activity cost pool.

Cost object–The reason for performing an activity. Cost objects include products, services, customers, projects, and contracts.

Performance measure–An indicator of the work performed and the results achieved in an activity. A measure of how well an activity meets the needs of its customers.

***Resource drivers*–**The links between resources and activities. They take a cost from the general ledger and assign it to the activities.

***Resources*–**Economic elements applied or used in the performance of activities.

References:

1. Peter B.B. Turney and Bruce Anderson, "Accounting for Continuous Improvement," *Sloan Management Review*, (Winter 1989), pp. 37-48.

2. Robert S. Kaplan, "Kanthal (A) and (B)," 9-190-002/3 (Boston: Harvard Business School), 1990.

3. Robin Cooper, "Winchell Lighting, Inc, Introduction, (A) and (B)," 9-187-073/4/5 (Boston: Harvard Business School), 1987.

4. Robin Cooper and Peter B.B. Turney, "Hewlett-Packard: The Roseville Network Division," 9-188-117 (Boston: Harvard Business School), 1989.

5. Robert S. Kaplan, "John Deere Component Works (A) and (B)," 9-187-107 (Boston: Harvard Business School), 1987.

Chapter 6

ABC INTELLIGENCE

Activity-based costing (ABC) provides a wealth of useful information. This may not be apparent, however, when you try to plow through the millions of pieces of data and many pages of printout found in a typical system. A wealth of information can be overwhelming if you don't know where to look.

Being able to find useful information depends, in part, on your background and training. There's no substitute for the knowledge born of experience with activity-based costing. Nor is there any substitute for reading books and attending training programs. Experience and training are just as important for activity-based costing as they are for any *world-class* tool.

But even the experienced user can benefit from two techniques that add *intelligence* to the information. The first technique is to *highlight* the information using attributes. The second is to *manage the level of detail* so that information can be used for different purposes.

These simple techniques make the information content of ABC "jump out" from the screen or off the page. They help meet the goal of empowering people with useful information about the work they do. The idea is to make a *positive difference* to the company, not design an elegant system that just gathers dust.

Means of adding intelligence to ABC are of interest to users as well as designers. They are techniques that designers use to make the system more "user friendly." But it's the users who take advantage of them and adapt them to their own unique situations.

This chapter describes how highlighting with attributes and managing detail works. It concludes with a description of an ABC model at TriQuint Semiconductor, Inc., that uses both of these techniques.

Highlighting Key Information

Information in an ABC system is highlighted using *attributes*. Attributes are labels that are attached to individual pieces of data to convey the characteristics of that data. For example, you may attach a label to an activity to signify that it's part of the engineering change process.

The value of attributes is that they enhance the meaning of activity-based information. Is an activity value-added or non--value-added? Is the cost of the activity fixed or variable with the volume of work done?

Attributes also allow you to identify common threads in the data. For example, you may wish to review all activities related to preventing, detecting, and correcting defects in products. A label attached to each activity associated with these purposes allows you to prepare reports about the cost of poor quality.

Attributes include information about the performance of activities, the level of activities, the type of activity and its cost behavior. Each of these types of information is described as follows:

Performance Information

Attributes are used to describe or measure the performance of activities. For example, *Figure 6-1* shows attributes for the activity *inspecting incoming materials* about cost drivers, performance measures and non-value-added activity.

Cost drivers, the factors that cause material receipts to occur, include the number of purchase orders issued, the number of regularly scheduled deliveries of incoming materials, and the percent of vendors who are uncertified. This latter cost driver reflects the progress of the company in certifying vendors for a level of quality that precludes the need for incoming inspection. It represents *an opportunity* for further improvement.

Performance measures for the activity include the number of inspections and the number of material-related problems discovered during manufacture. The second of these performance measures is also a cost driver for downstream activities that use the inspected materials.

Inspecting Incoming Materials

Cost Drivers
- Number of purchase orders
- Number of scheduled deliveries
- % of vendors uncertified

Performance Measures
- Number of inspections
- Number of material-related problems

Value Status
- Non-value-added

Figure 6-1. *Attributes about performance.* Attributes are used to describe the performance of an activity. In this example of an inspection activity, there are attributes for cost drivers, performance measures, and the belief that this activity does not contribute to customer value.

The incoming inspection activity is a *non-value-added* activity. That is its attribute. It's non-value-added because the inspection activity can be eliminated without diminishing the value received by the customer. Customers don't value inspection. They value high quality. If high-quality incoming materials can be assured, then inspection is no longer needed for providing customers with that high quality.

The value of attributes describing performance is that they make it possible to use ABC for process improvement. They allow nonfinancial information to augment the cost information within the ABC system. This facilitates judgements about the way the work is carried out and how it can be improved.

Level of Activity

Identifying the purpose of an activity is one way to make sense of the work going on. Even small companies have many different activities, and grouping them by common purpose is helpful.

There are two main categories of activities:

- Those that work on cost objects, and
- Those that sustain the organization.

Cost object activities benefit products or customers. Providing technical support to a customer is an example of a cost object activity (the customer is the cost object in this case).

Sustaining activities benefit different parts of the organization, such as the plant or the division. Maintaining the plant heating system is an example of an activity that sustains a plant.

Identifying activities by level has value for both designers and users of ABC information. The level of an activity is a reminder to the designer to match activities with an appropriate activity driver.

This value is demonstrated by the following scenario (typical of brainstorming sessions with members of the ABC design team):

> Someone in the group may ask, "What activity driver is appropriate for 'inspecting the first piece of each batch'?"
>
> "Let's use direct labor hours," someone else replies.
>
> "That can't be right," another pipes in. "First-piece inspection is a batch activity, and direct labor hours is a unit activity driver. How about using the number of production runs? That's a count of how many batches are produced."

In this common scenario, recognizing the level of activity helped guide the right design decision.

Grouping activities by level assists judgements about *why* activities are performed, *what* can be done about them, and *when* they are likely to change. For example, there's a big difference in the reason for department meetings and setting up a machine. Department meetings are a department-sustaining activity. Setting up a machine is a batch activity.

Improving the performance of different levels of activities requires different actions. Improving the *department meeting activity*, for example, requires careful study of the role of meetings in managing the department. How do meetings help effective decision making? How do they improve department communication?

Meetings are part of the bureaucracy, and there's probably much room for improvement. The managers of some companies, for example, seem to spend their entire time in meetings.

Cutting down meeting time, however, or even reducing the frequency of meetings, is an intangible management challenge. It's quite different from something like reducing machine setup time.

Reducing setup time is technically oriented and emphasizes such things as tool placement, training, and practice.

The need for activities varies depending on the level of the activity. For example, setting up a machine varies depending on how many different batches of product are scheduled. A production schedule that calls for 25% more batches inevitably translates into more work for the setup activity. This may have little or no impact, however, on the need for meetings in the production scheduling or setup departments.

The concept of cost behavior in ABC is radically different from conventional costing. The cost of the setup activity is treated as a fixed cost in conventional costing because it doesn't vary with product volume. It's a variable cost in ABC, however, because it varies with the number of production runs.

The difference? ABC shows that cost varies with changes in the work load of each activity. *Unit activities*, such as drilling a hole in a metal piece, vary with the number of units produced. *Batch activities*, such as scheduling a batch of production, vary with the number of batches. *Product activities*, such as maintaining the bill of materials, vary with the number of products. *Customer activities*, such as customer support, vary with the number of customers.

Cost also varies with *the quantity of cost drivers*. Let's say the number of defective parts received is a cost driver for a machining process. If the previous activity improves and reduces its defect rate (that is, it reduces the quantity of the cost driver for machining), there should be a reduction of cost in machining. Less rework is required, there are fewer repeated runs, and delays are eliminated.

Identifying activities by level allows you to understand how changes in your business affect the demand for activities. It takes the *fixed* cost of conventional costing and reveals that much of it does indeed vary.

Type of Activity

Activities can also be marked by type. This facilitates process management by identifying related activities wherever they are performed in the company.

For example, Dayton Extruded Plastics is a manufacturer of vinyl extrusions for windows. They were concerned about the time and cost required to get dies from engineering to production.

Engineering's job is to develop dies for new products, modify dies to reflect changes in product specifications, and overhaul dies at the end of their productive life. For each of these engineering initiatives there's a new or modified die. Each die is tried (checked for its ability to produce good quality product) prior to production. This involves manufacturing engineering, product engineering, die engineering, the material laboratory, and quality control.

Departments/Activities

Purchasing
  Setting up vendor
  Qualifying vendor
  Determine requirements
  Preparing POs

Receiving
  Receiving parts
  Processing receiving
    paperwork

Quality
  Inspecting & verifying
  Recording statistics

Storing
  Stocking
  Issuing

Performance Measures/Cost Drivers

1. # of vendors
2. # of part numbers
3. # of line items ordered
4. # of receipts
5. # of line items received
6. # of parts inspected

7. # of defects
8. # of inspection steps
9. # of work orders
10. # of bins filled
11. Time
12. Accuracy/conformance

Figure 6-2. *Information about cross-functional processes.* Attributes allow ABC to provide information about cross-functional processes. The material acquisition process, illustrated here, shows activities in four departments that work together to get material to production. Each activity is identified as a part of this process, so reports can be prepared about the process. Cost drivers and performance measures help interpret the performance of each activity in the process.

The first step in reducing cost and time was to understand the work involved in trying out dies. Accordingly, the attribute *trying out* was attached to all such activities (regardless of department). This allowed Dayton Extruded Plastics to prepare a report listing cost and other information about *trying out* activities.

This use of attributes adds power to ABC's ability to report information about cross-functional processes. It allows you to follow the chain of activities as it crosses organizational boundaries *(Figure 6-2)*.

Cost Behavior

Attributes can reveal important characteristics of cost elements. They show whether cost elements as fixed or variable, direct or indirect, or avoidable or unavoidable.

Attributes about cost behavior are used to support "what if?" decision analyses. These are simulations of cost impacts resulting from changes in the way activities are performed.

For example, the Business Products Division of Northern Telecom studied ways of reducing procurement costs. They looked at several alternative ways of procuring many thousands of low-cost, high-volume parts. They used information in their ABC system to model the cost impact of each procurement alternative.

Northern Telecom Limited

The Business Products Division of Northern Telecom Limited assembles the Vantage and Norstar telephone systems. Their Calgary plant used ABC as an analytical tool to help identify, prioritize and model improvement opportunities.

Some alternatives changed the level of work done in some of the procurement activities. For these, it was necessary to identify the *activity cost elements* that would be variable with the changes in work load.

One alternative eliminated several activities entirely. The requirement here was to identify those cost elements that would be avoided if the activity was eliminated. On average, they found that about 60% of the cost of these activities was avoidable.

The designation of attributes about cost behavior at Northern Telecom was done by the individuals doing the simulation. This makes sense because there's nothing black and white about cost behavior. The attribute is determined by the type of cost element and the circumstances of the change. Inevitably, it also depends on the user's judgment.

Managing the Level of Detail

Managing the level of detail in the ABC system is a key ingredient of successful use. When you dig deep into an organization to identify the work that's done, it's not hard to turn up hundreds of different activities.

At one level, all this detail is very useful. The manager of a process engineering department, for example, needs detailed information about the cost and performance of activities in that department. Each detailed activity represents real work that must be managed and improved.

But what about the cost of collecting all that detailed activity information?

Surprisingly, the cost is quite low. In some cases, it's even "free," because the detail is typically received directly from the department managers.

At another level, however, the detail is overwhelming. The plant manager, for example, cannot pay attention to the smallest activity. For one thing, there's not enough time. For another, the plant manager is not the one doing process improvement. The plant manager may provide coaching, may help move constraints preventing improvement, and may provide resources where necessary—*but the improvement is done by those who do the work.*

The marketing staff also has no need for detailed activity information. Their interest is in understanding the implications of product and customer strategies. For this purpose, information about broad groups of activities and their related activity drivers is sufficient.

This creates a dilemma in ABC. At the operating level there's a need for detailed information about the work going on, including cost and process information about each activity. At the strategic level, there's a need for summary information about activities. Additional detail would be unnecessary and burdensome at this latter level.

For example, at Dayton Extruded Plastics, 24 activities were performed in the process engineering department *(Figure 6-3)*. With minor modifications, these activities were the ones identified by the manager of the department during interviews. These activities represented the components of work in the department.

Cleaning dies	Measuring shrinkage
Cleaning areas	Monitoring wear of
Cleaning sizers	production equipment
Trying out new dies	Training
Setting up tools for production	Trouble shooting
Trying out reworked dies	Developing new processes
Assisting production	Recruiting
Trying out dies with engineering	Meeting
changes	Administering
Trying out materials	Researching rail coating
Trying out machines	Supervising
Fabricating production equipment	Evaluating scrap
Measuring die volume	Evaluating shrinkage

Figure 6-3. *Detailed activities.* Dayton Extruded Plastics included a lot of activities in their ABC system (such as in the process engineering department in this example). This detail reflected the level at which work was managed in the department.

At a strategic level, however, such detail was overwhelming. Across all the departments of the company, maintaining this level of detail meant there would be over 400 activities in the ABC model.

Managers above the department level had no interest in this amount of detail. Nor was this amount of detail necessary to support product and customer costing. (400 activities did not require 400 activity drivers to report reasonably accurate cost. Closer to 20 drivers would have been sufficient).

How do you resolve this detail dilemma?

The answer is to use *macro activities.*[1] Macro activities are summary activities. They are aggregations of several related detailed activities.

Detailed activities can be combined into one macro activity if they meet *three* rules:

1. *They must be the same level of activity.* (You can't combine a batch and a product activity.)
2. *It must be possible to use the same activity driver for all the detailed activities that comprise a macro activity.* (Remember you can only use one activity driver per activity.)
3. *The detailed activities must have a common purpose.* (Several activities that are all part of making engineering changes to dies can be combined. But engineering change activities should not be combined with customer engineering support. It would be difficult to interpret a "conglomerate" activity of this sort.)

Dayton Extruded Plastics used macro activities to reduce the burden of detail within their ABC system. In the process engineering department, for example, the 24 detailed activities were reduced to just five macro activities.

An example of how they did this is shown in *Figure 6-4*. This illustration shows three activities associated with *trying out* dies. These are the detailed activities of interest to the department manager.

The cost of each of the detailed activities was assigned to a single macro activity. This macro activity provided summary information for higher level management and for strategic purposes.

What is unique about Dayton Extruded Plastics is the presence of two tiers of activity detail in the same system. This avoided having to make a choice between a system that supported process improvement or one that supported strategy formulation. Their ABC system did both.

The macro activity concept avoids the need to make compromises in the design of an ABC system. You can have your cake and eat it too!

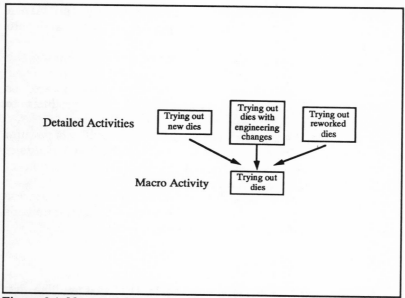

Figure 6-4. *Macro activities.* Dayton Extruded Plastics used macro activities to manage the detail in their ABC system. The detail is there for operational use, but strategic users need only see the summary information in the macro activities.

A Case Study

Let's take a look at an ABC system at TriQuint Semiconductor, Inc. This will illustrate the use of attributes and macro activities. It will also demonstrate just how easy it is to use activity-based costing for strategic *and* process improvement purposes.[2]

The Company

TriQuint is a manufacturer of gallium arsenide (GAS) integrated circuits (ICs). They produce a limited mix of standard and custom ICs for the high-performance end of the market. Their customers are primarily in the telecommunications and computer industries. Additionally, TriQuint is one of only a handful of companies that compete in the GAS IC market.

TriQuint is well known around the world for its ability to engineer high-quality ICs for custom applications. TriQuint is also well known for short engineering lead times—they can take a product from design, through the prototype stage, and into production rapidly.

TriQuint has been less successful, however, in making the transition from custom prototypes to standard products. Their customers love them for their engineering capabilities, but are less likely to dedicate long-term production of their products to TriQuint.

To a degree, the company is a victim of the inability of gallium arsenide to score inroads against the dominant silicon variants of ICs. The gallium arsenide industry remains a collection of "boutiques" struggling to mature.

The bottom line for TriQuint is that their engineering prowess has given them a dominant share of the market. Unfortunately it's also an unprofitable share of the market.

Terms of Reference

TriQuint set two objectives for their ABC system. The first objective was to provide information to support process improvement. It was believed that this would help eliminate waste, reduce process variability, and help them make the transition from prototype to production. An existing high level of cost provided a lot of opportunity for cost reduction (and profit improvement).

The second objective was to provide cost information for pricing purposes. Pricing was difficult for TriQuint because of the lack of published prices in a limited marketplace. It was also an important issue because cost was high, and the dominance of custom products meant that most products were unique.

The TriQuint ABC system focused initially on the packaging area of the plant. Packaging here refers to the high-speed, high-density IC housings that enabled the ICs to be attached to printed circuit boards.

The ABC Design Approach

Figure 6-5 shows the cost flow in the TriQuint system. Let's walk through each part of the ABC system design:

Micro Activities. The micro activities are the detailed activities at Triquint. *Figure 6-6* shows information for the laser-cutting micro activity. This is the use of a laser to cut sheets of laminate into individual parts.

The information for laser cutting shows that it's a batch activity–sheets are cut in batches not individually. Key performance measures include the number of cuts per part. (If you only do it once, it costs less and takes less time.)

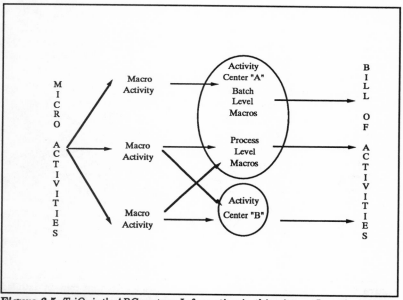

Figure 6-5. *TriQuint's ABC system.* Information in this picture flows from left to right. The costs are assigned from the general ledger accounts (not shown) to the micro activities. The micro activities are summarized into macro activities, and collected in departmental activity centers. Macro activity costs are then assigned to cost objects and listed in the bill of activities for each cost object.

The micro activity in *Figure 6-6* also shows the cost elements assigned to the activity. Salaries and benefits were traced to the activity via estimates of effort (obtained during interviews with the manager of the laser-cutting process). Materials were traced based on records maintained by the process manager.

Macro Activities. The costs of micro activities were assigned to macro activities. This was done to reduce the amount of information seen at higher management levels. Detailed activity information was also unnecessary for product costing purposes because several activities shared a common activity driver.

Activity: Laser Cutting
Activity Level: Batch
Cost Elements:

GL Acc. Account Description		Cost
6720	Operating Materials	$ 2,500
6654	Maintenance Materials	$ 3,500
6311	Salaries and Benefits	$15,075
	Total Activity Cost Pool	$21,075

Performance Measures:

Measure	Quantity	Cost per Unit of Measure
Number of parts cut	40,000	$0.53
Number of cuts per part	4	0.13
Cutting time	1,050 hours	20.07

Figure 6-6. *TriQuint micro activity.* Micro activities at TriQuint contain detailed cost and nonfinancial information about individual activities. The information is available to help improve activity performance.

Figure 6-7 shows the macro activity for cutting laminates. It includes the cost of three micro activities, including the laser-cutting activity in the previous discussion of *Figure 6-6.* Note that the total of each micro activity's cost pool is visible in *Figure 6-7,* but the detailed cost elements cannot be seen at this level.

A single activity driver is shown for this macro activity– the number of production runs. The ABC system designers omitted the process information in the belief that process improvement would focus at the micro rather than the macro level.

Activity: Cutting Laminates
Activity level: Batch

Micro Activities	Cost Pools
Setting up laser	$ 5,400
Laser cutting	$21,075
Testing cuts	$ 7,300
Total Activity Cost Pool	$33,775

Driver: Number of Production Runs
Driver Quantity: 450
Cost per Driver Unit: $ 75

Figure 6-7. *TriQuint macro activity.* Macro activities summarize the cost of several detailed activities. They reduce the detail seen by strategic users of the system. (Notice that the total cost of the micro activity from Figure 6-6 is listed here).

Activity Centers. TriQuint also used the *activity center* as a flexible tool for reporting activities in different ways. The primary grouping of activities was by function. For example, all activities associated with electroless plating were placed in an electroless-plating activity center. (Electroless plating is a chemical method of applying a metallic substance.)

Within each activity center, the activities were also grouped by level of activity. In the electroless-plating department, for example, there were groups of unit-, batch-, and process-sustaining activities. These groups were actually higher level macro activities that further reduced the amount of detail.

The power of activity centers at TriQuint was their ability to change structure *dynamically* to meet management's reporting needs. There were several processes at TriQuint that cut across department boundaries, and activity centers were used to report information about them.

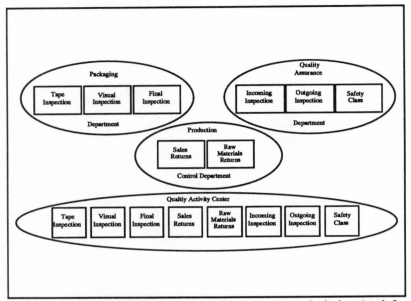

Figure 6-8. *TriQuint activity centers.* Activity centers are both functional (by department) and cross-functional (by process). In this example, quality related activities in three departments are shown. Also, a single activity center shows all these activities in one place (the "cost of quality").

Figure 6-8 shows information about quality related activities in three departments—one production department and two support departments. (There were other nonquality related activities in these departments, but they are not shown.)

At the bottom of the *Figure 6-8*, there is a single activity Center that contains all the quality related activities. The value of the quality activity center was that it reported in one place all pertinent activity information about preventing, correcting, and detecting poor quality.

Bill of Activities. Figure 6-9 shows an example of a bill for one of TriQuint's packages. A bill of activities reports cost for each product. It contains information about the activities, activity drivers, and cost of a product.

Let's take a moment now to think about how a bill of activities compares with the product cost report typical of a conventional cost system.

Part#: XYZ123		Volume: 10,000 Parts		
	Driver	Cost per Driver	Driver Quantity	Total
Unit Activities:				
Elect. test	# units	$ 0.15	10,000	$ 1,500
Inspect	# units	$ 0.20	10,000	$ 2,000
Batch Activities:				
Laser cuts	# runs	$36.91	150	$ 5,537
Laminate	# layers	$ 0.25	105,000	$26,250
Print	setup hours	$18.60	2,000	$37,200
Product Line Activities:				
MLC	# parts	$ 0.77	10,000	$ 7,700
Process Related Activities:				
Plating	# runs	$92.80	375	$34,800
Punching	# punches	$ 0.02	200,000	$ 4,000
		Total cost		$118,987
		Unit cost		$ 11.90

Figure 6-9. *TriQuint bill of activities.* The bill of activities shows all the activities, activity drivers, and costs associated with a particular product or customer. The activities in this bill are grouped by level to help direct management attention to areas of opportunity for cost reduction.

A conventional product cost report shows only the direct material cost, direct labor cost, and a big blob of "burden." In contrast, a bill of activities provides a pathology of the source of cost (the activities consumed by the product).

Additionally, a bill of activities can be structured in different ways and varying degrees of detail, depending on your preferences and needs. For example, activities can be *nested* according to their level (such as unit versus batch activities). Costs can be separated according to whether the activity is value-added or non-value-added.

TriQuint's bill *(Figure 6-9)* is nested by activity level. It shows that the major cost of the product comes from two sources. *First,* the cost of batch activities is heavy. Is this because the product was run in small batches? (Possibly the customer requires frequent *just-in-time* deliveries for this product.) Why is lamination so expensive?

Second, the product is a heavy consumer of an expensive plating process. Is this a reasonable charge for using this activity?

Is the cost high because some of the capacity of the plating process is currently unused?

TriQuint's bill shows the cost of macro activities rather than the underlying micro activities. This reduces the amount of detail in the bill and makes it easier to read.

If you wish to look further to answer some of the above questions, it's easy to go behind the macros to find out what detailed activities are represented by each macro. From the micro activity you can (if you wish) pursue the "trail" from the cost elements back to the general ledger accounts.

The value of TriQuint's bill of activities is that it supports *goal seeking*—identifying prospects for improvement and doing the research to confirm and define what can be done. Chapter 8 provides an in-depth example of a company that used the bill of activities to identify goal-oriented improvement opportunities.

Summary

Several simple techniques enhance the meaningfulness and usefulness of ABC information. These techniques are:

- *Highlighting the important information with attributes* makes it easy to extract the information you need. Attributes are labels that describe how well an activity is performed, what type of activity it is, and how its costs behave. You use them to prepare reports, to look for improvement opportunities, and to facilitate decision analysis.
- *Managing the level of detail* ensures that just enough detail about activities is available to support different purposes and different users of the information. Detailed activities are used for improvement purposes. *Macro activities* provide summary information for higher level management and strategic purposes.

Highlighting and *managing detail* are opportunities to extract the full potential of ABC. They turn ABC into a flexible system that meets varying needs.

Key Terms in Chapter 6

Attribute–Labels attached to data in an activity-based cost system to signify the meaning of the data.

Avoidable cost–A cost element of an activity that would not be incurred if the activity was not required. The depreciation cost of the insertion activity–but not the cost of space–is avoidable if the activity is no longer performed.

Bill of activities–A list of the activities and costs associated with a cost object. The bill may include additional information such as which activities are non-value-added.

Cost object activity–An activity that benefits products or customers.

> *Unit*–An activity performed on a unit of the product (e.g., tapping threads in the hole of a metal part).
>
> *Batch*–An activity performed on a batch of a product (e.g., scheduling production of a batch of parts).
>
> *Product*–An activity that benefits all units of a product (e.g., making an engineering change to a product).
>
> *Customer*–An activity that serves specific customers (e.g., supporting the technical needs of a customer).

Direct cost–A cost element that is traced to an activity or a cost object. The depreciation cost of the insertion machine is *direct* to the radial insertion activity. The engineering time devoted to a product is direct to that product.

Fixed cost–A cost element of an activity that does not vary with changes in cost drivers or in the volume of work performed by the activity. The depreciation cost of an automated part insertion activity will not increase with the number of insertions (except for large sustained increases in volume).

Indirect cost–A cost element that is allocated to an activity or a cost object. The cost of space occupied by the insertion machine is allocated to that activity and is therefore indirect.

Macro activity–A summary activity. An aggregation of several detailed activities.

Sustaining activity–An activity that benefits the organization (such as another activity or the department), but not a cost object.

> *Process*–An activity that sustains individual processes, cells, or functions (e.g., maintaining equipment and machinery).

Department–An activity that sustains the department (e.g., managing the department).

Plant–An activity that sustains the plant, (e.g., securing the plant).

Division–An activity that sustains the division (e.g., managing the division).

Company–An activity that sustains the company (e.g., preparing the company's financial statements).

Variable cost–A cost element of an activity that varies with changes in cost drivers or in the volume of work performed by the activity. The power consumed by a part insertion machine increases and decreases proportionally with the number of components inserted.

References:

1. Macro activities were first described by Anne Riley and Peter B.B. Turney in *TriQuint Semiconductor*, (Portland: Cost Technology), 1990.

2. This section is based on the TriQuint case written by Anne Riley and Peter B.B. Turney.

Part IV

HOW TO PUT ABC TO WORK

Part IV reveals how ABC information is used to achieve *the ABC performance breakthrough*. You'll learn the secrets of activity-based management and the "tools of the trade." You'll also learn about the many companies that have applied ABC to improve their business.

Activity-based management uses ABC information to help meet two important goals. *First*, it helps improve the value received by the customer. *Second*, it helps improve profits earned from providing this value. It meets these goals by helping improve where and how activities are performed.

Chapter 7 describes the activity-based approach to improvement. You'll learn:

- How activity-based management uses ABC information,
- The rules of activity-based management,
- How to improve the performance of activities,
- How *not to* reduce cost the "old-fashioned accounting way," and
- How to permanently reduce cost the *activity-based way*.

Chapter 8 showcases the tools of activity-based management. You learn to:

- Use strategic analysis to find profitable opportunities to reprice products or services, redirect resources, and change product strategy,
- Apply value analysis to improve business processes and reduce cost,
- Perform cost analysis to identify cost reduction opportunities and communicate what's learned from the improvements,

- Complete activity-based budgets to estimate work load and resource requirements and to direct resources and activities to the most strategically valuable purposes,
- Use life-cycle costing to make strategic judgements and identify cost reduction opportunities over the life of a product, and
- Use target costing to design products to meet a predetermined cost.

Chapter 8 describes how each of these tools have been used to improve performance in various companies. Companies included are General Electric, Northern Telecom, Dayton Extruded Plastics, and Tektronix.

Chapter 9 shows how activity-based management helped a company achieve *world-class* standards of business performance. ABC does this by identifying ways to *improve profitability* in meeting customer needs.

The experiences of the company in Chapter 9 are used to pinpoint the ways activity-based management can help improve competitive position and capability. This includes how this company used ABC information to:

- Set strategic priorities and help implement their chosen strategy,
- Manage performance to profitably meet business goals,
- Manage suppliers to achieve a long-term relationship emphasizing quality, short lead-times, and low cost, and
- Direct investments to the areas that would yield the greatest improvement.

This entire section of *Common Cents* brings alive the concept of *information empowerment.* Putting ABC information in the hands of those doing the improvement increases their power to improve performance.

Chapter 7

ACTIVITY-BASED IMPROVEMENT

To achieve continuous improvement, you must be informed. You need accurate and timely information about the work done (the activities) and the objects of that work (the products and the customers). That is what activity-based costing (ABC) is all about.

But gaining good quality information is only half the battle. The real key to success is putting ABC information to work to *identify* appropriate strategies, *improve* product design, and *remove* waste from operating activities.

In striving for these goals, you'll find numerous ways to improve your ability to profitably meet customer needs. Take the case of Stockham Valve and Fittings. Stockham used ABC to:

- Match parts to the lowest cost processes,
- Pick new parts patterns to reduce subsequent manufacturing cost,
- Initiate equipment modifications to reduce cost,
- Increase the price of products that were priced below ABC cost, and
- Drop unprofitable products from marketing's price sheet and the production schedule.

And Stockham Valve and Fittings has barely started to tap the potential of ABC!

Using ABC to improve a business is called *activity-based management,* or simply ABM. ABM is management analysis that brings the full benefits of ABC to your company. It guides efforts to adapt business strategies to better meet competitive pressures, as well as to improve business operations.

An increasing number of companies now practice ABM. General Motors, Hewlett-Packard, Siemens, Tektronix, Black and

Decker, General Electric, AT&T, and a host of other companies, large and small, have put ABC systems in place at various locations. All are managing activities as the route to business improvement.

In this Chapter you'll learn how you, too, can use ABM for business improvement. The keys to this include the following:

- How ABM uses ABC information,
- What ABM is,
- How to improve the performance of activities,
- How *not* to reduce cost *the old-fashioned accounting way*, and—
- How to permanently reduce cost *the activity-based way*.

The Link to ABC

Activity-based management and ABC are made for each other. ABC supplies the information needed to manage activities for business improvement. ABM uses this information in various analyses designed to yield this improvement.

Figure 7-1 shows this interrelationship. ABC is in the center, at the heart of activity-based management. Activity-based management encircles ABC, drawing its power from the ABC data base.

Basically, ABM consists of several analysis tools that use ABC information. These include value analysis, activity-based budgeting, and strategic analysis. All will be covered in the next chapter. For now, however, let's focus on the more basic element—*how activity-based management works*.

Activity-Based Management

Activity-based management aims directly at two goals. *Both* are common to any company. The first goal is to improve the value received by customers. The second is to improve profits by providing this value. These goals are reached by focusing on management of activities.

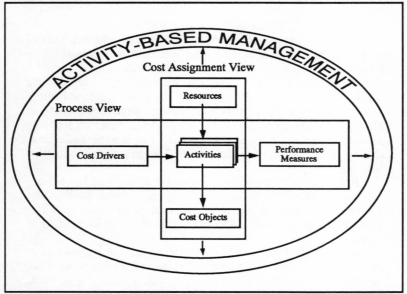

Figure 7-1. *ABC and activity-based management (ABM) are closely interlinked.* ABM focuses on business improvement, and ABC supplies the information needed for analysis.

This starts with a simple realization—customers have very simple wants. They want products and services that fit a specific need. They want quality. They want service. They want an affordable price. They want to be delighted. *And they want it now!*

Meeting customer wants is one thing. Meeting them profitably is quite another.

It's not enough to tell stockholders that your products have the highest quality in the industry. Or that customers consistently rate you highest in customer satisfaction. You must also provide an adequate return on stockholder investment.

There's really no conflict here. In the long run, your profitability is important to your customers. This is because your customers want you around for the "long haul" (which you won't be if you're unprofitable).

To support this, ABM adheres to the belief that managing activities is the route to profitably improving customer value. Each activity contributes in its own way to this overall goal. Each makes a measurable contribution to its customers—be it quality, timeliness, reliable delivery, or low cost.

What is Customer Value?

Customer value is about what customers get (the realization) and what they give up to get it (the sacrifice). Subtract sacrifice from realization and you have customer value.

Realization comes in a bundle. Included in the bundle are the features of the product or service. For a car, features include interior space; engine size; type of transmission; front-, rear-, or all-wheel drive; and so on. For a checking account, features include electronic bill paying, access to automatic teller machines, and twenty-four hour verification of your account balance.

But realization goes well beyond features. Whether buying cars or checking services, customers value good quality and service. In some cases, quality *is* the primary purchase consideration. In all cases, quality affects the cost of using the product or service.

Customers also buy future costs when they buy a product or service. Future costs are incurred to use and service a car. Fees are incurred for services associated with a checking account. Some products (such as nuclear fuel) also have disposal costs.

There's no realization without sacrifice. Many products and services require time and effort, both in initial purchase and in learning how to use them. It takes time, for example, to master a new software program.[1]

It's important to realize, too, that managing activities *is not* a custodial task. Rather, it's a process of relentless and continuous improvement of all aspects of your business.

This involves an on-going search for opportunities to improve. That search, in turn, involves a careful and methodical study of activities. What activities should be performed? And how should those activities be carried out?

Let's address those questions by looking at some examples of improving strategic position and capability.

Improving Strategic Position

Activities are determined by strategic choices. A successful business deploys resources to those activities that yield the highest strategic benefit.

The Rules of Activity-Based Management

Rule 1 Deploy resources to activities that yield the maximum strategic benefit.

Rule 2 Improve what matters to the customer.

Example: A hospital makes a strategic decision to be a certified trauma center. This deliberate choice determines the activities and resources needed. A trauma center requires a different set of medical activities—and resources—than other types of medical services.

What is needed: The hospital must analyze ABC information about the link between its strategy and the activities and resources needed to put the strategy into place. These analyses can guide strategic decisions prior to implementation, as well as help evaluate their on-going effectiveness.

As another example, Armistead Insurance Company used ABC to refine the strategy of a computer data services unit. This unit performed data analysis for fast-food franchisers. Unfortunately the operation was unprofitable, and the existing cost system provided few insights as to why.

ABC showed that Armistead customers differed in cost and profitability. Small customers were found to be unprofitable because of the high cost of acquiring and installing a new system for each of them. The result—Armistead raised prices on small franchisers and started a program to reduce the cost of acquiring new customers.[2]

Improving Strategic Capability

The key to implementing any strategy successfully is to improve what matters to your customer. This is not a new idea. The economist Ludwig Von Mises, for example, wrote about it seventy years ago. But it's never been more important than now.

What does matter to your customer? That's going to vary from business to business, and from activity to activity within the business.

Example: Ford Motor Company says "Quality is Job One." What Ford means is that good quality is the most important consideration for its customers.

What is needed: Ford needs to analyze information about quality. What does *quality* mean to their customers? Is it low faults on delivery or doors closing with a satisfying clunk? If it's faults on delivery, what's the defect rate? What has been the trend on this key performance measure? Which activities were responsible for the defects? How much cost is associated with this *poor quality*?

ABC can supply much of this information. It points out the cost of poor quality by revealing activity centers filled with detection and correction activities. Information on cost drivers and performance measures reveals opportunities for improvement and helps monitor progress. The impact of poor quality on product cost is revealed in each product's bill of activities. (This last piece of information is important because quality can vary significantly from product to product.)

Dayton Extruded Plastics is a case in point. It was widely believed at Dayton that scrap was "free." For one thing, very little material was lost. Scrapped extrusions were ground into powder and fed back to the extruders as raw material. For another, the existing cost system "confirmed" that scrap cost nothing—only good extrusions carried cost.

Implementing an ABC system brought Dayton Extruded Plastics face to face with the reality of scrap. They found it was expensive to run extruders just to produce scrap (including the cost of extra capacity). There were also many costly activities associated with detecting and correcting quality problems (such as inspecting, checking line work, and handling returns from customers). And grinding up reject extrusions required additional equipment and resources.

Dayton's ABC system also revealed the impact of quality differences from one product to another. Reviewing the bill of activities revealed the cost of poor quality for each product and identified candidates for quality improvement.

Activity-Based Improvement

There are three steps to improving activity performance. *First*, analyze activities to identify opportunities for improvement. *Second*, look for factors that cause waste (the cost drivers). *Third*, measure the things—time, quality, etc.—an activity should be doing well if it's contributing to the organization's success and profitable servicing of customers.

The Steps to Improvement

Step 1 Analyze activities
Step 2 Dig for drivers
Step 3 Measure what matters

Analyze Activities

Understanding why work is done, and how well it's done, is the key to eliminating waste. This can also strengthen strategic position, as many organizations can testify. Here are some analysis guidelines to follow:

1. Identify non-essential activities. If an activity *is not* essential, it's reasonable to ask "why do we do it?" If we ask *why*, it's an easy step to the next question, "how do we get rid of it?"

Activities with value fall into either of two categories. In the first, an activity has value if it's essential to the customer. Polishing a precision optic, for example, has value because the customer wants outstanding optical performance.

In the second, an activity has value if it's essential to the functioning of the organization. Preparing financial statements, for example, is not of immediate concern to customers. But it does satisfy an organizational need. (You must prepare financial statements to satisfy stockholders, bankers, and regulators.)

All other activities are non-value-added. These are activities that are judged unessential, and they are candidates for elimination.

How to Analyze Activities

Step 1 Identify nonessential activities.
Step 2 Analyze significant activities.
Step 3 Compare activities to the best practices.
Step 4 Examine the links between activities.

Expediting products is an example of a non-value-added activity. Customers don't care if products are expedited or not. They just want to receive the product by a certain time. So expediting really doesn't add value for the customer. It can be eliminated, without customers even noticing, if order and manufacturing lead times are reduced. This, in turn, permits reduced batch sizes and increased flexibility.

2. Analyze significant activities. A typical business can have two to three hundred activities. There simply isn't the time (or resources) to analyze all of them at once.

The key, then, is to focus on significant activities—the ones important to customers or operating the business. Moreover, these are the activities that provide the greatest opportunities for improvement.

In fact, I've yet to visit a business that didn't fit Pareto's rule: *80% of what you care about is determined by 20% of what you do.*

You can easily test this for yourself. Pick a department in your company. Then rank its activities in descending order of cost. You'll likely find that 20% of the activities cause 80% of the cost—and those activities are the ones worth analyzing.

3. Compare activities to the best practices. An activity should bear comparison to a similar activity in another company or another part of the organization. Just because an activity is value-added doesn't mean it's efficient or that its work is of good quality.

Comparing an activity to a benchmark of good practice helps determine the scope for improvement. Xerox, for example, has an extensive benchmarking program. Activities are rated on such factors as quality, lead times, flexibility, cost, and customer satisfaction. Each activity is rated against an identified best practice. In the case of distribution, for example, the best practice was the mail-order distributor, L.L. Bean.[3]

As another example, you may determine that *taking customer orders* is an essential activity. You find that it's being done manually. The best practice, however, uses electronic data interchange, costs less per transaction, has a lower error rate, and provides faster service. Clearly there's room for improvement over manual order taking.

4. Examine the links between activities. Activities work together in a chain to meet common goals. The links of this chain must be constructed to minimize time and duplication of work.

The product design process illustrates what can be accomplished here.

In the traditional approach, design activities are performed serially. Product designers prepare the product specifications without consulting production. When the design is finished, production tries to manufacture the product (often with difficulty). Not surprisingly, this approach is repetitive, time consuming, and costly.

Concurrent engineering is a better way to go. In this approach, activities are performed concurrently. Product design, manufacturing, marketing, and procurement work together toward a common goal. There's less repetition and duplication, and better quality products get to the customer faster.

Studying product or transaction flows can also reveal delay and repetition. *Ideally*, work should proceed in an uninterrupted, continuous flow. Each activity should process a transaction only once.

For example, a study in Pacific Bell's customer payment center found that 25% of the center's work was devoted to processing 0.1% of the payments. More than a third of all payments were processed twice and, in some cases, several times.

To improve on this, a new work flow was proposed to change how payments were processed. Individual work cells were proposed for each type of payment processing. The emphasis was to process each payment once in a continuous flow. It was estimated that these changes would reduce resource requirements by 25%.[4]

Dig for Drivers

Identifying nonessential and poor performing activities is the first step to improvement. The second step is to look for things that require you to perform nonessential activities or to perform below par. These things are the cost drivers.

For example, let's say you identified *moving the product* to be nonessential. The customer doesn't care about the product being moved from one process to another because that activity doesn't affect what's received. So *moving the product* is a non-value-added activity.

But how do you eliminate the activity? You can't, not while there's distance between the two processes. Failure to move the product would result in piles of inventory at the end of the first process and no work for the second process.

The distance between the two processes (or the plant layout) is the *moving* activity's cost driver. If you reorganize the plant to place the two processes next to each other, the cost driver is eliminated. It's no longer necessary to move the products over a distance.

Understanding and managing cost drivers is crucial to improvement. Simply understanding that waste exists doesn't result in automatic removal of that waste. Only when the causes of waste are addressed (the cost drivers) can it be removed.

Measure What Matters

Activity and cost driver analysis is periodic. But activity performance goes on day-in and day-out. How do you ensure that on-going efforts will successfully (and collectively) focus on what matters to the organization?

The answer is to develop a performance measurement system that fosters improvement in the right areas. Such a measurement system has three elements[5]:

1. Determine the mission. The first step is to determine what matters to the company. Generally this results in a statement of mission—the key objectives considered important to profitably meeting customer needs.

```
How to Measure Performance

Step 1    Determine the mission.
Step 2    Communicate the objectives.
Step 3    Develop the measures.
```

Zytec Corporation, for example, wrote a mission statement that focused on the following six objectives:

1. Improve total quality commitment.
2. Reduce total cycle time.
3. Improve Zytec's service to customers.
4. Improve profitability and financial stability.
5. Improve housekeeping and safety.
6. Increase employee involvement.

These objectives defined what was important to the success of the company as a whole. They articulate a vision of how the company should focus its improvement efforts.[6]

Partly as a result of this approach to performance measurement, Zytec's improvement program was extremely successful. Major improvements were seen in all areas of the mission statement.

2. Communicate the objectives. After specifying what matters, the next step is communicating it to the people in the organization. Each person should understand the importance of the company's mission and how each objective relates to their activity. With this understanding comes the possibility of a collective focus on a common goal.

3. Develop the measures. The final step is to develop performance measures for each activity. These measures should signify how each activity contributes to the overall mission. They also coordinate and motivate the efforts of the activity, and they provide facts about activity performance that direct improvement efforts.

Zytec did this by identifying improvement targets for all activities associated with each of six objectives. For example, the automatic insertion activity identified its total quality commitment as *improve yields by 2%*. It set its cycle time target as *reduce average cycle times by 5% in 1989*.

As another example, the Oscilloscope Group at Tektronix found ABC to be a fertile source of performance measures. Cost drivers were plotted against the cost of related activities over time. The intent was to prepare large charts of these graphs and to display them in the activity area. The idea was to draw people's attention to the relationship between the cost driver's quantity and the resources dedicated to the activities.

Figure 7-2 shows such a chart for the cost driver *number of modifications*. The number of modifications was a count of engineering changes made to products. It was believed that this affected several activities, including engineering and bill-of-materials maintenance.

While the graphs were being prepared, there was a significant drop in the number of modifications. There was also a reduction in resources used, but the effect was neither immediate nor proportionate to the drop in modifications.

Before any resources could be redeployed, a number of questions had to be addressed. Should there be "surge capacity" for a new product introduction? (There usually were many modifications associated with a new product.) What was the impact of the engineers learning to handle modifications with less time and fewer resources? How should they deal with the concern of some engineers that the analysis might result in layoffs?

Despite these questions, it was believed that the measurement exercise was worthwhile. The graphs stimulated a lot of discussion about managing activities and use of resources. This resulted in positive changes, which is the goal of ABC.[7]

Reducing Cost the Old-Fashioned Accounting Way

ABM is quite different from old-fashioned management accounting. Management accounting focuses on meeting cost targets. Standard costs and traditional expense budgets define the goal, and the analysis focuses on controlling variances (the difference between actual and budget). The emphasis is on "managing by the numbers" while paying little attention to the underlying activities and customers who benefit.*

Attempts to cut cost without restructuring the work is putting the cart before the horse and are doomed to failure. Many companies attest to cutting costs the "old-fashioned accounting way," but few achieve lasting savings. In some cases costs have gone up, while employees complain about stress and increased work loads.

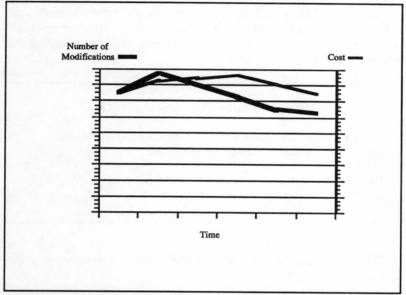

Figure 7-2. *This chart from Tektronix' Oscilloscope Group* plots the cost assigned to activities, such as maintaining bills of materials, against the cost driver, *number of modifications*. This stimulated extensive discussion over how to respond to a significant drop in the number of engineering modifications to products.

In contrast, the heart of ABM is the activity. Cost management focuses on the performance of each activity and its resulting use of resources. Managing activities better—*not some abstract measure of cost*—is the key to permanent cost reduction.

---

*   Budgets—if constructed using ABC information and used properly— can be an important part of activity-based management. Activity-based budgeting is covered in Chapter 8.

Reducing Cost the Activity-Based Way

Reducing cost is *only one* of several focal points of ABM. This is the first major difference compared to the old-fashioned accounting way. Improving quality, flexibility, and service–the importance of which vary from one business to another–is also central to ABM.

The second major difference is the way costs are reduced. Cost reduction is best achieved by changing the way activities are used or performed (managing the activities first), then redeploying the resources freed by the improvement.

How to Reduce Costs Permanently

Rule 1 Reduce the time and effort required by activities.
Rule 2 Eliminate unnecessary activities.
Rule 3 Select low-cost activities.
Rule 4 Share activities wherever possible.
Rule 5 Redeploy unused resources.

The following five guidelines show how to reduce cost the activity-based way:

1. Reduce the time or effort required to perform an activity. A key element of improvement is reducing the time and effort needed to perform an activity. This reduction can come from process or product improvement.

For example, the time to set up a machine can be reduced by improved training, eliminating conflicts in employee assignments, and placing tools and dies in convenient locations. Practicing the setup routine can create the manufacturing version of a "Grand Prix pit stop team." Reductions of 90% in setup time are not unusual.

Reductions in setup time can also come from changes in product design. Engineers at Dayton Extruded Plastics, for example, changed the specifications for the vinyl weatherizing material used in extruded window frames. This eliminated the need to add a weather-resistant coating to the frame. As a result, setup time was reduced because a simpler die could be used and a second extruder wasn't required.

Reductions in time and effort may come, not from the activity in question, but from the preceding activity. For example, the defect rate of parts received by a machining activity is a cost driver for that activity. Improving quality in the preceding activity reduces the quantity of this cost driver and the effort required by machining.

In another case, a retail distributor used ABC to highlight *breaking up packages* as a high-cost activity. This cost was reduced by asking suppliers to reduce the size of the packages and to design packages for easier break-up.[8]

2. Eliminate unnecessary activities. Some activities are candidates for elimination because they aren't valued by customers or aren't essential to running the organization. It's possible, for example, to eliminate material handling activities through changes to the processes or products.

There are a variety of possibilities here. Steps can be taken to ensure that all incoming materials and parts are fit for use. The parts can be delivered directly to the shop floor as needed. Changes can be requested in the vendor's production process to improve quality and increase responsiveness. And parts that cause quality problems can be redesigned to eliminate those problems.

Once these changes have been made, it's *no longer necessary* to inspect parts when they're delivered, or place the parts on the shelf in the stockroom. Eliminating these activities reduces overall cost and the cost of products that no longer use those activities.

Stockham Valve and Fittings, for example, used ABC to identify process changes that would eliminate scrap, rework, and other activities associated with poor quality. The design of the core box was changed on one particularly costly product. The improved quality was enough to reduce the product's cost by 20%.

Stockham also used ABC to identify a group of products that had potential for cost reduction. Among the changes made was an improvement to the tooling on one product. This single change eliminated several manufacturing operations and related setup, moving, and scheduling activities.

Prior to this, the product's ABC cost exceeded its selling price. Now it's competitive again.

Does Improved Quality Reduce Cost?

It used to be a common belief that improved quality meant higher cost. This seemed reasonable. Doesn't improved quality mean more inspectors, more rework, more costly warranties, and the like?

How wrong we were. It's *poor* quality that costs money (and loses customers). Poor quality is doing the job more than once. It's wasting materials. It's having costly systems to keep track of defective parts. It's paying salaries for hordes of inspectors. It's incurring the cost of warranties and customer returns. And it's suffering the anger of disgruntled customers.

Improving quality is a sure way to reduce cost. Do it right the first time. Work on reducing cost drivers that cause errors (such as frequent schedule changes, excessive process variability, or poor product design).

Paradoxically, reducing cost the activity-based way almost always improves quality. Eliminating unnecessary work, for example, reduces opportunities to "get it wrong" and tightens the linkages between activities.

Activity-based management fits well with any quality improvement program. It encourages the actions that improve quality, and directs attention to quality improvements with the greatest cost reduction potential.

3. *Select low-cost activities.* Designers of products and processes often have choices among competing activities. This offers a means of reducing cost by picking the lowest cost activity.

A designer of an electronics product, for example, may be able to specify the type of activity required for inserting components into circuit boards. Components such as resistors, diodes, and integrated circuits (ICs) may be inserted either manually or automatically. Depending on the design of the component, several automatic activities can be used to insert components, including axial, radial, and IC insertion. There may also be an option to place the components on the boards using surface mount equipment.

Each of these activities has a different set of resources associated with it. Manual insertion is predominantly a direct-- labor activity. Automatic insertion, however, requires equipment, software, setup for each batch of circuit boards that receives components, and additional process engineering and training. Each type of automatic insertion or placement also differs in resources required.

Because each of these activities has a different cost, the designer's selection has an important impact on costs. At Hewlett-- Packard's Roseville Network Division, for example, the ABC system showed that manual insertion cost about three times more than an automatic insertion.[9]

Process designers face similar choices. For example, a part designed for machine insertion might also be inserted manually. A process designer may chose to have the part inserted manually because a drop in the batch size makes it uneconomical to program and set up an insertion machine.

Stockham Valve and Fittings used ABC to identify parts that could be run at lower cost on different equipment. One product, for example, was sold for $9.68 per unit, but had an ABC cost of $12.63. Despite this loss, the product could not be dropped (it was a complementary product sold to a key customer). It's price couldn't be increased either.

The solution was to shift production to an automated machine more suited to the design and volume of the product. This shift reduced the number of operations required. It also reduced the need for batch activities, such as scheduling and moving, and reduced the cost to $9.86 per unit. While this represented a small loss on the product, the customer was now profitable overall.

4. Share activities wherever possible. If a customer has unique needs, it's necessary to perform activities specific to that customer. However, if customers have common needs, it's wasteful not to service those needs with the same activities.

For example, product designers can use common parts in new product designs. A common part is one that's used in several products to perform the same function (such as a gasket used in several car models). The only parts that need to be unique are those that add product differentiating functions valued by customers.

The activities associated with common parts—such as part number maintenance, scheduling, and vendor relations—are shared by all products that use them. This sharing increases the volume of parts served each time an activity is carried out, thus reducing the cost per part.

This insight was recognized by the Oscilloscope Group of Tektronix. This group introduced an ABC system that used *number of different parts* as an activity driver. This driver then assigned the cost of procurement activities to the parts.

The result was an increase in the reported cost of unique (and therefore low volume) parts and a reduction in the cost of common parts. The engineers responded over a three-year period by redesigning portable oscilloscopes to reduce part counts in these products from 3,500 to 2,500.[10]

Process designers can also cut costs by combining products into work cells. This is possible when products have similar designs (members of a product family) and when the manufacturing process is sufficiently flexible to handle any differences. Cost is reduced because the products in the cell share activities such as supervision, testing, training, scheduling, material handling, storage, and documentation.

5. *Redeploy unused resources.* In the final analysis, cost can only be reduced if resources are redeployed. Reducing the work load of an activity does not, *by itself*, reduce the equipment or number of people dedicated to that activity. There must be a conscious management decision to deal with the freed resources. This can be done by growing the business to take up the slack, redeploying the resources to other activities, or removing them from the company.

ABC can be used to calculate the type and amount of unused or under-used resources. Resource plans based on this information then become the basis for redeployment.

Summary

Activity-based management (ABM) uses ABC information to help meet two important goals. The first is to improve the value received by customers. The second is to improve profits earned from providing this value.

ABM also helps improve strategic position as well as strategic capability. It helps improve strategic position by showing how resources can be deployed for maximum strategic gain. It helps improve strategic capability by guiding improvements to the factors (such as quality, service, and low cost) most important to customers.

There are three steps to improving activity performance. The first step is to analyze activities in order to find opportunities for improvement. The second step is to look for factors that cause waste (the cost drivers) and for ways to remove them. The third step is to encourage and reinforce the right kind of improvement by measuring the important elements of performance.

ABM is quite different from old-fashioned accounting approaches to improvement. Accounting focuses on meeting cost targets. Costs are cut by eliminating staff and other resources without reference to the underlying work.

In contrast, ABM focuses on restructuring the work to *achieve lasting cost reductions*. This involves the following steps:

- Reducing the time and effort required to perform activities,
- Eliminating unnecessary activities,
- Selecting the lowest cost activity to perform work.
- Sharing activities wherever possible, and
- Redeploying resources made available by improvement efforts.

These efforts are as likely to improve quality as they are to reduce cost. ABM and quality management go hand-in-hand in any improvement program.

Key Terms in Chapter 7

Activity analysis—The evaluation of activity performance in the search for improvement opportunities.

Activity-based management (ABM)—A discipline that focuses on the management of activities as the route to continuously improving the value received by customers and the profit achieved by providing this value. This discipline includes cost driver analysis, activity analysis, and performance analysis. ABM draws on activity-based costing as a major source of information.

Benchmark—An activity that is *best practice* and by which a similar activity will be judged. Benchmarks are used to help identify opportunities for improving the performance of comparable activities. The source of a benchmark may be internal (such as another department in the same company) or external (such as a competitor).

Cost driver–A factor that causes a change in the performance of an activity and, in doing so, affects the resources required by the activity. For example, the quality of parts received by an activity is a determining factor in the effort required by that activity.

Customer value–The difference between customer realization and sacrifice. Realization is what is received by the customer. It includes product features, quality, and service as well as the cost to use, maintain, and dispose of the product. Sacrifice is what is given up by the customer. It includes the amount paid for the product plus the time spent acquiring the product and learning how to use it. To maximize customer value, maximize the difference between realization and sacrifice.

References:

1. This discussion of customer value is based on definitions found in M. Stahl and G. Bound, editors, *Competing Globally Through Customer Value: The Management of Strategic Suprasystems*, (Westport: Greenwood Publishing), 1991.

2. J.L. Colley, Jr, R.A. Gary IV, J.C. Reid, and R.C. Simpson III, "Data Services, Inc. (B)," UVA-OM-582 (Charlottesville: University of Virginia).

3. *Competitive Benchmarking: What It Is and What It Can Do For You*, Xerox Corporate Quality Office, Stamford, CT, 1984.

4. H. Thomas Johnson, Gail J. Fults and Paul Jackson, "Activity Management and Performance Measurement in a Service Organization," in Peter B.B. Turney (editor), *Performance Excellence in Manufacturing and Service Organizations*, (Sarasota: American Accounting Association), 1990.

5. Howard M. Armitage and Anthony A. Atkinson, "The Choice of Productivity Measures in Organizations," in Robert S. Kaplan (editor), *Measures for Manufacturing Excellence*, (Boston: Harvard Business School Press), 1990.

6. Robin Cooper and Peter B.B. Turney, "Zytec Corporation (B)," 9-190-066 (Boston: Harvard Business School), 1989.

7. For an extensive discussion of performance measurement issues, see Robert W. Hall, H. Thomas Johnson, and Peter B.B. Turney, *Measuring Up: Charting Pathways to Manufacturing Excellence*, (Homewood: Dow-Jones Irwin), 1990.

8.   J. Innes and F. Mitchell, *Activity-Based Costing: A Review with Case Studies*, (London: The Chartered Institute of Management Accountants), 1990.

9.   Robin Cooper and Peter B.B. Turney, "Hewlett-Packard: The Roseville Network Division," 9-189-117 (Boston: Harvard Business School), 1989.

10. Robin Cooper and Peter B.B. Turney, "Tektronix: The Portable Instrument Division," 9-188-142,143,144 (Boston: Harvard Business School), 1988.

Chapter 8

THE TOOLS OF
ACTIVITY-BASED MANAGEMENT

Now you understand what activity-based management (ABM) is all about. It helps improve your ability to profitably deliver value to your customers. It relies on managing activities better to achieve this improvement. It differs markedly from *old-fashioned accounting approaches to improvement*. And it draws heavily on information in the ABC system.

Now the question is, how do you do it?

To answer that, let's look at the following "tools of the trade" for ABM:

- Strategic analysis,
- Value analysis,
- Cost analysis,
- Activity-based budgeting,
- Life-cycle costing, and
- Target costing.

Some of these tools of the trade have been practiced for a number of years. General Electric, for example, has practiced value analysis for at least a quarter of a century. Others have come about more recently. All of these tools, however, can make contributions to increasing the competitiveness of your business.

Strategic Analysis

The strategic value of ABC is easily recognized. When ABC reveals that 80% of your products are unprofitable (as is typical of many ABC studies), the implications for pricing policy and product mix are loud and clear.

But strategic analysis using ABC information goes far beyond product pricing and mix considerations. It includes customer value analysis, competitive studies, sourcing, and product strategy analysis. Let's look at each of these in turn.

Pricing

ABC is invaluable for pricing decisions. Some organizations—including defense contractors—base their prices exclusively on cost. Others use cost in combination with competitive factors to set price.

For example, the Oscilloscope Group of Tektronix used ABC to help win a military contract. This was a strategically important contract that Tektronix did not wish to lose.

It was believed that the contract would be won if Tektronix had the lowest price. It was important, however, to ensure that the bid did not fall below cost.

ABC provided the baseline for setting the price. A bid was made that was low enough to win the contract, and yet exceeded the contract's ABC cost.

ABC may reveal many hidden opportunities to adjust prices. One company, for example, found that most of its low-volume specialty products were losing money, often by orders of magnitude. Some products were obvious candidates for the axe, but others were important to their customers. Was there any opportunity for increasing prices on any of those products?

The answer is *yes*. The price was increased on a select number of products. In several cases, the customer response was one of inevitability: "We're surprised you haven't done it before."

The company's competitors also followed the new prices without hesitation. That's a *sure sign* that prices in the industry had failed to follow true cost.

In some cases, the customers weren't willing to pay the higher price. Even this was an important opportunity. Clearly the company was unable to provide value to these customers at a price they could afford. These customers could be served with other products, or lost to competitors. Most importantly, however, there were opportunities to reduce the cost of these products via continuous process improvement and product redesign.

In some cases, ABC may reveal opportunities for repricing, but the market may not allow unilateral price changes. A local warehouse, for example, implemented ABC—the only warehouse in the area to do this. The ABC system revealed a systematic pattern of underpricing and overpricing services, yet the warehouse didn't have the market clout to change industry prices.

The solution? The warehouse intensified its marketing efforts on services that were currently overpriced, and reduced its emphasis on underpriced services. This produced a significant increase in profitability. And as a nice bonus, that increased profitability was invisible to the competition.

Customer Value Analysis

The central goal of ABM is to improve profitable delivery of value to your customers. To do this, customer value analysis focuses directly on the activities and activity-based cost of the customer.

The Oscilloscope Group of Tektronix, for example, analyzed differences in profitability between different types of customers. It was found that small customers were generally unprofitable or had been ignored by the sales force.

The ABC information showed *why* the small customers were unprofitable. It was the high cost of marketing and distributing products to these customers.

One reason for the high cost was that the cost of marketing and distribution activities exceeded nonmaterial manufacturing costs. A second reason was the expense associated with the dominant channel of distribution.

Oscilloscopes were distributed using a direct sales force. These sales engineers were well qualified (and therefore well paid). They also required an expensive infrastructure to support them.

The relatively high cost of distribution was less of a burden for large accounts. Large customers had sufficient volume to cover the cost. They also typically bought high-priced, top-of-the-line products having large profit margins. Small customers, however, didn't purchase enough product to justify the time and cost of the sales engineers. Small customers also preferred the lower margin, low-end products.

The solution? A new distribution channel, *Tek Direct*, was introduced. This channel emphasized telemarketing with a focus of selling low-priced oscilloscopes to small accounts.

Not only did this new approach substantially lower the cost of serving small accounts, it opened a potentially huge market that had previously been neglected. This consisted of customers not directly targeted using the traditional high-cost distribution channel. It was estimated to number in the hundreds of thousands of customers.

Competitive Studies

Strategic analysis can be used to understand competitor profitability as well as your own. The knowledge gained can be used to make selective price changes, change marketing emphasis, enter new markets, or counter unfair competitive actions.

Strategic analysis can be used to *understand competitor profitability* as well as your own. The knowledge gained can be used to make selective price changes, to change marketing emphasis, to pinpoint required reductions in cost, to enter new markets or to counter unfair competitive actions.

The Oscilloscope Group of Tektronix, for example, used ABC to study the manufacturing and distribution costs of products sold by competitors. ABC provided the insights for determining the likely activities to build and distribute these competing products.

Costs were built from the activity information, and cost data from annual reports. They did "reverse engineering" ABC style!

The analysis helped Tektronix understand their position *vis-a-vis* the competition. The knowledge gained from the analysis was used to assess the relative price of Tektronix products, the potential for market-share gains, and the need for reductions in the cost of distribution activities.

Sourcing

Deciding who does what is strategic for any company. Which parts do you manufacture, and which do you source from outside suppliers? Which services do you provide yourself, and which do you contract to a third party?

A plumbing fixture manufacturer, for example, completed an ABC study that showed major swings in cost from one process to another and one product to another. Among other things, the study revealed that costs assigned to the autopolishing activity increased by $1 million, while inner-assembly cost decreased by $300,000. Also, the cost of some low-volume parts increased by thousands of percent.

The company used ABC information to review its sourcing policy. Based on the insights provided by ABC, low-volume parts and high-cost activities were sourced to outside vendors. This was a completely new–*and profitable*–approach for a vertically integrated company that had traditionally done everything in-house.[1]

Product Strategy

ABC vividly portrays differing patterns of profitability among products. Analyzing these patterns may show, for example, that products fall into quadrants that differ by profit and volume *(Figure 8-1)*. Each quadrant will require a different product strategy.

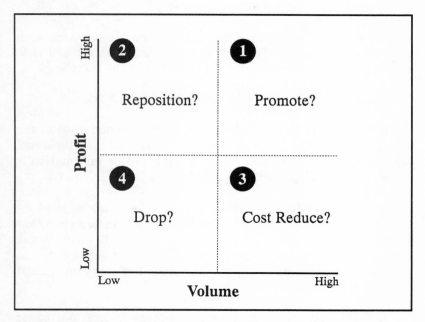

Figure 8-1. *Product strategy.* ABC may show products falling into distinct categories of profitability and volume. These insights are useful because each category requires a different strategy.

This type of analysis was done by a retailer with hundreds of stores in the United Kingdom. The retailer first placed each product into the appropriate quadrant based on the results of ABC. Then strategies for each of the four product types were evaluated.

Quadrant 1 products were candidates for extra promotion and more prominent display. Quadrant 2 products received additional advertising, improved shelf location, and price reductions to boost volume. Quadrant 3 products were studied for cost-reduction opportunities. Quadrant 4 products were reviewed for possible elimination from the line.[2]

In summary, strategic analysis helps you deploy resources to activities yielding the highest benefit. It helps you choose the best way to profitably serve your customers.

Value Analysis

Value analysis is the intense study of a business process with a view to improving the process and reducing cost. Its goal is to ensure that you perform the right activities in the right way.

Value analysis works with the following information:

1. Activities. Value analysis focuses on the activities in the process—what they are, what resources they consume, their cost drivers, and how they work together. Most of this information is found in the ABC system.

2. Activity analysis. Value analysis uses knowledge about activities gained during activity analysis. This is information that describes *why* and *how well* the work is done. It includes the designation of activities as value-added or non-value-added, whether they are significant, and how well they stack up against benchmark performance.

3. Cost drivers. The cost drivers—*those factors that cause work*—are the key to putting value analysis to work. Reducing the impact of negative cost drivers is the key to eliminating nonessential activities and removing waste from essential activities.

As an example, General Electric applied value analysis to an electromechanical assembly department and obtained dramatic results. This department assembled large products in small volumes.[3]

General Electric had previously implemented world-class manufacturing concepts in this department. This included just-in-time inventory flow. But the efforts had failed to improve performance significantly. Value analysis was viewed as the missing catalyst for improvement.

To understand how value analysis was applied, let's take a closer look at the activities in the department. *Figure 8-2* shows a partial list of those activities. Also shown are the equivalent number of people working in each activity (such as 3.9 people accumulating material).

Each activity in *Figure 8-2* is designated value-added, gray, or waste. Value-added activities are important to the customer, while non-value-added are not. The customer *wants* an assembled product, so assembly is classified value-added. Waiting for material, however, is clearly of no benefit to the customer, so it's non-value-added.

A third category—*gray*—is used for activities of no value to customers, but that may be essential to the functioning of the department. Assigning work and communicating with employees fall into this category.

Value analysis was focused on the significant activities in the department. These were the five activities with the most waste, making them candidates for the greatest improvement. These activities are shown in *Figure 8-3* along with their cost drivers.

As the next step, the cost drivers were divided into those internal and external to the department. Internal drivers were factors that could be changed by the department without outside involvement. The activity of *accumulating material*, for example, was affected by the way stock was laid out, by the procedures in the stock room, and by the flow of material in assembly.

External drivers also caused work, but were largely determined outside the department. *Accumulating material*, for example, was affected by the number of different parts—the more parts, the more difficult and time consuming the work.

The project team identified stockroom layout and material flow in assembly as the department's key cost drivers. The team then attacked these drivers to achieve performance improvement.

Activity	Equivalent People	Value Added	Gray	Waste
Assemble	10.7	10.7		
Accum. Material	3.9			3.9
Expedite Material	2.1			2.1
Wait for Material	1.2			1.2
.				
.				
Assigning Work	1.2		1.2	
Employee Communication	0.3		0.3	
Total	31.5	10.7	4.7	16.1
Percent		34%	15%	51%

Figure 8-2. *Activity distribution.* This is a partial listing of the activities in an electromechanical assembly department at General Electric. Each activity is classified according to whether it is valued by the customers of the department.

The results of the value analysis effort were dramatic. Productivity was improved by over 20%. Inventory levels and the time required to move a product through the process were cut in half. Also, quality improved as the number of defects fell.

More importantly, customer satisfaction increased with improved quality. Customers were also pleased with the improvement in on-time delivery and drops in order lead times.

Value analysis has been applied in many different business settings with similar positive results. General Electric has used it to improve performance in small departments as well as in businesses with thousands of employees. Value analysis also has been used successfully in a beverage company, a telephone company, and a bank.

In all cases, the purpose of value analysis was to *improve the ability to profitably serve customers.* In General Electric's heavy mechanical and electrical assembly business, for example, value analysis was followed by an increase in market share, a rise to *number one* in the market, and a significant return on investment.

Activity	Accum Mtl (Floor)	Expedite Material	Move Material	Rework	Test/Verify	Total
Equivalent People	3.9	2.1	2.1	1.9	1.8	11.8
Internal Drivers	Stock layout	Scrap	Material flow	Assembly errors	Interpretation of design	
	Stocking procedures	Stock errors	Handling equipment	Large batches	Training	
	Material flow	Ordering errors		Damage	Quality problems	
		MRP lead times		Methods/procedures		
External Drivers		Engineering change notices		Engineering change notices		
		Schedule changes		Supplier quality		
		Supplier/delivery & quality				
	Volume of part numbers		Labor classification	Quality of design	Design	
					Regulations	

Figure 8-3. *Highest waste activities.* This value analysis focused on the five activities with the most waste. Improvement (and cost reduction) was made by eliminating the negative effects of key cost drivers.

Cost Analysis

ABC supports cost reduction efforts in two ways. First, it helps find opportunities with the greatest cost reduction potential. ABC is a navigational aid that helps quantify the size of the hidden "rocks"—and pick the biggest ones as cost reduction targets. We'll look at *goal seeking* and *Pareto analysis* as ways of doing this.

Second, you can use ABC to simulate the impact of cost reduction actions. *Cost simulation* helps build commitment in advance and subsequently confirms positive results.

Goal Seeking

One way to identify cost-reduction targets is *goal seeking*. Goal seeking starts with the bill of activities. This is a listing of activities and activity drivers associated with a product or service. The idea is to use the information in the bill to identify a cost-reduction opportunity for improving the competitiveness of the product or service.

Oregon Cutting Systems used goal seeking to identify products with lower than acceptable profit margins and as a way to improve their profitability. For example, *Figure 8-4* is the *bill of activities* for a component of the chain used in chain saws. This Component was the high-cost part in a low-margin product.

The bill of activities reveals sources of highest cost. For example, the batch-process activity center in *Figure 8-4* accounts for about a third of the cost of the part. What goes on in this activity center?

Oregon Cutting Systems
Component, Part #AB343

Type	Activity	Level	Driver	Unit Cost
Macro	Procuring	Batch	# Times requisitioned	$ 4.29
Center	Initiating			6.35
Center	Batch process			12.41
Center	Individual process			8.19
Macro	Planning	Product	# of Part #s	3.79
Macro	Changing specifications	Product	# of ECNs	2.98
Total				$38.01

Figure 8-4. *Goal seeking (1).* Goal seeking uses a bill of activities to look for opportunities to improve a product's competitiveness. This bill shows the main groupings of activities needed to make this component at Oregon Cutting Systems. Notice that the *batch-process activity center* is the highest cost activity area.

The batch process is a central activity to which parts are moved from the product cells. The activities in this process are shown in *Figure 8-5*. The process is first set up to produce each batch of parts. The pans containing parts are then dipped into a chrome bath. After the batch process, the parts are inspected for defects, then transported back to the product cells.

There are three non-value-added activities in *Figure 8-5* that are candidates for improvement. They are setting up, inspecting, and transporting. Which one would you improve for the greatest cost savings?

Oregon Cutting Systems
Components, Part #AB343
Batch Process Activity Center

Type	Activity	Level	Driver	Value-Added	Non-Value-Added
Micro	Setting Up	Batch	# of Setups		$2.94
Micro	Processing	Unit/Batch	# of Pans	$6.04	
Center	Inspecting	Batch Unit/Batch	# of Setups # of Pans		1.14
Micro	Transporting	Unit/Batch	# of Pans		2.29
Total				$6.04	$6.37

Figure 8-5. *Goal seeking (2).* This detailed bill of activities reveals the activities and activity costs in the batch-process activity center. It shows three non-value-added activities, each a candidate for elimination or improvement.

A review of the cost drivers for these activities revealed that plant layout was the most important factor. The plant was laid out in product cells, yet the batch process was a large central activity serving several product cells. This layout required that parts be moved to and from the process, and the variety of work affected both quality and setup time.

The ideal solution was to replace the large central process with small ones dedicated to each product cell. This would eliminate the transporting activity entirely. The number of setups would be less because each small process would be dedicated to a product family. The time required for setup would likely go down, as well, because of the similarity of parts in each cell and the improved opportunity for learning.

In practice, installing small local processes requires a capital investment. If funds aren't available, cost reduction should focus instead on improving the existing process. This might include reducing the time required for setup or improving quality so parts inspection can be eliminated.

Pareto Analysis

Another way to identify cost-reduction targets is to look for the activity drivers that account for most of the cost traced. Pareto analysis involves arranging activity drivers in descending order of the amount of cost assigned.

Figure 8-6 shows a Pareto analysis prepared at the Business Products Division of Northern Telecom. Each bar in this figure represents the proportion of cost assigned by activity drivers of a common type. For example, 25% of the cost is assigned via material-type drivers. These include *number of receipts, number of purchase orders, number of material inspections*, and *number of movements*.

Based on this Pareto analysis, the division selected material-- related activities as targets for cost reduction. Not only was this the second highest area of cost, but in many cases the activity cost exceeded the components' material costs by orders of magnitude.

A look at the cost drivers associated with these activities shows why the cost was so high:

- The large *number of vendors* created high demand for vendor development and maintenance activities;
- The large *number of different part types* increased demand for purchasing, receiving, inspection, stocking, and other activities; and
- *Procurement procedures* were cumbersome and involved numerous people. The purchasing department used a computerized shop-floor scheduling system to determine what needed to be purchased. On-hand quantities in the stockroom were verified and phone calls placed to vendors. Purchase orders were prepared and mailed. Once the parts were received they were inspected, counted, moved, stored, and paid for.

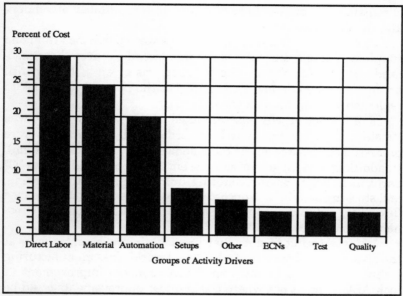

Figure 8-6. *Pareto analysis at Northern Telecom.* Northern Telecom's Business Products Division grouped its activity drivers into "common" types such as procurement and quality. Each bar on this chart represents the cost assigned via each group of drivers. It shows that labor, material, and automation drivers account for most of the cost—and the major opportunities for improvement.

Cost Simulation

ABC is an economic *and* performance model of a business or process. It provides building blocks for simulating the impact of changes in operating a business or process or the impact on the type of business conducted.

For example, the Business Products Division of Northern Telecom used cost simulation to identify *the best way* to reduce the cost of material-related activities. The simulation focused on alternative ways of procuring "C" parts (low-cost and high-volume parts). There were thousands of these parts, and they accounted for the bulk of the activity.

The cost of each alternative was computed using the ABC model. The activity driver quantities for each one were multiplied by the cost-per-unit of the activity drivers.

The analysis showed that the lowest cost alternative totally changed the way "C" parts were procured. This alternative also eliminated two of the three cost drivers (the number of vendors and the procurement procedures themselves).

Under this alternative, all "C" parts were purchased from one supplier. A single purchase order was issued to cover the plant's needs for an entire year. The supplier was given a three-month production schedule and agreed to visit the plant once a week to replenish *kanban* bins on the shop floor.

The impact on cost–as computed by the ABC system– was substantial. Only one purchase order and 12 invoices were processed each year (versus thousands under the current system). In addition, several activities were entirely eliminated for the "C" parts, including receiving, counting, unloading, inspecting, moving, and stocking activities. Noncost improvements included increased flexibility, reduced lead times, and reduced likelihood of component obsolescence.

It's interesting to note that previous improvement efforts at the division–applications of traditional world-class manufacturing techniques–turned up only small increments of improvement. It took ABC to point out where the greatest improvements could be found, and to focus efforts on successful waste elimination and simplification.

The ability to simulate the cost impact of improvement programs has benefits in addition to identifying the lowest cost alternative. Improvement programs may now proceed on the basis of analysis rather than faith alone. Management commitment to improvement is easier to obtain, and the ability to communicate the results helps transfer the learning across the company.

For example, one manufacturing plant was unable to persuade its parent company to allow it to drop some complex low-volume products. The plant knew these products required excessive effort *not rewarded* by revenues (even though their conventional cost system revealed the opposite).

An ABC study confirmed the intuitions of the plant–the products did cost a lot more than they generated in revenues. These results were presented to the parent company.

The parent company's first response was dismissal of the ABC product costs as invalid. But they did permit the plant to seek an outside supplier bid to manufacture the products.

The bid turned out to be higher than the ABC cost. This was enough to convince the parent that the ABC cost was *indeed valid*. Permission was granted to remove the products from the plant.

The lesson is clear. Cost-reduction analysis using ABC does not reduce cost. Cost can only be reduced if changes are made in performing activities and if the redundant resources are redeployed. Cost analysis does help identify cost-reduction opportunities, garner management support, communicate the learning associated with the improvement, and generally reinforce the entire improvement effort.

Activity-Based Budgeting

ABC's power to simulate cost impacts of proposed changes in activities can be extended to planning, too. Why not prepare a budget based on ABC data?

ABC helps the budgeting process in two ways. *First*, the mix of activities, and degree of emphasis on particular activities, can be linked to the business strategy. Resources can be assigned to those activities that are the most important for delivering value to customers.

Second, the ABC model provides a foundation for creating a realistic budget. It does this by providing information to link projected sales to work load and work load to resources required.

Activity-based budgeting starts with the cost objects and works up in the following way:

- Projections of sales volume and product and customer mix for the coming period create a potential demand for activities,
- The activity drivers measure the use of the activities by the cost objects,
- The volume of the activity drivers determines the work level of the related activities,
- The cost drivers of each activity determine the effort needed to meet the estimated demand, and
- The level of effort for each activity determines the resources required.

Figure 8-7 shows how this might work to budget the activity of *setting up a machine*. The company in this example has scheduled 1,000 products for manufacture in the coming period. This production schedule requires 3,750 production runs (the number of production runs is the activity driver that helps determine work load for the activity). A setup is required each time there's a production run, so the activity is also performed 3,750 times.

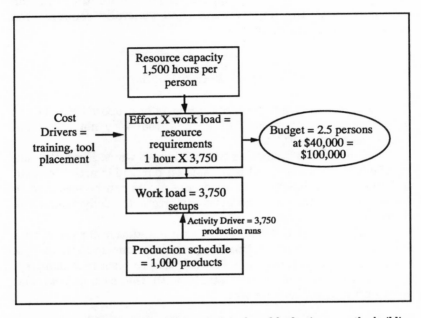

Figure 8-7. *Activity-based budgeting.* Activity-based budgeting uses the building blocks of ABC to prepare estimates of work load and resource requirements. Illustrated here is creation of the staff budget for the activity of *setting up machines.* The ability to model changes in operations and type of business is a far cry from the traditional "let's add 10% to last year" approach to budgeting.

In the preceding year it took, on average, two hours to complete a setup. During the year, however, operators were trained in setup time reduction, and tools were placed more readily at hand. This reduction in key cost drivers brought the average time down to one hour.

One hour per setup for 3,750 setups requires 3,750 hours of effort. If each person is available to perform setups 1,500 hours per year, 2.5 people are required to do the work. (It would have been 5 people if the cost drivers had not been reduced.)

The budgeted cost of the activity is $100,000. This is 2.5 people at $40,000 total salary and benefits for each person.

Of course, it's not possible to assign 2.5 people exclusively to the setup department. (One person may have to be assigned to other work for half of the time.) Nor may it be possible to immediately reassign the two individuals who are not needed during the coming year.

But the information allows *conscious* and *deliberate decisions* about resource deployment. These decisions are based on understanding the demands placed on the activity by the cost objects and the role of cost drivers in determining the effort required.

A number of companies have used activity-based budgeting to help plan work loads and resource requirements. For example, a retailer in the United Kingdom used ABC to set the budget for distribution activities.[4] Caterpillar, Inc., has used activity-based budgeting for several years, too.[5]

Dayton Extruded Plastics designed its ABC system specifically to support activity-based budgeting. Detailed activities were grouped into activity centers paralleling departments in the organizational chart. These included process engineering, the materials laboratory, customer service, and accounting.[*]

There are no assignments at this level of detail that would introduce costs incurred for work under someone else's responsibility. (The assignment of the cost of sustaining activities to the departments that benefit is done in a different part of the ABC system.)

This way of organizing detailed activities aids budgeting because the responsibility for budgeting is at the department level. All the activities for one manager's responsibility are in one place—the department where the work occurs. (Not coincidentally, *the same information* supports managing the performance of their activities.)

Activity-based budgeting uses the building blocks of ABC to prepare estimates of work load and resource requirements. Its

---

[*] These same activities can be regrouped by key processes. Engineering change activities, for example, occur in several departments. To indicate this, the engineering change activities are *tagged with an attribute* that identifies their inclusion in this process. This allows an activity center for engineering change activities to be created on demand. This also makes activity interdependence highly visible.

power is its ability to estimate the impact on activities and the cost of changes in operations and type of business. This is a far cry from traditional budgeting that relies on incremental adjustments to last year's budget.

Life-Cycle Costing

Life-cycle costing looks at products over their life cycle rather than just for one year. A product's life cycle encompasses initial research and development, proceeds through introduction and growth in the market, and ends with maturity, decline, and abandonment.

A life-cycle perspective yields insights to product cost and profitability that are not available from viewing a single year. A product that has just been introduced has a low volume. It's incurring start-up costs and may look uncompetitive from a one-year view. A product that's mature, however, may be reaping the rewards of hard work in previous years. So it appears highly profitable.

But it's misleading to compare the cost of a new product with a mature product in a single-period model. It's possible that incorrect conclusions will be drawn from the relative cost and profitability of the two products.

Dayton Extruded Plastics illustrates why a life-cycle perspective is important. This company develops new window systems, designs the dies required to manufacture the vinyl components of the windows, and then manufactures the dies. All this work occurs over one to two years before any production occurs. The development effort requires as much in the way of resources as the production itself.

What is critical, however, is the strategic nature of window and die development. This is where the company commits itself to the customers it will serve, and the products it will provide, over the next few years.

Can ABC be Used by Defense Contractors?

Defense contractors face a dilemma. On the one hand, they face intense competitive pressures. Reductions in government defense spending are accompanied by dual sourcing of major weapons systems. A leader/follower arrangement ensures that the lowest cost supplier gets the lion's share of the business.

On the other hand, government procurement regulations have (in the past) required contractors to use conventional cost systems, and to base their prices on the costs reported by these systems. But these systems inhibit the improvements that are necessary to win and maintain leadership positions on government contracts.

Can a defense contractor use ABC? The answer is a qualified yes. You can replace your existing cost system with ABC if you proceed cautiously and obtain the necessary approval. According to Jack Haedicke and David Feil at Hughes Aircraft[6], the key to obtaining such approval is to inform, educate and involve:

INFORM: Inform the Defense Contract Audit Agency (DCAA) of your plans. This avoids any possible suspicion as to the intent of implementing ABC.

EDUCATE: Educate your local audit staff about the purpose and design of your ABC system. They may not be familiar with ABC, and education is necessary for proper communication. It's an on-going task starting with implementation planning and ending with the evaluation of the results.

INVOLVE: Involve your local audit staff in the implementation process. This gives them an opportunity to provide input and to influence the direction of the project. It also ensures they have "ownership" when the ABC system is complete.

Does a defense contractor need ABC? *The answer is a resounding yes.* Hughes Aircraft, for example, used ABC to determine what should be manufactured internally and what should be subcontracted to achieve the lowest cost. Hughes has also used ABC to identify opportunities for process improvement and to identify the lowest cost processes across the company. ABC supports more accurate estimates of contract costs. It's used by Hughes' engineering staff to "design to cost." And it supports improvement efforts all over the company.

Intelligent strategic decisions—and the commitment of scarce engineering resources—require a life-cycle perspective. Each customer has different requirements. Some customers, for example, may stick with the same window design for years and buy the product in high volumes. Other customers, however, may request constant changes to the design, buy low volumes, and phase out the product quickly.

Clearly the cost of serving each of these customers over the product's life cycle is quite different. And unless the prices charged are different, the economics will be quite different, too.

Life-cycle costing also highlights the activities and resources needed to take a product from development to abandonment. Indeed, the analysis may show that the product is uncompetitive and that a reduction in life-cycle cost is in order. The life-cycle costing information pinpoints which activities can be improved and shows the impact of this improvement on product cost.

A major defense contractor, for example, used life-cycle costing to look for ways of reducing the cost of a large subassembly. The life cycle of this product included a transition phase where production was moved to a lower cost facility.

The study confirmed that moving production did reduce cost over the life cycle of the product. The transition itself required various activities and resources, but this cost was more than offset by lower production costs in the new facility.

The defense contractor also did an analysis of activities across the phases of the life cycle. This analysis identified activities with superior performance and common cost drivers. It was discovered, for example, that cost drivers relating to shortages and poor quality accounted for more than a fifth of total life cycle cost.

How does life-cycle costing work? In its simplest form, it's the accumulation of a product's development and start-up costs and applying these costs to units over the product's life *(Figure 8-8)*. This includes costs incurred prior to introduction, such as initial die manufacture, and anticipated costs such as replacement of the die during the product's life.

In *Figure 8-8*, the product's development and start-up costs are $20,000. These costs are placed in a special life-cycle account. The cost in this account is then divided by an estimate of production over the product's life. In this example, the estimated volume is 10,000 units and the unit cost is $1.

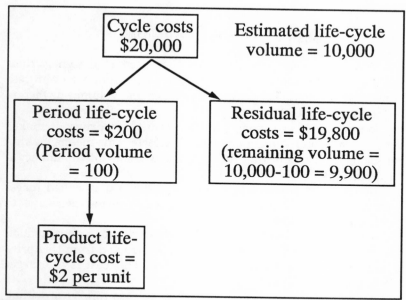

Figure 8-8. *The mechanics of life-cycle costing.* Life-cycle costing requires estimates of life-cycle costs and volume.

In the first year of production, 100 units of the product are made. A cost of $2 is added to the current period's cost of each unit to give the life-cycle cost.

The cost in future periods may need adjustment. For example, the estimate of life-cycle volume may be revised. Additional life-cycle costs may be incurred at levels other than those anticipated. Also, depreciation may need to be computed on a replacement cost basis.

A key to the success of life-cycle costing is the accuracy of the estimates of product life and costs. Some companies have developed elaborate systems for estimating these data. Boeing and British Aerospace, for example, use sophisticated statistical models.

Life-cycle costing involves all functions of the company. Dayton Extruded Plastics involves marketing, engineering, and manufacturing in the estimating process. Marketing receives feedback on actual sales versus estimated sales. They initiate the sales, so are held responsible for significant differences.

Target Costing

Operating managers often say that product design is their most important cost driver. They point to the number of process steps, product complexity, and parts types and volumes as factors beyond their control.

If product design is such an important cost driver, it makes sense to work on reducing its negative effects. This means making conscious decisions during the design process about the impact of design on cost.

Designing a product to meet a specific cost is called *target costing*. This is a device for linking engineering decisions to market requirements.

It involves setting the planned market price for a new product. Distribution costs and profits are then subtracted from this price to leave the required manufacturing cost. This cost is the target the engineers shoot for.

ABC makes target costing possible. It does this by providing the framework for estimating the impact of design decisions on cost.

Engineers at Hewlett-Packard, for example, use ABC to pick the least expensive activities for a product. They build up the cost of each alternative design using the activity driver rates from the ABC system. Then they pick the design with the lowest cost (and the proper functionality).[7]

Engineers at some companies have even developed "rules of thumb" based on ABC. The Oscilloscope Group of Tektronix did this to prepare its *cost guidelines* for design. These guidelines summarized the relative cost of key design alternatives. The placement of a part using surface-mount technology, for example, costs 1.5 times that of machine insertion.

These guidelines were also a reminder to engineers of the impact of their decisions on cost. It was estimated, for example, that 80-90% of the cost of an instrument was frozen when it left engineering *(Figure 8-9)*.

Tektronix also used *target costing* in their cathode ray tube (CRT) division. This division supplies CRTs for use in analog oscilloscopes.

1. Cost of insertion and placement activities relative to machine insertion:

Placement (surface mount)	1.5X
Robot insertion	3.0X
Hand insertion (pre-solder)	6.0X
Hand insertion (post-solder)	10.0X

2. Purchasing and inspecting parts from a qualified vendor is three times more expensive than from a nonqualified vendor.
3. Engineering modifications cost $2,500 each.
4. Many costs vary with the number of part types rather than the volume of parts.
5. Ninety percent of nonmaterial manufacturing costs vary with the complexity of the instrument.
6. An automatic test on a circuit board costs $3.00 per board.
7. The cost of a product is 80-90% frozen when it leaves engineering.

Figure 8-9. *Cost guidelines for product design.* Cost guidelines developed from ABC at the Oscilloscope Group of Tektronix highlight important cost information. These guidelines influence engineers in their design choices and remind them of the impact of their decisions on cost.

In one example, an internal Tektronix customer set a target transfer price for a new CRT. The CRT division would get the business if they could meet the target price.

The CRT engineers used ABC to examine the impact of several design alternatives on activities and resources. For example, a new design for a major component of the CRT–the CRT gun–was proposed. The new gun would require an additional production operation, but the improved quality would reduce the testing needed versus existing guns. Overall, ABC showed that the cost of the new gun would be less.

This design review continued until the CRT target cost was met. The business was won and the new CRT is now in production.

Summary

The tools of ABM are ways of applying ABC information to improve performance. They work in the following manner:

- *Strategic analysis* helps you deploy resources in activities that yield the highest benefit. It helps you choose the best way to profitably serve your customers.
- *Value analysis* is the intense study of a business process with a view to improving the process and reducing cost. Its goal is to ensure that you perform the right activities in the right way.
- *Cost analysis* supports cost reduction efforts in two ways. First, it helps find the opportunities with the greatest cost reduction potential. Second, it helps build commitment to improvement in advance, and it communicates what's learned from the improvement.
- *Activity-based budgeting* uses ABC's framework to estimate work load and resource requirements. It can help direct resources and activities to the most strategically valuable purposes.
- *Life-cycle costing* looks at cost over a product's life cycle rather than just one year. It facilitates judgements about cost and profitability that just can't be made from a single-year perspective.
- *Target costing* is use of ABC information to design products to meet a predetermined cost. It links engineering decisions to market requirements. It's also a reminder to engineers of the important role their decisions play in determining cost.

Key Terms in Chapter 8

Activity-based budgeting–Preparation of cost budgets using ABC to help estimate work load and resource requirements.

Cost analysis–Simulation of cost-reduction opportunities. Cost analysis helps you select opportunities that yield the greatest improvement. It also helps build commitment for improvement actions and helps communicate the knowledge gained through the improvement.

Customer value analysis–Study of customer activities directed at finding ways to improve customer value and reduce the cost of delivering that value.

Goal seeking–The search for ways to improve the competitiveness of a product or service. The search starts with identifying high-cost activities in the bill of activities. It then proceeds through the causes of high cost and finishes with actions to reduce or eliminate the effect of these causes.

Life-cycle costing–Costing products over their entire life cycle rather than for a single accounting period. The product life cycle spans development, introduction, growth, maturity, decline, and abandonment. Life-cycle costing helps assess product profitability.

Pareto analysis–Arrangement of activities or activity drivers in descending order of cost. The activities or drivers accounting for the majority of cost are targeted for cost reduction.

Strategic analysis–Analysis of products, services, and customers for strategic opportunities. Strategic analysis may point out opportunities for repricing, redirecting resources to more profitable opportunities, and changing product strategy.

Target costing–Setting cost targets for new products based on market price. The analysis starts with an estimate of the selling price and subtracts profits and distribution costs to arrive at the target cost. Engineers then use ABC to help design a product for this cost.

Value analysis–Intense study of a business process with the intent of improving the process and reducing cost. Its goal is to ensure that you perform the right activities in the right way.

References:

1.   Michael O'Guin, "Focus the Factory with Activity-Based Costing," *Management Accounting*, (February 1990), pp. 36-41.

2.   J. Innes and F. Mitchell, *Activity-Based Costing: A Review with Case Studies*, (London: The Chartered Institute of Management Accountants), 1990.

3.   Thomas O'Brien, "Improving Performance Through Activity Analysis," *Performance Excellence in Manufacturing and Service Organizations*, Peter B.B. Turney, editor, (Sarasota: American Accounting Association), 1990.

4.   J. Innes and F. Mitchell, *Activity-Based Costing: A Review with Case Studies*, p. 56.

5.   C.J. McNair, "Interdependence and Control: Traditional vs. Activity-Based Responsibility Accounting," *Journal of Cost Management*, (Summer 1990), pp. 15-25.

6.   Jack Haedicke and David Feil, "Hughes Aircraft Sets the Standard for ABC", *Management Accounting*, Vol. LXXII, No.8, February 1990, pp.29-33

7.   Robin Cooper and Peter B.B. Turney, "Hewlett-Packard: The Roseville Network Division," 9-188-177 (Boston: Harvard Business School), 1989.

Chapter 9

BUILDING THE WORLD-CLASS COMPANY

Activity-based management helps companies become—*and continue to be*—world class. World class is achievement of high standards of business performance, profitably meeting customer needs, and continuous improvement of performance.

There's nothing "business as usual" at a world-class company. The things that matter are different (they are the things that matter to the customer). It's managed differently (decision making is pushed to the lowest levels of the organiza tion). And it uses different tools to improve business (such as total quality control and ABM).

ABM brings *information empowerment* to aspiring world- class companies. Putting ABC information in the hands of those doing the improvement increases their power to improve.

Analyzing ABC information, for example, helps reveal the causes and magnitudes of poor performance. It also helps focus efforts to improve quality or eliminate waste in areas where the payoff is the greatest.

This Chapter shows how *information empowerment* worked in a printed circuit board plant (PCB). We saw in an earlier Chapter how this plant's ABC analyses revealed a dramatic pattern of unprofitable products and customers. Now we'll see how the PCB plant put knowledge gained from ABC to work in creating a world-class plant.

The contribution of ABM at PCB was as important as ABC's new perceptions were dramatic. This plant is now the benchmark facility in the printed circuit board industry—the world-class plant against which all others compare themselves. And ABM was a key reason for this success.

PCB's general manager sums it up this way:

We could not have achieved our success without ABC. It has helped us focus on what we do best and has accelerated our improvement efforts. Its influence extends to all corners of the plant and governs short and long-term decisions alike. And you can see clearly the positive impact of ABC on the bottom line. All told, I would estimate that at least a third of our improvement is due to ABC.

The case of the PCB plant illustrates how ABM fosters world-class performance. It describes how the plant used ABC for:

- Strategic management,
- Performance management,
- Supplier management, and
- Investment management.

Strategic Management

Strategic management is the use of ABC and market information for two purposes:

1. To help set strategic priorities and
2. To help implement the chosen strategy.

PCB learned from their ABC study that many products and customers were unprofitable. But *which type* of products and customers were unprofitable? How should they change their strategy as a result of this knowledge? And how should they implement the changes once they'd been identified?

Product Strategy

A close look at the ABC data showed that product profitability varied by technology, volume, and life cycle. From this, PCB learned the following:

1. Technology decision—focus on high-technology products. ABC showed that product functionality had an enormous impact on the amount and type of production and support activities required. Boards varied by number of layers, circuit density, and fineness of printed metal lines.

High-technology boards—ones with more layers, more density, and finer lines—were far more expensive to manufacture than low-technology ones. One high-technology board, for example, required more tools (film) from engineering, more materials and sequence scheduling, more expensive drills with shorter lives, and more inspections than a low-technology board of the same size.

But high-technology boards commanded a much higher price than low-technology ones. This made them more profitable. Boards with ten layers or more carried an average profit margin of 46%, whereas two-sided boards earned a *negative* 49% margin *(Figure 9-1)*.

PCB decided on high-technology products as their strategic priority. These boards were well suited to the plant's engineering and production capability, and they promised excellent profitability.

2. *Volume decision—focus on low-volume boards*. PCB also found that, in general, high-volume products were less costly (and more profitable) than low-volume products. This was because activities associated with a product would cost less per product unit when shared over a larger volume.

For example, the cost of creating a board-test program for use with automated testing equipment did not vary with volume. As a result, if two boards were of equivalent design, but of different volume, the test program development cost per unit for the higher volume board would be less.

There was a similar effect for activities associated with taking a customer's order. These activities included order processing, order entry, credit checking, scheduling, and maintaining the data base. The activity demand was generally the same for each order, but the volume per order varied from high to low. The cost per unit of high-volume orders, therefore, was much less than that of low-volume orders.

This created a dilemma for PCB. Many low-volume boards were also high-technology boards. (Companies at the leading edge of their markets typically ordered in low volumes.) A strategic decision to drop low-volume boards would conflict with the decision to focus on high-technology boards.

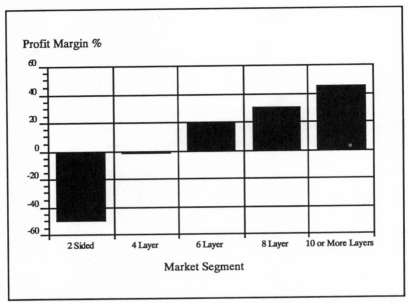

Figure 9-1. PCB's market choices. PCB participated in five distinct market segments. ABC helped decide which segments to focus on by revealing wide disparities in profitability between segments.

It was clear that PCB had to sell low-volume boards to complement the high-technology focus. But how could this be done profitably?

The first step was to institute a minimum-order charge. This covered the cost of order- and batch-related activities. It also made customers conscious of the impact of their order size on PCB's activities and costs. The minimum-order charge was a short-run solution, and it got the attention of customers.

The long-run solution was to reduce the cost of low-volume production. To do this, PCB introduced computer integrated manufacturing (CIM). This reduced the costs of order- and batch-related activities. For example, CIM allowed customers to use an electronic link to transmit engineering drawings directly to PCB. This reduced the engineering cost and time associated with placing an order.

PCB also acquired a production facility that specialized in high-volume, low-technology production. An ABC study showed that the costs of high-volume, low-technology boards dropped as much as one-third in this facility. The facility met PCB's need to fill a minimum level of demand for these types of boards. It also freed up capacity in the main facility, which was then filled with high-margin, high-technology products.

3. *Product life-cycle decision—acquire products early in their life cycle; dispose of products late in their life cycle.* A review of product profitability could not be done without reference to the product's life cycle. This was because cost (and profitability) varied considerably in each phase of a circuit board's life cycle. *Figure 9-2* shows this life cycle. The circuit board is designed, and a few boards are produced for design verification during the prototype phase. This prototype production typically has short lead times and frequent engineering changes.

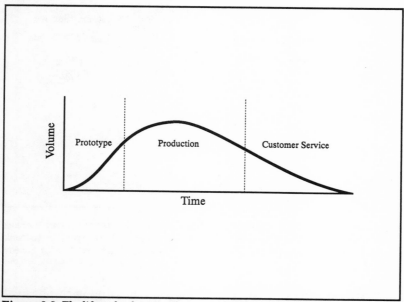

Figure 9-2. *The life cycle of a printed circuit board.* Boards go through three phases. The prototype phase is where the design is verified and, if necessary, revised. The production phase sees the tested product shipped to the customer in quantity. The customer-service phase covers sales after the board has been discontinued.

The production phase is when actual customer orders are placed and filled. It's characterized by repetitive orders and infrequent design changes.

The third phase is customer service. This is a period of declining sales after the product has been phased out. Orders from customers to replace boards that have failed in the field typically are received infrequently, in low volumes, and over a number of years.

	Prototype	Production	Customer Service
Production Activities	$ 378	$ 130	$534
Support Activities	184	3	86
Total Cost	$ 562	$ 133	$ 620
Volume	6	500,000	10

Figure 9-3. *Variation in product cost over the life cycle.* The cost of a board changes dramatically over its life. The most profitable life-cycle strategy was to seek business early in the product's life cycle and "hand off" customer-service boards wherever possible.

Figure 9-3 shows the costs of a typical board in each phase of its life cycle. The intense use of engineering and support activities, and low-volume, is reflected by the high cost during the prototype phase.

The cost per unit plummets during the production phase. This reflects the stability of the product (its reduced need for activities) and the high volume over which cost is spread.

The customer-service phase sees costs return to prototype levels as volume falls and demand for activities picks up. For example, boards in this phase commonly require additional engineering to accommodate changes in the production process.

A review of ABC information showed that boards were typically profitable during the prototype and production phases, but not during the customer-service phase. On balance, boards acquired during the prototype phase were profitable over their entire life cycle. Boards acquired late in the production phase were unprofitable.

What was the appropriate response to this knowledge? The first response was to reemphasize the prototype business. The earlier a product was contracted for in its life cycle, the more profitable it would be.

The second response was a three-part strategy to reduce product costs in the customer-service phase. To do this:

- Customers were offered reduced prices for a single "last buy."
- PCB located suppliers specializing in low-volume production of obsolete parts. Customers, if they were willing, took their service needs to these suppliers.
- Customer-service orders were subcontracted to the specialized suppliers. This alternative was the most costly of the three, because additional activities were needed to order, schedule, track, and pay for the subcontract work.

In short, PCB used *life-cycle cost data* to help formulate a strategy to maximize profitability over the product's life cycle. The decision to acquire board contracts early in the board's life fit well with the plant's technical skills with prototype boards. Eliminating much of the customer-service work was also done without abrogating commitments to customers.

Customer Strategy

PCB's review of product strategy showed that the marketing emphasis should be on customers needing high-technology, low-volume boards at the prototype stage. Were there any other customer characteristics that should be reviewed?

An analysis of ABC information on customers revealed two groupings, each with different profitability profiles:

Group 1.   This customer group followed "good business practic-es." They maintained a long-term relationship with PCB and obtained all of their needs from the plant.

Group 2.   This customer group had no loyalty to any one suppli-er. These customers moved their business from one supplier to another, constantly searching for the lowest price.

PCB decided to serve the first customer group, the ones following "good business practices." This was done for two reasons. *First*, PCB's strategy emphasized quality and customer service. It was easier to do this when there was a stable relationship with the customer.

Second, the ABC information made it quite clear that the cost of serving loyal customers was a lot less. There was less sales effort, less order processing effort, less engineering effort, less material handling effort, and less effort associated with higher quality.

The decision to seek customers with "good business practices" increased PCB's profitability. It also fit well with the plant's desire to focus efforts on providing quality and service on an on-going basis to a small group of customers.

Strategy Implementation

ABC information allows you to pick a strategy with confidence. You take your bearing from an accurate compass setting.

The next step is to follow your chosen course. This requires you to take steps to implement your chosen strategy, and ABC can help here, too.

PCB used ABC to persuade sales to sell products that fit best with the chosen strategy. When a customer called in for a bid, the product was costed using ABC. This was done by building up the cost from the characteristics of the product, such as number of layers, number of holes, and the *activity driver rates* in the ABC system.

Sales staff performance and compensation were tied to profitability based on ABC cost. This gave sales a strong incentive to pay attention to the profit impact of their sales.

Sales staff response to this performance measurement and incentive program was immediate. In the first month after program introduction, there were substantial changes in product mix. This quickly moved the PCB plant in the direction of its chosen strategy.

Performance Management

Performance management applies activity-based management to meeting goals of improved performance. This is aided enormously by the array of available ABC weapons, such as cost analysis and performance measurement, for waging war on waste.

Performance management at PCB focused on four areas. *First*, ABC was used to guide product design. *Second*, ABC helped prioritize cost reduction opportunities. *Third*, ABC was used to guide total quality control (TQC). *Fourth*, ABC data were used to measure performance in the plant and monitor on-going improvement.

Product Design

An important ABC application was guiding product designs for lower cost. In doing this, PCB was right in step with Hewlett-Packard and the Oscilloscope Group of Tektronix. What was unique about PCB was the customer involvement in the cost reduction efforts.

Figure 9-4 provides an example of ABC's cost reduction power. It compares the design and cost of two circuit boards. Notice that there are three differences in the design of the two boards. However, these differences do not affect the functionality of the boards.

The differences between the boards in *Figure 9-4* are minor adjustments in board size, hole sizes, and board thickness. Yet these minor design adjustments yielded a 15% cost reduction (as estimated by ABC).

PCB went straight to the customer to achieve these design-based cost reductions. This was necessary because customers often did their own board design.

Involving the customer in this way soon became a competitive weapon for the PCB plant. Customers clearly saw the impact on cost (and their purchase price) of making changes in their boards.

The changes increased the net value received from PCB and encouraged customers to send more business to PCB. In some cases, entire product families were sourced at PCB because of design and cost improvements made to a single product. Some customers moved their engineering data base to PCB and turned over the design work to PCB or did the work jointly with them.

Trade off	Design 1	Design 2
1. **Size of Board**	36.72 sq. inches	38 sq. inches
Impact:	9 boards/flat	10 boards/flat
2. **Size of Holes**	2% of holes > .021"	Alll holes > .021"
Impact:	Larger holes use lower cost drill bits	
3. **Thickness of Board**	.022"	.021"
Impact:	Thinner board uses 2 parts versus 3	
Cost:		
Production Activities	$ 94	$ 80
Support Activities	$ 10	$ 9
Total Cost	$104	$ 89

Figure 9-4. *How design affects product cost.* Small changes in design can have a major impact on a product's cost. The three changes shown here affected the use of activities and resources enough to reduce cost by 15%—with no sacrifice in board function.

The result was *customer entrenchment.* Cost reductions, single sourcing of product families, and joint engineering created a long-term incentive for customers to stay with PCB. It was a powerful competitive weapon when played alongside PCB's leadership in quality and customer service.

Improvement Prioritization

The trip to *world class* is not made in one nonstop journey. Rather, it consists of many small trips, each making a small (but important) contribution to improvement.

But which route gets you to your world-class destination the fastest?

There are many improvement opportunities in the typical company. Some return more improvement for the effort than others, and there usually aren't enough resources to travel all routes at once.

PCB used ABC to help identify the improvement projects with the greatest cost impacts. This was a good use of ABC analysis because improvement projects can vary widely in their impact on activities and resources.

Figure 9-5 shows examples of four types of improvement projects and the associated cost savings. Some projects actually eliminated the need to perform activities. Moving inspection equipment into a work cell, for example, eliminated the need to move the boards.

Other projects substituted lower cost activities for higher cost activities. An example, is using punching rather than routing to remove boards from flats.

A third type of project reduced the resources needed to perform the activities. Changing the layout of the imaging area, for example, reduced the space and supplies required by imaging.

The fourth type of change allowed activities to be combined or shared to achieve cost savings. For example, using standard materials in lieu of nonstandard materials allowed products to share data base, purchasing, scheduling, inspection, and handling activities.

Total Quality Control (TQC)

High quality was an important goal for PCB. As with most improvement goals, however, there were usually more quality projects to be completed than the available resources could handle.

Quality improvement and cost reduction go hand-in-hand. The cost reduction potential of a quality improvement project is, therefore, a good indicator of that project's potential.

Eliminate Activities
1. Modify solder mask equipment to apply mask to both sides simultaneously
Savings: $ 47,000
2. Move inspection equipment into work cell to eliminate handling activities
Savings: $ 32,000

Substitute Lower Cost Activities
1. Punching instead of routing high volume parts   Savings: $ 16,000
2. Use long life drill bits, reduces the need to change bits   Savings: $ 9,500

Reduce the Resources Required by Activities
1. Change layout of imaging area to reduce distance between the location of activities and supplies   Savings: $ 93,500
2. Bevel edges of material prior to issue to reduce incidence of rework caused by scratches   Savings: $ 71,000

Combine or Share Activities
1. Substitute standard for non-standard materials, allows sharing of many activities such as data base maintenance and handling   Savings: $238,000

Figure 9-5. *Examples of improvement projects.* There are many opportunities for improvement. Each project has a different impact on activities and cost. But they all save money. The key is to pick the ones with the greatest savings—and this is where ABC is invaluable.

The PCB plant applied ABC to TQC in two ways. First, the defects associated with each activity were costed for each of the three daily shifts.

A report on the *cost of poor quality* for each activity was prepared immediately after each work shift. A graph showed the trend in physical defects *and* cost. The report allowed each activity in the plant to focus immediately on the quality problems with the biggest cost impact.

Second, a *top ten offenders* list was prepared daily *(Figure 9-6).* This reported the ten products with the highest *cost of poor quality* on the previous day. It riveted attention on the products that were guiltiest, had the costliest sins of poor quality, and provided the greatest potential for redemption.

When a product unit on this list was scrapped, a report was prepared that showed the cause of the problem (such as machine or operator error) as well as the cost. This report was sent to the person or activity most likely to correct the problem.

	Total Units	Rework Units	Scrap Cost	Total Cost	Cause
1	35	32	$1.201	$5,279	A7
2	8	8	$1,007	$2,118	E1-3
3	23	21	$ 871	$2,109	56-9
4	12	5	$ 732	$1,650	A7
5	32	32	$ 687	$1,587	JE-6
6	390	387	$ 642	$2,874	L4
7	25	25	$ 596	$1,298	GC-1
8	14	11	$ 298	$ 986	EI-3
9	10	10	$ 256	$ 754	H1
10	7	7	$ 228	$ 635	A6

Figure 9-6. *The top ten offenders list.* PCB prepared a *top ten offenders* Pareto report daily. This report identified the products with the highest *cost of poor quality.* These were the products that would benefit the most from corrective action.

This use of ABC made quality problems visible within a matter of hours, or even minutes. Under the previous system, it took weeks before quality problems were identified, and even then it wasn't possible to estimate each problem's cost.

These cost-of-quality reports could not have been prepared daily without linking ABC with computer integrated manufacturing (CIM). For the PCB plant, ABC plus CIM equalled real-time and cost-effective quality control.

Performance Measurement

ABC provides a boost to performance measurement. Performance measurement, in turn, reinforces the benefits of ABM.

Performance measurement wasn't initially a goal of PCB's ABC system, but it was a natural development. As people became accustomed to thinking about activities, they developed their own measures of performance.

They typically chose measures that helped them manage their own activities better. These were measures that tracked customer oriented goals such as quality and lead times.

The tooling department, for example, learned about the high cost of rework from ABC. They used ABC to calculate and monitor two performance measures in physical and dollar terms:

1. The number of film packages reworked, and
2. The number of sheets reworked per package.

Focusing on these two measures led to rapid and significant reductions in rework. This reduced tooling costs and freed resources for more productive work. It also had a "waterfall" effect as quality improvement cascaded across the organization.

Performance measurement helped make ABC a "local" tool at PCB. ABC wasn't just a plaything of the finance department. It was the basis for *information empowerment* in all corners of the plant.

Supplier Management

Partnerships with suppliers are just as important as partnerships with customers. All activities have customers and suppliers. Some suppliers are outside the company and some inside. Those outside suppliers are just as important as internal suppliers in determining levels of cost, quality, and customer service.

PCB's first application of ABC to supplier management was to model the activity cost of two very different supplier strategies. The first strategy was to buy each material from several different suppliers. The second was to buy materials from a single source.

The ABC analysis showed that single sourcing was by far the cheaper strategy. This was because activity use was less with one supplier.

For example, adding a second supplier for laminate (the basic raw material for printed circuit boards) included:

- Setting up and maintaining dual processing specifications,
- Setting up and maintaining two bills of materials,
- Managing dual safety stocks,
- Receiving and warehousing two part numbers,
- Inspecting incoming materials twice as often,

- Dual troubleshooting of quality problems at each process step, and
- Analyzing process changes and additions twice.

This list of additional effort doesn't include indirect effects. These indirect effects included increased obsolescence, increased human error due to confusion, and increased scrap.

PCB used ABC to prepare some interesting "rules of thumb" about the cost of multiple suppliers. *Figure 9-7* illustrates the full drama of these rules. For example, the cost of maintaining and managing a supplier averages $37,000 per year.

---

1. The average cost of adding a new supplier is over $800 if no engineering, manufacturing testing, or qualification is needed.

2. The cost to maintain and manage a supplier averages $37,000 per year. This cost *does not* include additional testing and inspection for criticial manufacturing processes.

3. The total cost of maintaining a back-up supplier "just-in-case" of a shortage, or if the main supplier is lost, was over $180,000 per year.

Figure 9-7. *Rules of thumb for the cost of maintaining multiple suppliers.* If you don't believe multiple sourcing is costly, take a look at these dramatic rules of thumb. They were prepared by PCB with the help of ABC.

The news that single sourcing costs less was timely for PCB. It reinforced the belief that single sourcing was better for their more immediate goals—better quality and service.

PCB's second application of ABC to supplier management centered on creating a new relationship with their laminate supplier. ABC was used to model a new supplier relationship that would dramatically reduce the cost and time for procuring laminate and would also improve laminate quality.

The current approach was shipment of bulk laminate sheets from the supplier's plant in one state to another supplier in another state. This second supplier cut and packaged the material to PCB's specifications. The packaged material was then shipped to PCB where it was unpacked, inspected, and stocked.

This approach had a negative impact on time and activities. The average lead time, from placing an order to receipt on the manufacturing floor, was eight weeks.

ABC showed why it took so long—there was a lot of work required in PCB and the supplier plants. Activities such as maintaining, ordering, scheduling, receiving, unpacking, inspecting, warehousing, and releasing parts were needed for over 200 different laminates. These were in addition to a similar list of activities for each supplier.

All that work represented a lot of non-value-added activity. Just look at the cost drivers.

The main cost driver was the supplier's location in a different state many miles from PCB. A secondary cost driver was the need to ship the laminate to a second supplier for cutting to size.

The key to eliminating the waste, and cutting cost, was to eliminate those two cost drivers. Arrangements were made with a supplier to build a plant to manufacture laminate adjacent to PCB's plant. Laminate was then transferred in bulk through the adjoining walls of the two plants.

Part of the raw material section of the warehouse was converted into a cutting operation. (The space was no longer needed to store laminate.) The laminate was then cut to the proper shape as required and just-in-time for processing.

The impact on activities—and cost, quality, and lead times—was dramatic:

- Gone was a whole set of activities at both PCB and the supplier. These included purchasing, scheduling, inspecting, packaging, moving, warehousing, shipping, and handling.
- Cutting the laminate cost less because parts were cut only when needed and in the right size and quantity.
- Shortening the supply pipeline reduced the resources needed for transporting and holding inventory.

- PCB now purchased only one type of laminate (bulk sheets). Activities associated with this single part, such as maintaining the part data base, ordering, tracking, and scheduling, were now shared by the entire volume of laminate purchases.

ABC proved to be the perfect tool for a plant looking for ways to get closer to its suppliers. It was the impetus to move to a single supply source for each type of material. And it was the inspiration behind relocating a major supplier to a spot adjacent to PCB's plant.

The benefits in reduced cost, improved quality, and customer service were real. It was the kind of performance breakthrough that ABM is all about.

Investment Management

Capital spending's role at PCB was to improve their ability to meet customer demand, improve quality, and reduce lead times. ABC played a major role in determining how these objectives could be met with limited funds.

To do this, ABC was applied in two ways. *First*, ABC was used to load the plant based on profitability and available capacity. This increased profitability and identified bottlenecks. *Second*, ABC was used to determine which bottlenecks should be removed (via capital spending).

This is how the plant was loaded:

1. The plant production schedule was prepared. Initially, this was the most profitable mix of products that could be produced.
2. The schedule's product mix and volume were translated into actual demands on each activity in the production process. This was done via the activity drivers in the ABC system. The number of holes to be drilled in the products, for example, determined the work load for the hole-drilling activity.
3. Each activity's required capacity was compared to available capacity. This identified bottlenecks.
4. Schedule adjustments were made to accommodate the bottlenecks.

This worked well in the short term. The plant was balanced to produce the most profitable mix.

In the long-run, however, it was possible to eliminate bottlenecks with judicious capital investments. For example, it was difficult to get products through final inspection. The inventory piled up in front of this activity equalled three days of production.

Analysis showed that 35% of this inventory was eventually routed back to previous activities in the process for rework. An additional 6% of the boards were scrapped after final inspection.

It was clear that poor quality was the major cost driver as far as capacity was concerned. The key to eliminating bottlenecks was to improve quality and eliminate scrap and rework.

An ABC study showed that over $300,000 would be saved if poor quality were caught in the activities where the problems originated. The size of the savings was sufficient to justify a capital investment to solve the problem.

An investment was made in automated optical inspection equipment for the tooling activity. The investment ensured that quality problems originating in tooling would be caught and corrected in tooling. This eliminated a major cause of rework and scrap at the earliest point in the production process. Gone was an entire chain of poor quality, scrap, and associated activities and resources.

The result was elimination of the bottleneck in the final inspection activity. Capacity was now available for additional revenue-generating production, lead times were reduced, and on-time delivery enhanced. On the cost side, there was a significant reduction in the need for activities such as inspection, rework, handling, and warranty servicing.

ABC was therefore an important investment management tool. It helped identify key bottlenecks that caused lost revenues. It also helped identify the causes of these bottlenecks and guided capital investments to places of greatest benefit.

Summary

ABM brings *information empowerment* to companies aspiring to world-class status. It puts ABC information in the hands of the people doing the improvement. And analysis of this information increases their power to improve.

The PCB plant used ABM to:

- *Set strategic priorities and help implement their chosen strategy.* ABC identified profitable products and customers and focused sales attention on those targets.
- *Manage performance to profitably meet their business goals.* ABC was used to improve product design, target cost reduction and quality improvement opportunities with the greatest payoffs, and encourage continuous improvement via activity-based performance measures.
- *Manage suppliers for a long-term relationship that emphasized quality, short lead times, and low cost.* ABC revealed waste associated with multiple and remote suppliers. It helped develop new strategies that emphasized close, on-going relationships that yielded better service, improved quality, and a substantial drop in cost.
- *Direct investments to the areas that yielded the greatest improvements.* ABC revealed bottlenecks in the plant and identified which ones cost the most in lost profits. This knowledge helped direct investments to the areas that increased profits the most.

ABM was the single most important factor in turning PCB into the world's benchmark circuit board plant. PCB is a testimony to the ability of ABM to create improvements that go straight to the bottom line.

Key Terms in Chapter 9

Investment management–The use of ABC to manage capacity for maximum profitability and to direct capital spending to the most profitable improvement targets.

Performance management–The use of ABC to improve profitability. It includes searching for low-cost product designs, identifying cost reduction opportunities, guiding efforts to improve quality, and measuring performance.

Strategic management—The use of activity-based analysis to set and implement strategic priorities. Supplier management—The use of ABC to identify waste in supplier relationships and to develop supplier partnerships that help eliminate this waste.

Part V

HOW TO DO IT

By now, you're probably convinced that activity-based costing is a valuable tool. You've seen how and why conventional cost systems not only fail, but may even be dangerous. You know what ABC systems look like. You know what they can do. Now you need to know how to do it, *how to put an ABC system to work for you*.

Doing it—and doing it well—requires careful planning and attention to technical details. *First*, management must be convinced that ABC should be introduced. *Second*, a strategy (and plan) need to be developed to take full advantage of ABC's potential. *Third*, the required data must be collected. *Fourth*, the ABC model must be designed. And, *Fifth*, the use of ABC information in the improvement process must be managed carefully.

Chapter 10 shows you how to win management "buy-in" to activity-based costing. This is where you get answers to the following questions:

- How do I create interest in ABC?
- What are the barriers to acceptance?
- Is my company a good candidate for ABC?
- Where do I look for evidence that our existing systems don't work well?

Chapter 11 walks you through creating a strategy for using ABC. You'll see how to develop an implementation plan based on this strategy. And you'll find answers to these questions:

- What should the ABC objectives be for my company?
- What should the deliverables be?
- What should ABC's scope be?
- How should the implementation project be organized?
- Who'll design the system?
- What training is required?

- What tasks need to be done, and how long will they take?
- What will it cost?

Chapter 12 covers ABC's information requirements and guides you through collecting that data. It answers the following questions:

- How do I collect the needed information?
- Who should be interviewed?
- How do I prepare for an interview?
- How do I conduct an interview?
- What documentation is required?
- What should an interview schedule look like?
- How do I get the data into the ABC system?

Chapter 13 shows you how to design an ABC system by following the six steps to success:

- Identifying activities,
- Reconstructing the general ledger,
- Creating activity centers,
- Defining resource drivers,
- Determining attributes, and
- Selecting activity drivers.

Then in Chapter 14, you'll learn how to ensure successful use of the ABC system. This is extremely important since the completion of an ABC model is only the beginning of the improvement process. To make positive changes, the ABC system must be used. But, for this to happen, you need to develop a plan for use and carefully manage the process of change.

All the rules, steps, and guidelines in this section go well beyond just the theoretical. They're based on the experiences of many different companies that have already implemented ABC. These experiences cover a wide range of industries. They also range from limited "back of an envelope" studies to company-wide, two-dimensional activity-based costing.

Chapter 10

CONVINCING MANAGEMENT TO CHANGE

You're convinced that activity-based costing (ABC) is a valuable tool for fostering positive change. Now you want to introduce it into your company.

To do this successfully, you must first convince management to change. Remember, *ABC is quite different from existing systems.* For a successful change to ABC, management must believe in it, must want to do it, and must be willing to commit the effort and resources required to do it.

The question is, how do you convince management? How do you make sure ABC is seen, not as just another fancy system, but as a necessary and valuable tool for improvement.

Well, there's good news...and there's some bad news.

First the bad news.

Acceptance of ABC is not always won without effort and care.

The problem is, ABC signifies change. It's a different way of doing business. And, like any other change, the path to acceptance, successful implementation, and wise use is not without pitfalls.

Management may not be fully prepared for what ABC reveals. At Schrader Bellows, for example, ABC revealed that over 80% of the products were losing money. However, despite months of effort designing the system and analyzing results, management still could not accept the changes necessary to address the situation.[1]

Management may oppose the introduction of ABC. As an example, one company's approach to management buy-in, planning, and implementation was beautifully "text book." The ABC system was completed. Everything was ready to go.

Then the company hired a new Chief Financial Officer.

As it turned out, this person was adamantly opposed to ABC. Management meetings on ABC were referred to as "the gunfight at the OK corral." Ultimately, the well-wrought ABC system was shot down.

The system may be too complex to understand and use. One company, for example, designed an ABC system with hundreds of activity drivers. No one knew what to do with all the information. So the system was never used.

The system may be too simple. One company designed an ABC system with only four activity drivers. The reported cost of one important product went up significantly. Based on this new information, marketing de-emphasized that product. The next year, however, the ABC system was redesigned to include more activity drivers. This caused the reported cost of the product to go back down. Marketing was irritated and refused to the use activity-based costs for any further strategic decisions.

Now, for the *good* news.

Many companies have introduced ABC and put it to good use. From these experiences, a method for successful ABC introduction has been developed. It all begins with three crucial steps:

- Generate interest in ABC,
- Remove any barriers that may exist to the introduction of ABC, and
- Obtain management's commitment to embark on an ABC project.

Step 1–Generating Interest

You're convinced that ABC is a valuable tool. But are your colleagues also convinced? Has top management been briefed on (and bought into) ABC?

It's important to have support–*ABC champions*–at all levels of the company. These champions should include top management, plant management, engineering, finance and accounting, and marketing. Success in a service company, such as a hospital, requires support from both administrators and professionals.

Without broad endorsement, it's unlikely that you'll be able to place ABC at the top of anyone's agenda.

The key issues for top management are what can ABC (and the activity-based management that ensues from it) do for the company, and what will it cost to do it. ABC must be perceived as a strategic and cost-effective tool that yields competitive dividends.

Marketing is sometimes defensive. They have a light— the light of conventional cost information—that casts a distorted image on their world. When they get their new precision ABC light bulb, however, they'll need to make radical adjustments in perception. And they will need to be convinced that this new perception is close to reality.

In contrast, engineering has been completely in the dark. Turning on the lights for them may be perceived as a blessing. Plant management may also be so disenchanted with conventional cost information that they are happy to turn off the conventional lights.

Finance and accounting must be handled with *kid gloves*. They're the ones who are responsible for the existing cost system (and the distorted images it presents), as well as the knowledge to design it. If their support is not carefully cultivated, ABC can appear to be a threat to both their "turf" and their expertise. But win them over, and finance and accounting will be a willing and invaluable source of technical assistance and support.

Successful introduction of ABC begins with three steps:

Step 1.   Generate interest
Step 2.   Remove barriers to acceptance
Step 3.   Obtain management commitment

The first step in generating support among your important constituencies is to *expose them* to ABC. They need to be shown why conventional cost systems fail and why ABC systems succeed. You can do this by circulating materials on ABC and by organizing in-plant seminars. You should also look for *benchmarks* to use in this exposure process. Benchmarks are companies similar to your own that have implemented ABC. Their experiences are valuable for answering proof-of-performance questions.

Circulating Materials. Managers without prior exposure to ABC need a short executive summary that tells them:

- *What* ABC is,
- *Why* it's superior to conventional costing,
- *Why* it's important, and
- *How* it can be used.

You can lay the groundwork by putting together an information package for circulation. Videotapes are a quick and easy means of providing basic ABC knowledge. This can be built on with a collection of short articles that can be read and digested rapidly. And for those wishing to expand their knowledge even further, you can recommend or provide books such as this one.[2]

In-Company Seminars. There's no substitute for the voice of experience. This can be provided via in-company presentations from ABC specialists.

Such presentations are an opportunity to get the key players together in one room for an exchange of ideas and information. The specialist can address concerns about ABC and can lead the group in a discussion of how ABC might be applied in your company.

Benchmarks. "What has ABC done for other companies?" That's a common question asked by potential ABC converts. It's probably best answered with published case studies. A visit to a company using ABC can be an even more dramatic and convincing experience.

The Schrader Bellows case study is a good place to start. It shows the dramatic changes in reported product costs that can occur when ABC is used. These changes—*which can be in orders of magnitude*—should make anyone using a conventional cost system extremely nervous.

The effectiveness of the Schrader Bellows study is illustrated by an experience following an ABC seminar. One of the people attending, a manager from a local manufacturing company, rushed up to the speaker. "Your description of Schrader Bellows could have been my company," this person exclaimed. "No question about it. We desperately need ABC."

The experience of the Oscilloscope Group of Tektronix is another good example to use. This study shows how ABC can become part of a continuous improvement program. Specifically, the Oscilloscope Group used ABC to show its engineers the expense of designing products with low-volume components. As a result, the count of different parts used in the division's products decreased by over 50%.

It's more difficult to find case studies of service organizations—most of the early applications of ABC were in manufacturing companies. But if you look carefully, you'll find good write-ups on health-care, financial-services and other service organizations.[3]

The best case study, though, is an actual visit to a company that's using ABC. The people there can tell you firsthand why they adopted ABC, how they implemented it, and how they're using the information. Such visits make an excellent follow-up to an in-company seminar.

Step 2—Removing Barriers

A key decision maker's negative comments can be a major barrier to ABC implementation. Unless these comments are overcome, the entire ABC project can be held up.

The danger in anti-ABC comments is that they typically hold a grain of truth. They are true in certain limited circumstances. But they are not general truths for the entire world of ABC.

Myth 1   ABC is too difficult to implement and use.
Myth 2   Improving the existing system will do the job.
Myth 3   We do not need more accurate product costs.
Myth 4   Cost systems play a limited role in process improvement.

Myths are beliefs about the cost and value of ABC systems. While they contain grains of truth, they are not general truths. Unless addressed, myths may bar successful introduction of ABC.

These comments are heard often enough that they are called "myths" about ABC. These myths generally follow one of four different themes. Being able to recognize these myths and their themes allows you to remove them as barriers to ABC implementation.

Myth 1: ABC is too Difficult to Implement and Use

This myth is based in the observation that ABC systems use more activity drivers than conventional systems. The logic, albeit ill directed, is that more drivers mean a more costly and complex system.

Additional activity drivers do create additional data requirements. Data points must be determined for each product or part that consumes an activity driver. The activity driver *number of receipts*, for example, requires estimates of the number of receipts for each type of part. As a result, the number of data points can easily reach into the millions for a modest system.

Experience shows, however, that most people overestimate the cost of ABC data tracking. Much of the needed data already exist in the plant or can be easily captured. The number of holes punched in a printed circuit board, for example, is probably already stored in the manufacturing data base.

Some people also believe that additional activity drivers make ABC too complex to understand. This may be true if the ABC system is designed with more drivers than necessary to report accurate costs.

Concerns about complexity, however, usually stem from experience with complex conventional systems rather than from experience with multiple-driver ABC systems. Consider, for example, the complexity of the cost system at Tektronix' Oscilloscope Group prior to redesign. This conventional system was costly to operate and difficult to understand. This system:

- Generated 21 different cost variances each month,
- Required as many as 50 performance measurements by each operator each day (over 30,000 measurements per month on one product line alone),
- Processed more than 25,000 inventory transactions per month, and
- Divided the plant into more than 100 cost centers.

The perception that ABC systems are too costly to use, and too complex to understand, is a myth born of conventional cost systems. This myth is not reflected in the experiences of companies that have implemented ABC systems. In fact, the cost of an ABC system is surprisingly modest, and ABC is easier to understand because it matches economic reality.

The best way of dispelling this myth is to demonstrate how simple, direct, and effective ABC methods can be. For example, a small pilot project covering a couple of product lines or one department is an economical way of providing this demonstration.

Myth 2: Improving Existing Systems Will Do the Job

ABC critics often push improvements to the existing system as a better alterative to a completely new system. Improvements may work to a limited extent, but certainly not as comprehensively as putting an ABC system in place. The following reminders explain why.

Yes, conventional systems can often be improved—*but only up to a point*. For example, creating multiple cost centers where only one or two existed before may reduce some cost distortions.

This would be true, for example, where plating and painting activities are combined into one cost center. This also distorts reported product costs if some products are routed through one activity and some through the other. Creating separate cost centers solves the problem.

But even good conventional systems cannot cope with product diversity. Nor can they cope with situations where a significant amount of cost is associated with nonunit activities.

The most common activity driver in conventional systems is direct labor hours. This measure assumes that the cost of non-direct labor activities is proportional to the labor hours required to build a product. That assumption is false if products are at different stages in their life cycle, or are designed differently, and there are nonunit activities such as engineering.

For example, two products may require equal amounts of direct labor hours. Product A, however, may be a new product that requires engineering attention. Product B, in contrast, requires no engineering attention at all. It's a mature product from which all bugs have been eliminated. But direct labor hours assigns equal engineering costs to each of these products. This is an assignment that's clearly not consistent with reality.

One way of dispelling this myth is to look for miscosted products that will not be helped by engineering changes to the conventional cost system. Another possibility is to emphasize the other benefits of ABC such as information about activities and customers.

Myth 3: We Do Not Need More Accurate Product Costs

Some people retort that conventional systems report product costs that are *sufficiently* accurate. Some add that additional accuracy is unimportant because managers know intuitively what products cost. Others believe accuracy is unnecessary because the cost to produce a product is not used to set prices. These beliefs are important because they challenge one of the major ABC benefits—*more accurate product costs*.

Managers may be able to identify products that are overcosted or undercosted. These managers know, for example, that a difficult to manufacture product must cost more than one that's easy to manufacture. They recognize this reality even when their unit-type conventional cost system reports that the two products cost the same.

However, *managers often do not realize the size of the cost problem*. Experience has shown that managers typically underestimate product cost distortions. They may believe, for example, that the true cost of a difficult to produce item is 50% greater than the reported cost. In reality, the true cost may be 500% greater.

Some companies use cost to set prices. This is particularly true in regulated industries and for defense contractors. But there are other companies who price to market, or price based on what the customer is "willing to pay." In these latter cases product cost may not figure into the pricing equation.

However, it's dangerous to believe that accurate product costs are unnecessary even if they are not needed for pricing: *Managers chase profits, and profits can be phantoms of the cost system*. It's only natural for managers to devote attention and resources to the products they perceive to be the most profitable. And it's the cost system that reports the absolute and relative profitability of products.

For example, it was quite natural for a printed circuit board manufacturer to emphasize the sale of two-sided circuit boards when the cost system showed they were profitable. In fact, the majority of their sales were two-sided boards.

But when an ABC system revealed the "awful reality"—two-sided boards were not profitable at current prices—a new strategy was adopted. The two-sided business was de-emphasized, and a market for complex multi-layer boards was built up.

Such experiences have shown time and again that improved accuracy is an important benefit of ABC. Managers may be able to identify products that are incorrectly costed, but they need ABC to judge the size of the distortion. Even when pricing strategy isn't based on product costs, ABC allows attention to be focused on products based on relative profitability.

Documenting case histories like this may be enough to dispel this myth. If not, try completing a "back-of-the-envelope" study such as the one completed at DeVilbiss in 48 hours. This study was enough to demonstrate the inaccuracy of product-line costs and to obtain acceptance for a full implementation of ABC.

Myth 4: Cost Systems Play a Limited Role in Process Improvement

Another school of thought maintains that ABC plays a limited role in fostering process improvement. This school views ABC as a strategic product costing tool, but not as a source of information for improving the performance of activities. For those subscribing to this opinion, any decision to implement ABC must be based on strategic benefits rather than cost reduction.

This school is right—ABC is an invaluable strategic tool. It reports accurate product costs for product mix and pricing purposes. This helps guide companies in their choice of markets and customers.

But ABC also provides useful information for cost-reduction programs. Product designers, for example, can use information about the cost of activity drivers, and products' consumption of those measures, to help design products that have a lower cost. Hewlett-Packard and Tektronix have implemented ABC systems specifically for that purpose—*to help engineers design products with a lower cost.*

ABC also provides information for simulating cost-reduction alternatives. One company, for example, used its ABC system to determine the cost of engineering change activities. Careful study showed that the engineering change process could be redesigned to reduce the time and cost required to complete an engineering change. The ABC system was used to model the proposed change and to confirm the cost savings that resulted.

ABC also provides a wealth of *nonfinancial* information about activities. For example, information about *cost drivers* provides opportunities to manage the factors that cause work. Information about activity *performance*, such as a measure of the quality of the activity's output, provides feedback on how well the activity is performed. Designation of activities as *non-value-added* provides opportunities for eliminating waste.

Overall, there is no justification for the myth that ABC plays a limited role in process improvement. ABC is, in reality, a rich source of information for managing activities. In some cases, firms have implemented ABC solely for that reason.

How to dispel this myth? Try implementing a value analysis similar to the one at General Electric described in Chapter 8. Pick a department where you expect to find waste. If you can cut costs successfully, you will find ready converts to your cause.

Step 3—Obtain Commitment

Generating interest in ABC is an important first step. But actual commitment to an ABC project requires evidence that ABC will yield substantial benefits for the organization.

Commitment will be forthcoming if you can demonstrate two things: *first*, that your company is the type of company that can benefit from ABC; and, *second*, that there is evidence that your company's existing cost system is not doing the job.

The Type of Company that Benefits the Most

The truth is, any company can benefit from ABC—large or small, manufacturing or service. Even if you are making a 20% return, 25% would be better. Even if you are ahead of the competition today, leadership in a market can change hands quickly.

Organizations with a lot of *complexity* and *diversity* are prime candidates for ABC. The more complexity, the more overhead there is, and the greater the potential for inaccurate costs. More complexity also means more opportunity for waste elimination. Either way, ABC provides improved information.

Diversity in products or volumes also increases the value of ABC. If your product line has products of different designs, chances are these products will require different activities and will cost different amounts. ABC helps you understand and deal with this diversity.

If your products vary in volumes (some high, some low), a conventional cost system usually overcosts the high-volume products and undercosts the low-volume ones. If the range of volumes is considerable, the cost errors can be thousands of percent. You definitely need ABC to correct these errors, or you'll leave yourself vulnerable to the competition.

Companies with only one product or service can still benefit from ABC. This single product may be sold to customers in different ways. For example, a software company may sell a single software program. For a $1,000 the customer receives a disk and a manual in a box. For $2,000 the customer receives the box and a service contract. For $5,000, the customer also receives training in how to use the software.

Nonplant costs in a manufacturing company—and all the costs in a typical service company—are outside the scope of conventional product cost systems. However, these costs are likely to be significant. And it's important to understand customer profitability and to improve marketing and other customer-oriented activities.

Then there's the issue of *competitive pressure*. To remain competitive, you must have good information. The more accurate it is, the more competitive you can be.[4]

The Japanese, for example, are famous for entering markets with high-quality products priced below competitive levels. This can send shock waves through an entire industry and reveal patterns of waste and misallocation of effort—the very targets of activity-based management (ABM).

However, don't wait for the Japanese to enter your markets. You won't retain your market position unless you improve continuously in every aspect of your business. ABC—and its application in an activity-based improvement program—is an insurance policy for the future.

Symptoms of a Broken Cost System

Can you find symptoms suggesting that your company is indeed suffering from inadequate cost information? There are numerous symptoms of a "broken" cost system. Here are some to look for:[5]

Symptom 1:   *Management believes the cost information is distorted.* There's a simple test for this. Talk to your plant manager. Ask, "Do you believe that the reported product costs accurately reflect the actual work necessary to move those products through the plant?"

The plant manager's answer may surprise you.

Symptom 2:   *Marketing and sales are unwilling to use cost information for product pricing, market entry, and product portfolio decisions.* Sales people, especially those on commission, tend to be sensitive to competitive pricing and quality issues. Ask them how they feel about your company's approach to these issues.

Symptom 3:   *Sales go up, yet profits go down.* This one can be a real shocker. It's a clear sign that reported product profit margins are in error. Time to check your product mix and prices!

Symptom 4:   *There's a bootleg cost system in your company.* A "bootleg" system is an *unofficial* cost system (one not blessed by accounting). It's usually found on a personal computer on the shop floor, in engineering, or in marketing. Its existence is a clear vote of no confidence in the *official* cost system.

Bootleg systems have been found at several companies, including Hewlett-Packard and Tektronix.

Symptom 5:   *An improvement project fails to yield expected cost reductions.* When this occurs, it is usually the cost system that gets the numbers wrong. For example, a labor productivity improvement may show a substantial reduction in direct labor cost, but may be accompanied by increases in engineering and information system costs.

Symptom 6:   *Customers "cherry pick" your products.* If customers love your low-volume specialty products, but buy their high-volume standard products elsewhere, it's a sure sign of improper pricing. This "cherry picking" strategy can be a problem for anyone who relies on conventional cost information to set prices.

Symptom 1:	Management believes the cost information is distorted.
Symptom 2:	Marketing and sales won't use cost information.
Symptom 3:	Sales go up, yet profits go down.
Symptom 4:	There's a "bootleg" cost system in the company.
Symptom 5:	An improvement project fails to yield expected cost reductions.
Symptom 6:	Customers "cherry pick" your products.

Keep your eyes open for these six symptoms of a broken cost system. If you find any of them in your company, chances are your cost system is creating real damage.

Identifying the symptoms of a broken cost system really drives the message home. It's one thing to observe the predicaments of others. It's quite another to know that your own systems are failing.

If you do all the right things, and can pinpoint the value of ABC in your company, management commitment will be forthcoming. But it may take longer in some companies than others.

Sometimes it's agonizingly slow. At one company, the management team attended an ABC seminar and then spent the next year gaining commitment and completing a plan for their ABC project.

Sometimes it happens very quickly. A similar ABC presentation was given at another company. The management team had full commitment the same week. Beyond that, they also had resources identified and an implementation plan and training completed within one month.

Summary

Creating change in your company–however positive the eventual results–isn't easy. You must deliberately create an environment in which ABC cannot fail to succeed.

Enough experience has been gained with ABC to establish the initial steps to success:

- *Generate interest* in ABC. Cultivate "champions" everywhere you can, but particularly among top management.
- *Remove any barriers* that may exist to the introduction of ABC. People can develop many misconceptions about a new tool. Ask them what their concerns are and be ready with the answers.
- *Seek management's commitment* to embark on an ABC project. It's one thing to support ABC in principle. It's another thing to commit time, money, and reputations to an implementation project. If it takes some time to get this commitment, just "hang in there." Nobody can oppose something as valuable as ABC indefinitely. Experience has shown that the most vehement opponents often become the strongest supporters.

Key Terms in Chapter 10

Benchmark–A case documenting another company's experiences with ABC. You can learn from their experiences and use them to demonstrate the benefits of ABC.

Myth–A belief about ABC that is a barrier to acceptance. Demolishing these myths increases the chances of a successful ABC implementation.

Symptom–A visible sign of a broken cost system. Symptoms provide ammunition to advocates of ABC.

References:

1. Robin Cooper, "Schrader Bellows," 9-186-272 (Boston: Harvard Business School), 1986.

2. A recommended video is Peter B.B. Turney, *An Introduction to Activity-Based Costing*, (Portland, OR: ABC Technologies, Inc.), 1991. A recommended article is Peter B.B. Turney, "Using Activity-Based Costing to Achieve Manufacturing Excellence," *Journal of Cost Management*, (Summer 1989), pp. 23-31.

3. See, for example, William Rotch, "Activity-Based Costing in Service Industries," *Journal of Cost Management*, (Summer 1990), pp. 4-14; and Richard Zimmerman, "Health Care—an Industry in Need of Realistic Cost Measurement," *As Easy as ABC*, (Fall 1990), p. 3 (Portland, OR: ABC Technologies, Inc.).

4. The impact of diversity and competitive pressure on the need for reliable product cost information is discussed in Robin Cooper, "The Rise of Activity-Based Costing—Part Two: When Do I Need an Activity-Based Cost System?," *Journal of Cost Management*, (Fall 1988), pp. 41-48.

5. Symptoms 1, 2, and 3 are from Robin Cooper and Peter B.B. Turney, "Powell Electronics: The Printed Circuit Board Division," 9-189-054 (Boston: Harvard Business School), 1989. An example of symptom 4 is Robin Cooper and Peter B.B. Turney, "Hewlett-Packard: The Roseville Network Division," 9-188-177 (Boston: Harvard Business School), 1989. Symptom 5 is documented in Robin Cooper and Peter B.B. Turney, "Tektronix: The Portable Instrument Division," 9-188-142,143,144 (Boston: Harvard Business School), 1988. An example of symptom 6 is Robin Cooper, "Schrader Bellows," 9-186-272 (Boston: Harvard Business School), 1986.

Chapter 11

DEVELOPING THE GAME PLAN

Do you know the rule of the "seven P's?"

Here it is—**P**roper, **P**rior, **P**lanning, **P**ositively, **P**revents, **P**oor, **P**erformance.

Activity-based costing is no exception to this rule. In fact, some ABC failures are directly attributable to poor planning.

Yes, ABC can fail, especially when it's not properly planned to meet the specific needs of your company. And who best knows the specific needs of your company? Why, you do, of course. And that makes you the best person for planning your ABC implementation.

Also, the experience of many companies during ABC implementation shows that doing your own planning has several major benefits:

It enhances the chances of successful implementation. Implementing ABC is not overly difficult. But it's not a trivial task either. It takes time and effort. Approaching it in an organized manner—*the seven p's*—ensures that your time and efforts are well directed.

Since you know your company's organization and resources best, you are the best person for planning how those resources can be applied to an ABC implementation. Moreover, if you do the planning yourself, you'll be *intimately familiar* with the plan. This means you'll be better able to monitor and smooth the implementation process. And a tool that flows smoothly into place has a far better chance for *quick acceptance* and *successful use*.

You gain more knowledge about your company. Anyone who plans and designs an ABC model gains an enormous amount of knowledge about their company's products and activities. If a consultant does the bulk of the planning, that knowledge leaves with the consultant when the job is done. But if you're the primary planner, *even under the guidance of a consultant*, the knowledge stays with you, in your organization. It then becomes an information base for strategic and cost-reduction decisions.

There's a greater sense of ownership. By creating the model yourself, you gain the pride and commitment of ownership. That sense of ownership increases the chances of ABC being accepted and used. That in turn increases the chances of achieving true ABC success, **results that bring about positive change**. For that to occur, ABC has to be accepted and used.

The *game plan* for ABC planning and implementation varies from one company to another. Companies differ in needs, size, complexity, types of activities and processes, technology, information systems, products, and customers. All of these factors require careful study in order to develop a *successful ABC game plan*. And, because the factors differ, game plan specifics differ from company to company.

However, the steps in formulating a game plan remain the same regardless of differing factors. Briefly, these eight steps are:

1. **Formulate the objectives.**
   Define what ABC is to accomplish.
2. **Describe the deliverables.**
   Describe the improved information that will satisfy each of the objectives.
3. **Set the scope.**
   Determine how extensive a project you will pursue.
4. **Describe the organization structure.**
   Determine how the project will be organized.
5. **Identify the team membership.**
   Select the individuals and functions that will comprise the design team.
6. **Determine the training requirements.**
   Determine the type and scope of training.
7. **Complete a project schedule.**
   Determine what tasks need to be accomplished and how long the project will take.
8. **Budget the costs of the project.**
   Estimate the resources required to complete the project.

Let's take a closer look at each of these steps and how to successfully complete each one.

Objectives

ABC can be used for any of several purposes. It's important to select the specific purpose (or purposes), and then design a model that serves those specific purposes or objectives

Selecting the purpose of activity-based costing requires a *needs assessment*. This is the process of identifying where ABC can help. The following are some typical examples:

Manufacturing cost is too high. This results in an inability to make profits at competitive prices. It appears that production costs are higher than the competition's. *Requirement:* an ABC system that provides information (such as key cost drivers) about manufacturing activities to motivate and support waste elimination programs.

Nonmanufacturing cost is too high. The culprits in this case are excessive marketing, administrative, engineering, and other non-manufacturing costs. *Requirement:* an ABC system that provides information about nonmanufacturing activities and cost objects (such as customers and distribution channels) and that supports cost reductions in these areas.

Products are too complex and too different from one another. The competitive problem in this case stems from product designs that are too difficult and too costly to produce. *Requirement:* an ABC system that provides design engineers with cost information that guides selection of low-cost product designs.

Market share is being lost in several key markets. You're faced with a declining market share and don't know how to respond. *Requirement:* a high-level ABC study of market profitability to guide market focus and dedication of marketing resources.

It's unclear which type of customer is best suited to your way of doing business. Different customers place different demands on your company. Unfortunately, your pricing strategies or sales efforts make no distinction between customers. *Requirement:* an ABC system that costs customers, allows calculation of customer profitability, and supports development of appropriate customer and pricing strategies.

Market share and profitability need to be improved in one key market. Despite continuing efforts to improve manufacturing capability, market share and profitability fail to expand. *Requirement:* an ABC system that costs products, facilitates studies of relative product profitability, and guides product portfolio decisions and future improvement efforts.

There's uncertainty about which parts to make and which to source from outside suppliers. This is really an uncertainty about where manufacturing effort should be focused. *Requirement:* an ABC system that costs the parts and subassemblies going into products and guides make-or-buy decisions.

From the above examples, it's clear there are numerous possible purposes that an ABC system can be designed to address. As a result, the ABC systems, themselves, are usually as different as the purposes they address. This also means that there will be different levels of necessary effort for their design and use.

An ABC system for cost reduction purposes, for example, requires detailed information (nonfinancial as well as cost) about activities. In contrast, a system to support strategic marketing decisions needs accurate information about the cost of products and customers, but less detail about activities.

As for effort, a system that reports cost to the lowest part number level may take weeks or months to complete. A high-level study that costs a few markets or product lines may be completed in as little as a week.

Deliverables

After determining ABC's objectives, a statement of deliverables should be prepared. This contains the purposes of the system and the improved information that will support each purpose.

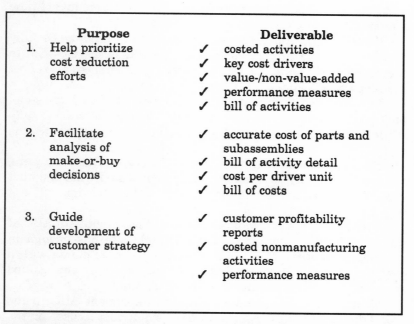

	Purpose		Deliverable
1.	Help prioritize cost reduction efforts	✓ ✓ ✓ ✓ ✓	costed activities key cost drivers value-/non-value-added performance measures bill of activities
2.	Facilitate analysis of make-or-buy decisions	✓ ✓ ✓ ✓	accurate cost of parts and subassemblies bill of activity detail cost per driver unit bill of costs
3.	Guide development of customer strategy	✓ ✓ ✓	customer profitability reports costed nonmanufacturing activities performance measures

Figure 11-1. *Example statement of ABC deliverables.* Deliverables vary from one implementation to another. Make sure you know what ABC will accomplish before you begin.

For example, *more accurate product costs* is a deliverable that guides product portfolio analysis. Other examples are shown in *Figure 11-1*, which is also typical of a statement of ABC deliverables.

Scope

There are several choices regarding scope that affect the time and effort required to complete an ABC project. Some choices relate to the degree of management commitment to the project. Others are affected by the project's purpose.

For example, each purpose has a different set of tasks associated with it. A customer-focused ABC study requires analysis of nonmanufacturing activities. This is quite different from make-or-buy decision studies, which require costing parts at the lowest level of the bill of materials. These two different ABC purposes have different tasks that take different amounts of time and effort to complete.

Whatever the purpose, management may already be fully committed to the process. Or management may merely wish to "dip its toe in the water." These commitment differences also affect the scope of ABC implementation.

In most cases, though, ABC is initially implemented as a small pilot project. This allows management, *whether skeptical or fully committed*, to evaluate ABC's potential contributions to the company.

Pilot projects are usually limited in scope. But even here, scope can still vary considerably. This depends on what the pilot project encompasses, which may be any of the following:

One or more sites. Most companies experiment with ABC at one site. This is appropriate if that single site has enough in common with other sites in the company (such as plants with a common technology). When that's the case, the experience gained in one site can be generalized to the other sites.

Cellular One, for example, chose to implement ABC in the credit department at one location. This small pilot focused on the cost of serving customers through different distribution channels. The results of this pilot were sufficiently interesting to justify expanding ABC to the rest of the company.

Large companies with many different types of operation, however, may chose to run pilot projects in several locations. General Motors, for example, set up ABC pilot projects in 19 different plants. Each plant was carefully chosen to represent a particular type of manufacturing and was used to test a specific use of ABC (such as design for manufacturability or investment evaluation).

All cost objects or a subset of cost objects. It's easy to limit the number of cost objects to be costed. This cuts down development time and effort. It also allows the pilot project to focus on the products, services or customers that will yield the most interest-ing—*and convincing*—results.

Oregon Cutting Systems Division of Blount, for example, selected two representative product lines to demonstrate the value of ABC. The particular product lines were chosen because they had competitive problems and their costs were too high. It was also felt that results from these lines would be the most interesting (primarily big changes in reported product costs).

All activities or a subset of activities. The most common way to limit the number and range of activities that need to be studied is to focus on one area of the company first. Manufacturing companies typically implement ABC in the plant and leave nonmanufacturing activities for a later time.

Oregon Cutting Systems limited its pilot project to plant activities. This allowed completion of data collection and modeling within the time limits set by management. However, subsequent adoption phases will extend the scope to include order entry, marketing, and other nonplant activities.

It's also possible to focus a pilot project on just part of the plant. For example, the procurement area could be studied intensively. This is appropriate if the objective is to eliminate waste in procurement activities. However, it's not feasible if the objective is to cost products in the plant. For this, it's necessary to study all plant activities.

An entire or partial accounting period. It's common, even in pilot projects, to cost the last accounting period. This makes sense. Most people still remember what they did during this period, so it's easy to get information about their activities. It also provides results for a complete accounting period and facilitates *benchmarking* the new information against the existing cost system.

In some situations it's better to limit the study to several months, such as the last six months. Consider the case, for example, where the production process or product mix has changed substantially over the last year. For this situation, only the most recent months reflect the current business and activity.

Historical or budgeted costs. Most companies start by using historical costs in their ABC system. This makes sense. An historical perspective is the easiest way to develop a model of the company.

Once the ABC model is complete, historical costs can be replaced with budgeted costs. Activities that will be eliminated can be removed from the model. New activities can be added. Projected changes in the product mix and volumes can also be factored in.

Single-period or life-cycle perspective. Most pilot projects focus on a single accounting period, even though activities and cost objects may affect several accounting periods. A single-period focus is easier because existing cost and accounting systems are in single-period form.

Dayton Extruded Plastics, for example, chose a single-period perspective for its initial model. This allowed rapid development of its ABC system.

The single-period model, however, didn't provide a complete picture of the company. This was because product and die engineering, as well as die use in manufacturing, extended over several years. Once Dayton Extruded Plastics completed the initial model, efforts were focused on developing a multiperiod, life-cycle version.

Positive results from a pilot study usually lead to adopting ABC as the official company methodology. This typically is a process of *phasing in* ABC over time.

Official adoption may also mean extending the scope of ABC. Activity-based information may become the *information of choice* for all decision making. This, of course, extends the scope from that of the pilot program. However, the existing standard cost system may still be retained for financial reporting purposes.

Some companies, such as Hewlett-Packard, go a step further. They completely replace the standard cost system with ABC. Here the ABC system's scope is further expanded to include valuing inventory on a month-by-month basis as well as financial reporting processes.

Organization Structure

Structuring the project's organization is more than just identifying responsibilities and reporting relationships. It's an opportunity to enhance commitment to ABC.

First, there are three parts to the project organization structure. As shown in *Figure 11-2*, these are the project team, the project manager, and the steering committee.

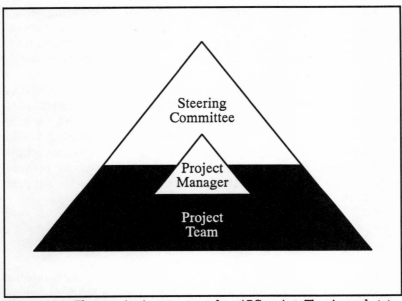

Figure 11-2. *The organization structure of an ABC project.* The size and status (full-time or part-time) of the project team depends on project requirements.

The *project team* does the actual implementation. Its members serve part-time or full-time, depending on the project requirements. A large project with a short time-line for completion requires full-time commitment. A small pilot project with a less pressing completion date can be handled on a part-time basis.

The leader of the team is the ABC *project manager*. This person is responsible for successful completion of the project and needs leadership skills, a solid understanding of ABC, and knowledge of the company's activities and products. Ideally, the project team leader should also have prior experience in implementing ABC. This will be rare, however, given the newness of the field.

The project manager reports to a *steering committee*. The steering committee is typically composed of upper management. It oversees planning and implementation of the ABC system and ensures that ABC objectives are met. It also provides an important link to the president of the company.

The steering committee should review the project plan prior to its acceptance. It should then meet with the project team every other week to review progress.

Membership of the steering committee is determined by interest in ABC and the need to build commitment in key areas. It's common to include vice-presidents of finance, marketing, production, engineering, and information systems on the committee.

At Stockham Valve and Fittings, for example, the marketing vice-president was appointed to chair the steering committee. This reflected the marketing VP's strong interest in ABC. It also reflected a desire to *increase the likelihood* that marketing would accept—and respond to—the study's results. This was important because the ABC system's primary objective was to provide marketing with *accurate* product cost information to support product portfolio decisions.

Design Team Membership

Design team size and composition depend on the project's purpose, size, and urgency of completion. Design team membership also depends on availability of staff.

A small project focused on costing a limited number of product lines can be handled by one or two part-time staff from accounting or marketing. In contrast, a plant-wide study that costs parts at the lowest level of the bill of materials will require more help and broader experience.

A cross-functional team is ideal for large projects. *Figure 11-3* shows such a membership for a manufacturing company. A *production supervisor* provides knowledge of the production process. A *product designer* understands the products. An *accountant* allows the team to interface with the existing accounting systems. A *marketing analyst* knows customers and is familiar with nonplant activities. And a *materials (or other support department) manager* brings knowledge about plant activities to the team.

ABC projects are completed faster with full-time team members. But in practice, it's difficult to pull people from their current assignments. As a result part-time commitment works better if project completion isn't urgent.

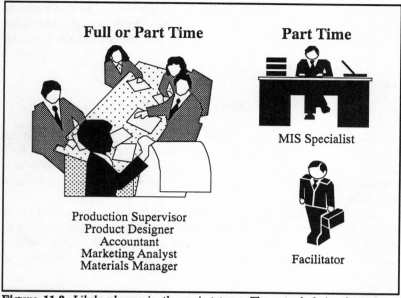

Figure 11-3. *Likely players in the project team.* The actual choice depends on availability of qualified staff as well as the project's purpose, size, and urgency.

The team should also include part-time consultants. For example, an internal *information systems specialist* develops interfaces to the shop floor control system, bill-of-materials system, and other company systems. This specialist also helps select and use ABC software. Additionally, an internal or outside facilitator can bring ABC system design experience to the project.

Training

Training is crucial to proper implementation, execution, use, and acceptance of an ABC system. There are different types of training required, depending on the audience. These are:

- *Management* should be exposed to ABC concepts. The objective is to achieve a high level of "buy-in."
- *Implementers* need skills that ensure a successful design. This includes technical design skills, software modeling capabilities, and project organization.

- *Users* should understand what information is available from activity-based costing and how that information should be used in decision making. The objective is to train them to use ABC in a program of ABM.

Project Schedule

It's now time to put a project schedule together. This is where you summarize the tasks that must be accomplished to complete the project, the estimated time needed for each task, and the overall time required by the project. *Figure 11-4* shows a project schedule.

The tasks, and the time required to complete them, differ from project to project. Most projects take from three to six months to create the first system. However, a simple *desk study*, which makes a rough estimate of the cost of a limited number of products, may take only a few days.

Creating an ABC system has its own *cost drivers*. These are factors that determine the effort required to implement the system. This effort, and the cost, varies from company to company depending on the cost drivers shown in *Figure 11-5*.

For example, the number of people interviewed is an important cost driver. In one plant with a limited support staff, a team of two completed interviewing in just two weeks. In another plant, it took over three months for a team of six to complete the interviews. This latter plant designed and manufactured defense products. It was very complex and had over 200 departments.

The overall time to complete the project can be reduced if tasks can be overlapped. The task of linking ABC software to the company's information systems, for example, can proceed during the interviewing phase.

Project Costs

Achieving ABC benefits requires incurring costs. Internal and external costs should be budgeted up-front. This will allow a careful comparison of the costs and deliverables.

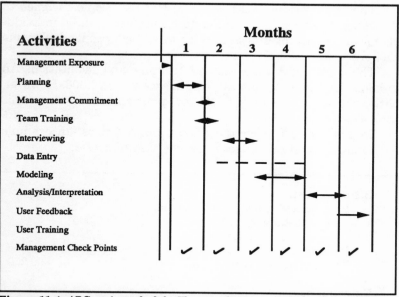

Figure 11-4. *ABC project schedule.* The actual time scale depends on objectives, number of cost objects, number of different activities, number of interviews, etc.

Number of products
Number of part numbers
Number of customers
Number of bill-of-materials layers
Number of processes
Number of departments
Number of activities
Number of people interviewed
Prior experience
Existing knowledge

Figure 11-5. *Cost drivers of ABC implementation.* These drivers determine just how much effort must be expended to complete the project. If you estimate the magnitudes of these drivers during project planning, you'll have a good idea of how long implementation will take.

The major *internal cost* is the cost of the people assigned to the implementation team. You need bright, experienced individuals for an important project such as this. Such people don't come cheaply.

The major *external costs* are training and facilitation. An in-house training program can cost in excess of $20,000. However, participation in a publicly offered program can reduce this somewhat.

To give you a feel for the different cost factors, an example ABC implementation budget is shown in *Figure 11-6*.

Internal costs:		
Salaries and benefits for 3 months:		
• Full-time: 4 staff	$50,000	
• Part-time: 1 staff 50%	6,250	
Resources:	10,000	
Total internal costs:		$66,250
External costs:		
Seminars	$ 5,000	
In-house training program	20,000	
Books and videos	1,000	
Computer hardware	10,000	
Software	5,000	
Facilitation	20,000	
Total external costs:		$61,000
Total project costs:		$127,250

Figure 11-6. *Example ABC implementation budget.* This is for a three-month project in a medium-size plant. The scope is plant-wide, all products are included, and costs are carried to parts at the lowest level of the bill of materials.

Lessons

With a good game plan and some effort, you'll reap the rewards of a successful ABC implementation. The system will be completed, and the information can be used to foster improvement all over the company. But, to reach this goal, you need to include all of the eight key steps in your game plan:

- Formulate the objectives of your project,
- Describe what tangible outputs the project will deliver,
- Set the scope of the project,
- Describe the organization structure of the project,
- Identify the individuals and functions that comprise the implementation team,
- Determine training requirements,
- Complete a project schedule that shows what tasks must be completed and how long the project will take, and
- Estimate the costs of implementation.

Key Terms in Chapter 11

Deliverable–A tangible benefit of activity-based costing.
Pilot project–A test of the applicability and utility of activity--based costing.
Project team–The individuals who plan, design, and implement the ABC system.
Steering committee–An upper management group that oversees planning and implementation of the ABC system.

Chapter 12

GATHERING THE INFORMATION

The information required by an ABC system is defined by the conceptual model described in Chapter 4. From this model, you know that you need information about resources, activities, and cost objects. You also know that you need information about the linkages between those items.

Now you need to know where to go for this information. As it turns out, there are three primary sources for ABC information:

1. The accounting department has information about the cost of resources. This information is in the general ledger account balances. The account balances are the starting point for assigning costs to activities.

2. Information about activities comes from the people who do the work or are knowledgeable about the work. What are the activities? How do they consume resources? What are the cost drivers and performance measures?

3. Information about cost objects, activity drivers, and some performance measures is found in the company's information systems. For example, the number of material receipts (a potential activity driver) is found in the inventory control system.

You'll be surprised at how much information *is readily* available to design an ABC model. In addition to the official data sources, it's common to find data files in desk drawers or personal computers. These unofficial information sources may be unknown outside of the work area, but are often useful for ABC.

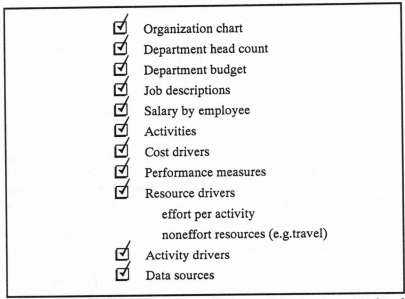

☑ Organization chart
☑ Department head count
☑ Department budget
☑ Job descriptions
☑ Salary by employee
☑ Activities
☑ Cost drivers
☑ Performance measures
☑ Resource drivers
    effort per activity
    noneffort resources (e.g.travel)
☑ Activity drivers
☑ Data sources

Figure 12-1. *Information checklist.* You need a lot of information for activity-based costing. Make sure you know what you want before you conduct an interview or send out a questionnaire.

The focal point for information gathering is the place where the work is performed (the department or the process). This is where you obtain information about activities and learn where data about cost objects and activity drivers can be found *(Figure 12-1).*

Knowing the location of data is one thing. Successfully gathering it—and seizing the opportunity to teach the users about ABC—can be quite another. There are, however, some secrets that make the task substantially easier. These secrets include:

- How to collect the information,
- Who to interview,
- How to prepare for the interview,
- How to conduct an interview,
- What documentation should be completed,
- What an interview schedule should look like, and
- How to get the data into the ABC system.

The goal of this chapter is to reveal those secrets to you.

The Tools of Data Collection

You know *what* information you want. That's largely determined by the ABC model you're about to build.

You also know *where* to find the information. You've checked your company's organization chart, and you've identified the departments and processes to be investigated.

The next issue is the *how* of collecting the information.

There are five major information collecting techniques—*observation, timekeeping systems, questionnaires, storyboards, and interviews*. Let's take a closer look at each method.

1. Observation

Observation is a fast and low-cost way to obtain information about the work being done. Just look around. What do you see going on? What conclusions can you draw from your observations?

Observation may be fast, but it's not always easy. It requires experience and knowledge about the type of work going on. It benefits from experience within the organization. And its success depends on an uncanny ability to draw correct and relevant conclusions from what's observed.

Observation won't be enough to obtain everything you need. But it can supplement the information you obtain from other sources.

2. Timekeeping Systems

Timekeeping systems provide records of the work done and the time spent on each activity. For example, the engineers in one company maintained records of their work and the products they were working on. This information was then used to develop an activity-based model for engineering.

Timekeeping can provide a reasonably accurate record of time spent. It's also a low-cost source of data—at least to the ABC design team, to whom it's *free*.

It's unusual, however, to find time records already available. The exception is direct labor, where daily time recording is common. But there's no such timekeeping tradition for most nondirect labor activities. Consequently, a timekeeping system must be instituted.

This can be a problem, though. Managers and support staff aren't likely to be enthusiastic about filling in time cards on a daily basis. Some may even look upon time cards as being intrusive. Often they won't be filled out properly through lack of attention or suspicion of their purpose.

In such cases, the design team may need to use some other source for information. If timekeeping was not in place during the previous year, it's impossible to go back and recreate the records.

It is possible, however, to use timekeeping on a sample basis. One company, for example, instituted timekeeping for a one-week period. This was done primarily to validate data obtained previously during interviews.

The results from these time records were somewhat different from those obtained during the interviews. In some cases, the differing records were discarded because their one-week coverage wasn't representative of the entire year. In other cases, the time records were used in the model in lieu of the interview information.

In some areas, timekeeping may be an ideal source of ABC information. Keeping track of time spent on engineering projects is one example. For such areas, a request can be made to institute timekeeping as a future source of ABC information.

3. Questionnaires

Questionnaires can be used to elicit information about the work going. This is done by sending lists of appropriate questions to individual department heads or others knowing about the targeted work areas.

In general, questionnaires can be used in the three following ways:

Pre-interview questionnaire. This questionnaire *(Figure 12-2)* is sent to department heads prior to an interview. It's sort of an interview preview. It allows department heads to gather their thoughts in preparation for the interview. The responses also provide the ABC design team with "food for thought" prior to the interview.

Questionnaires as a primary data collection tool. A questionnaire may be used exclusively in lieu of interviewing or timekeeping. This is faster than an interview. A questionnaire is also less intrusive than timekeeping, and it can be filled out by managers at their convenience and in the privacy of their offices. If you have hundreds of managers to interview, questionnaires may be the only feasible alternative.

To be effective, however, such questionnaires must be carefully designed. They must be complete, and they must ask the right questions in the right way. For example, if the question asks for data about cost drivers, and the question is not absolutely clear what a cost driver is, the answer may be wrong.

Questionnaires, unlike interviews, provide no opportunity for feedback. You miss the spontaneous questions and dialogue that often lead to important insights into the department's activities.

---

1. What are your primary activities?

2. How many employees do you have? Please list your employees and the time each spends on their specific activities.

3. Do you provide services to other departments? If so, please specify the type of activity and the providing department.

4. To perform your activities you need material and supplies:
   a. Where are they obtained?
   b. In what activities are they used?

Figure 12-2. *Example pre-interview questionnaire.* Questionnaires are efficient ways of obtaining information, but they lack the "human touch" of an interview.

Follow-up questionnaires. Questionnaires can also be used following the interview. One purpose is to confirm the accuracy of conclusions drawn from the interview. In other words: Have we recognized the right activities? Are our estimates of the effort devoted to each activity reasonable?

If there are disagreements over the correctness of the ABC design, it's better to find out before the design is finished than after.

Another use is to update the previous period's design. The questionnaire is used to find out if anything has changed in the intervening period. For example, are there any new activities? Has the relative effort shifted from one activity to another?

4. Storyboards

Another possibility is to use storyboards to obtain a department's activity information. Storyboarding migrated to ABC from quality management, although its roots go back further to Walt Disney, Leonardo Da Vinci, and others. It uses group problem solving techniques to create a picture—the storyboard—of relevant information.

Johnson and Johnson Medical, Inc.

Johnson and Johnson Medical, Inc., is a subsidiary of Johnson and Johnson, a Fortune 50 corporation. Their mission is to provide products that help prevent infection and manage the healing of wounds. Headquartered in Arlington, Texas, they manufacture and distribute products worldwide.

Johnson and Johnson used storyboarding in their ABC project. A facilitator (a member of the ABC design team) held three sessions with the manager and entire staff of each department to accomplish the following things:

- The first session covered basic ABC concepts, defined activities, the flow of work, and activity drivers. Each person was given ten dots (each dot represented 10% of their time) and asked to estimate how much time each activity required. These estimates were used to define the resource drivers—each person in the group received one vote for this purpose.
- Session two focused on the relationships between activities as suppliers and customers of each other. Cost drivers and performance measures were identified for each activity.
- Session three linked activity information to activity-based management. A red triangle was attached to the picture of each activity the group felt should be improved. (On average, each department attached 20 red triangles, a sure sign of the scope for improvement). From this, a plan for change was prepared for each tagged activity along with ten action steps for the department. All this was accomplished in a session that lasted less than three hours *(Figure 12-3)*.

Figure 12-3. *Storyboards at Johnson and Johnson.* This picture shows storyboards being prepared during a group design session at Johnson and Johnson. Each card represents an activity. Red triangles signify activities that need improving.

A storyboard was created for each session summarizing the group decisions. A photograph was taken of each storyboard, with one copy made for the department and another for the design team. The design team maintained a photo album of the company's design.

Storyboarding was a positive experience for Johnson and Johnson. It took less time than interviewing, yet it involved every person in the company, not just the managers. Its impact was felt not just on the design of the model, but on activity-based management as well.

5. Interviews

Interviewing is a key element in the ABC process. In fact, many companies use interviews as the primary investigative tool during initial ABC model design.

But interviewing is more than just a data collection tool. It's a dialogue. Information flows both ways. This provides an opportunity to involve ABC users in the design process itself. Users learn about the ABC project—how it works and what it is to accomplish. Such involvement makes it more likely they'll be supporters of ABC and use it to foster positive change.

In short, interviewing has three key purposes:

- *Gathering information from reliable sources.* It's a tool for collecting much of the data used to build a model of the activities and their relationship to resources and cost objects.

- *Educating users.* It's an opportunity to teach potential users about ABC.

- *Building Ownership.* Interviewing is an opportunity to answer questions, address concerns, and build ownership of the project.

Interviewing, however, is likely to be the most time consuming information gathering task—at least the first time through. So it's worth spending some time to learn how to do it well. This begins with *determining who to interview*.

Who to Interview

A major purpose of interviewing is to obtain information. Thus, the first step is to:

Identify those individuals with the most potential for providing the information you need.

These people are usually managers and supervisors. They have the broadest knowledge about the activities performed in their departments. True, subordinates actually perform the activities and usually know more about the fine details. But there are more subordinates than managers, and it would take too much time to interview them all.

You'll find some managers who can't provide the needed information. This is often the case in nonproduction areas that are less procedurally rigid. These managers may not know what each subordinate is doing or the time spent on each activity. Subordinates may also maintain input and performance data that isn't used by managers. To obtain information from such areas, you'll need to schedule additional time for follow-up interviews with selected subordinates.

How to Prepare for the Interview

There are two aspects to preparing for an interview. One is to prepare yourself. The other is to prepare the interviewee. The objective in both cases is to increase the chances of gaining all the information needed in the shortest possible time.

Remember, people are busy. They may not have time to grant you a second interview. Also, it'll probably take several weeks to interview all the people on your list. Any second round of interviews will delay the project that much more.

Preparing to conduct the interview. You can prepare yourself by doing some advance research. For example:

- Learn what you can in advance about the department's operations.
- Make sure you know what information you are looking for, and formulate your questions in advance.
- Know what level of detail to ask for (if the ABC is to be used for value analysis, for example, you will need detailed activity information)
- Understand the project's objectives and scope (you are an ambassador of the project and will inevitably be called on to talk about it).
- Be familiar with the concepts of ABC and activity-based management (so you can teach people about ABC and pave the way for positive change).

Preparing the interviewee. The interviewee needs to know what ABC is, what the project is to accomplish, and what information is needed. This knowledge can be communicated in the three following manners:

1. *Kickoff meeting.* A "kickoff" meeting is a good forum for presenting information to the interviewees. At Oregon Cutting Systems, for example, the design team invited all interviewees to a presentation that covered basic concepts, discussed the project, and described the purpose of the interview. This eliminated the need to individually brief each interviewee at the start of the interview.

2. *Interview orientation.* An alternative to the kickoff meeting is to do the orientation during the interview itself. While this may take more time, *it is a private meeting*, and the interviewee may be more willing to express concerns about the project. Orientation can also be tailored to the particular background of the interviewee. If the interviewee has attended an ABC exposure program or has participated in the planning or design process, orientation will be quite short. If the interviewee has scant knowledge of ABC, a half hour or more may be required.

3. *Material distribution.* Distributing materials in advance is valuable—if you can get the interviewee to read the information. A brief executive summary of ABC concepts, the project, and the interview guidelines are most likely to be read.

Articles, books, and videotapes are useful sources for those willing to take the time. One company, for example, circulated the videotape *An Introduction to Activity-Based Costing* to each manager prior to the interview.[1]

Other materials that should be distributed are:

- A "Pre-interview To Do" list for the interviewee. This may include preparing or copying relevant material such as a staff list, organization chart, data source list, and so forth.

- A questionnaire that should be filled out and returned to the design team prior to the interview.

- A notice stating the time and place of the interview. If possible, arrange to have the interview in the interviewee's office. This interviewee will be more relaxed there. A second choice is the safe, neutral ground of a conference room.

How to Conduct an Interview

The goal is to make the interview a positive experience. It's an opportunity to ensure quality design of the ABC model *and* to pave the way for positive change.

Success is most likely when the interviewer plays the role of coach. The ABC coach is a teacher, a motivator, and a facilitator of the ABC model's design and successful use.

Playing the role of a coach helps communicate to interviewees their ownership of ABC, their responsibility for its success, and the help they can expect to receive from the ABC team. A coaching role creates an atmosphere of trust in which open communication is possible.

Substantial experience has already been gained in conducting interviews for designing ABC models. This experience has yielded a recommended series of ABC coaching steps:

INTERVIEWING GUIDELINES

1. Explain the purpose.
2. Review the benefits.
3. Describe the project.
4. Explain the process.
5. Ask key questions.
6. Facilitate the answers.
7. Provide feedback.
8. Communicate responsibility.
9. Offer support.
10. Express appreciation.

---

1. Explain the purpose. Begin the interview by explaining why you are there. You want to brief the interviewees about ABC and the ABC project. You want a chance to address any concerns they may have. And you want to help them gather the data and design the model.

2. Review the benefits. Here's a chance to sell the ABC concept. Show how activity-based information can help focus strategy and improve operations. Give examples of how ABC may benefit the interviewee's own work area.

3. Describe the project. Talk about the ABC project and its importance to the company. What will be the deliverables? What's the scope? Who is involved? What is the role of the interviewee? Who is giving support? What progress has been made? And when will the project be completed?

4. Explain the process. Tell the interviewees about the data requirements of ABC. Go over the process of model design, emphasizing its dependence on the knowledge and input of the interviewees. Make it clear that you are not looking for absolute precision, just good quality information at a reasonable cost, information that meets the needs of ABC users (such as themselves).

5. Ask key questions. Ask a set of questions designed to yield all the data you need about each process. What work is done? What resources are required? How should the use of resources be measured? Why is work done? How well is it done? Which cost objects or other activities benefit from the work, and how should this be measured? Where can the data be found?

You may need to supplement this list of questions depending on the project's deliverables. For example, you may want to know the level of each activity or whether it is value-added or nonvalue-added.

6. Facilitate the answers. Help the interviewees answer the questions. Ask follow-up questions if you sense that an answer is incomplete or reflects misunderstanding of the original question. Provide technical assistance if the interviewees cannot respond because of a lack of ABC knowledge. Keep the interview on track (it's easy to go off on a tangent).

7. *Provide feedback.* Tell the interviewees what you have learned about each key discussion area. This gives the interviewees feedback on what has been communicated and a chance to correct any misunderstanding. It also gives them a chance to change their mind.

As a matter of procedure, explain that a copy of the finished model of the process will be forwarded to all interviewees for review. This provides further opportunities for feedback and reinforces the notion that each interviewee owns a part of the model.

8. *Communicate responsibility.* The interviewees have primary responsibility for the design of the model of the process and for updates. The interviewees are also responsible for explaining ABC to other members of the department, for ensuring that they are trained to use the information, and for fostering positive change.

9. *Offer support.* Make it clear that the interviewees are not alone in carrying out their responsibilities. Offer them software and information systems support. Offer technical support to resolve model design and data analysis issues. And describe how you can help train their staff.

10. *Express appreciation.* Don't forget to thank each interviewee for the time and support they are providing the ABC project. Remind them how important they are to the success of the project. Congratulate them on their contributions to improvement of the organization.

The Required Documentation

Background documentation serves as reference material during the modeling process. Examples are organization charts, budgets, position descriptions, transaction tracking reports, head-count listings, and salaries by employee.

Interview documentation is a summary of what was learned during the interview. It's part of the design process record and is available to subsequent designers or users.

What an Interview Schedule Should Look Like

An interview schedule should allow time to absorb, document, and model the results of each interview. A reasonable schedule covers no more than two or three interviews per day with one to two hours per interview *(Figure 12-4)*.

No.	Interviewee	Date	Time	Day	Interviewers	Comments
			Interview Schedule			Date Page of
14	Sandra Booth	8-10	8:30 a.m.	Mon	Peter/Mary	Check data sources
15	John Kershaw	8-10	1:30 p.m.	Mon	Peter/Mary	
16	Brian Hutton	8-12	9:30 a.m.	Wed	Vic/Nancy	
17	Susan Moody	8-12	3:00 p.m.	Wed	Vic/Nancy	
18	Bob Edwards	8-14	8:30 a.m.	Fri	Peter/Vic	Interfaces with Sandra Booth Dept
19	Mike Roberts	8-14	2:00 p.m.	Fri	Mary/Vic	
20	Roy Peterson	8-17	9:00 a.m.	Mon	Peter/Nancy	
21	Kathy Smith	8-17	2:30 p.m.	Mon	Peter/Mary	

Figure 12-4. *Take care in setting the interview schedule.* Don't set too fast a pace—leave time for modeling and evaluation. Two interviewers per interview is recommended.

Time should be set aside for modeling the results of the interviews. Time should also be available for follow-up interviews with subordinates or repeat interviews with managers.

Interview assignments should be based primarily on knowledge of the department. A secondary consideration is the availability of people on the design team.

It's always wise to have two people conduct each interview. This ensures proper coverage of the important issues. One person can do the job. But two people can reinforce each other and exchange notes.

Getting the Data into the ABC System

How you get data into the ABC system is always a *practical* design concern. Also, there is a cost associated with data entry. This cost varies with the design of the system and the source of the data.

Basically, there are two ways to get data into the system. These are *downloading* and *hand entry*.

Downloading. This is electronic transfer of data from one computer system to another. It's the ideal way to move data into the ABC system when data already exist in electronic form. The only additional cost is setting up the download link.

Creating the download link usually requires support from the information systems department. For example, data formats may need to be changed to make the two systems compatible. The effort to do this can be substantial the first time through. But once the link is made, the data are *free* to activity-based costing.

Stockham Valve and Fittings, for example, completed an ABC system with 58 activity drivers. This was a rather complex design that matched the tremendous variety of products and range of activities in the company.

Thanks to a well-developed information system, Stockham Valve found that data for 57 of the activity drivers were stored electronically. This allowed the bulk of the data to be electronically downloaded from the main computer to the ABC system *(Figure 12-5)*.

Making the electronic connection required help from an information systems specialist. But this was the only incremental cost for activity driver data, and primarily a nonrecurring, first-year cost at that.

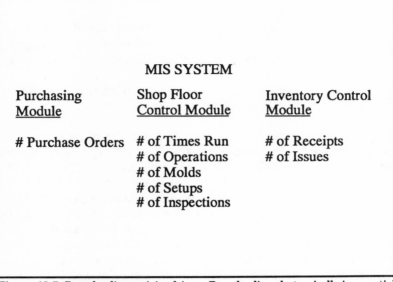

MIS SYSTEM

Purchasing Module	Shop Floor Control Module	Inventory Control Module
# Purchase Orders	# of Times Run # of Operations # of Molds # of Setups # of Inspections	# of Receipts # of Issues

Figure 12-5. *Downloading activity drivers.* Downloading electronically is essential if you have many cost objects. There are just too many pieces of data to enter by hand. For example, Stockham Valve and Fitting's ABC system costed about 80,000 different parts, but most of the data for the activity drivers were downloaded from the mainframe computer system.

If the data had to be hand entered, it would have been impossible to implement such a complex design. (The company's ABC system costed over 80,000 parts, each of which required data about the activity drivers.)

Hand Entry. The time-consuming alternative to electronic entry is hand entry. This is necessary when the data is not available in electronic form.

For example, it's common to hand enter information about activities. Decomposition of functions to create activities in the system is typically done by hand. Designation of cost assignment measures—such as which resource driver to use for a particular resource—is also done by hand.

However, hand entering activity driver data is an uncommon practice. This is because there are just too many pieces of data, even in moderate size systems. Stockham Valve and Fittings did hand enter data for one activity driver. However, this driver affected fewer than 50 products during the year, and the data only took a few minutes to enter.

Summary

Information gathering can be the most time consuming aspect of building an ABC system. It involves scouring the company for information about resources, activities, and cost objects. This is done by learning:

1. How to collect the information. There are five ways to collect information:

- *Observation* is a quick way to learn what is going on. Take a walk around the plant and see what's going on. But this does require good observational skills.
- *Timekeeping systems* are convenient sources of time data, but are not usually available, nor popular with those who must fill in the time-cards.
- *Questionnaires* are packages of questions soliciting information. They are used before interviews to obtain preliminary information, or they can be used in lieu of the interview entirely. They can also be used following the interview to confirm the ABC model's quality. Questionnaires are efficient, but lack the *personal* touch of interviews.
- *Storyboards* use group problem-solving techniques to create a picture of each department's activities and related information. It's relatively fast and involves everyone in the company in the ABC project.
- *Interviewing* is the most common ABC information collection technique, even though it is time consuming. It allows two-way communication—the interviewer gathers knowledge about activities, while the manager learns about activity-based costing.

2. Who to interview. The rule is to interview those most likely to have the information you need. Department managers are the choice under this rule—they generally have the broadest knowledge of the activities in their departments.

3. How to prepare for the interview. The interviewer prepares for the interview by doing "homework" about ABC, the ABC project, and the department in question. The interviewer also prepares the interviewee by supplying information on ABC concepts, the project, and the information required.

4. How to conduct an interview. Success in conducting an interview requires basic communication skills and careful attention to the "do's" and "don'ts" of interviewing.

5. What documentation is required. Important documentation includes material that guides the modeling process and summarizes what was learned during implementation.

6. What an interview schedule looks like. An interview schedule should set a pace that allows time to absorb the knowledge acquired and create a model from that information.

7. How to get data into the ABC system. The data can be downloaded from the company's information systems, from spreadsheets, or entered by hand. Downloading is the easiest, but requires technical information systems support.

Information gathering gives you a knowledge of your company's activities and people such as you have never had before. It's also fun once you "get the hang of it." If you learn to ask the right questions and get the right information, it makes the ABC modeling process that much easier.

Key Terms in Chapter 12

Interviews–In-person question and answer sessions. This is the method of choice in ABC. It's time consuming, but interviews yield a wealth of reliable information.

Questionnaire–Compilations of questions about the work that goes on in the company. Questionnaires don't have the *personal* touch, but they can be an efficient way to collect data.

***Storyboards*–A** group problem-solving technique that creates a picture of each department's activities and related information. An efficient data gathering technique, it extends the reach of ABC to everyone in the organization.

***Timekeeping system*–A** record of the time devoted to activities or cost objects. Not commonly used outside of tracking direct labor, may be costly and intrusive, but can still be a useful data gathering device.

References:

1.   Peter B.B. Turney, *Introduction to Activity-Based Costing*, (Portland, OR: ABC Technologies, Inc.), 1990.

Chapter 13

DESIGNING THE MODEL

Designing an ABC model is a critical stage of the implementation process. It's where the structure of the system is created and the *intelligence* added.

This is similar to playing chess. Each piece of the model has a specific purpose, and there are some clearly defined rules to follow. But many judgements are also involved, and it's often difficult to immediately measure the impact of each decision.

The designer's job is to meet the system objectives at minimum cost and complexity. At the same time, the system should provide the *right kind of information* at the *right level of detail*. This is necessary for ABC system success in supporting strategic and process improvement decisions.

The model should be as simple as possible—*but no simpler*. If it's too simple, it will report inaccurate costs. The model's activity information may also be insufficient to support improvement processes.

At the same time, the model should be as complex as necessary—*but no more complex*. If it's too complex, it will be too costly to design, implement, and maintain. It will also burden users with unnecessary detail and possibly reduce understandability.

The key is to strike a proper balance. To help you do this, let's look at some "tried and true" rules for success and how they can be applied in following the major steps of the design process. Briefly, these steps are:

- Identifying activities,
- Reconstructing the general ledger,
- Creating activity centers,
- Defining resource drivers,
- Determining attributes, and
- Selecting activity drivers.

Identifying Activities

The task of identifying activities is governed by the chosen purpose, or purposes, of the ABC system. If the purpose is strategic (e.g., choosing how specific markets or customers are to be served), the primary job is to accurately assign costs to cost objects. If the purpose is to improve the process (e.g., to better meet customer needs), the job is to provide information about activities as well as cost objects.

In either case, activities must be defined. This is done with a process that's referred to as *functional decomposition*.

To identify activities with functional decomposition, start with an organization chart for the company. Then divide (decompose) each box in the chart into smaller units. This decomposition of larger functions into smaller functions is continued until you meet the purpose of the ABC system.

In performing functional decomposition, you need knowledge about activities. This required knowledge will have been gained during the data gathering process discussed in the previous chapter.

Rules for Identifying Activities

1. Match the detail to the purpose of the model.
2. Use macro activities to balance conflicting objectives.
3. Combine insignificant items.
4. Describe activities clearly and consistently.

To see how functional decomposition works, suppose your organizational chart has a box called *manufacturing support*. Closer inspection shows that this box is made up of several departments—production scheduling, process engineering, receiving, etc.—such as shown in *Figure 13-1*.

You've finished interviewing the managers of each of these support departments. That means you have the information necessary for the next step in the decomposition. This next step is breaking out the activities.

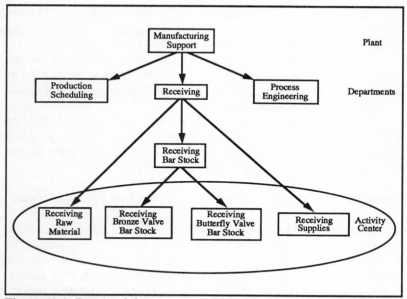

Figure 13-1. *Functional decomposition.* The process of functional decomposition leads naturally to departmental activity centers. In this figure, you can see how a receiving department activity center is created.

For example, let's say you found that three activities are performed in the receiving department. This department processes receipts of raw materials, bar stock, and supplies (such as parts for the maintenance department). You identify each of these activities separately because the effort required to process a receipt varies depending on what is received.

You've also found out, however, that the effort to process bar stock varies depending on the type of bar stock received. Bronze valve bar stock is received in bulk and requires more effort than the small boxes of butterfly valve bar stock. So the last step is to decompose receipts of bar stock into those two component activities.

This is illustrated in *Figure 13-1*, which is a *graphical* representation of functional decomposition. Such diagrams are invaluable to understanding and communicating the design of an ABC model. They should be used wherever possible. (Make sure the conference room where you hold design meetings has a drawing board or a flip chart for this purpose.)

Notice that the decomposition in *Figure 13-1* has three levels. The number of levels can vary from one to many, depending on your starting point and the level of activity detail required.

For the above example, the decomposition could have started at the division level. Additional steps would then be needed to decompose the division into its component plants and each plant into its main functional areas.

Overall, there are four main rules to follow in identifying activities. These rules are listed briefly in the accompanying box entitled *Rules for Identifying Activities*. Let's take a closer look at each of these rules and how they are applied.

Rule #1:   Match the detail to the purpose of the model.

Activities can be defined broadly or narrowly. *Figure 13-2*, for example, lists the activities in a customer service department. The first four activities are just different aspects of processing customer orders. Do you want all four of these activities in your model? Or do you want just one activity called *processing customer orders*?

	Cost	
Activity	**$**	**%**
Receiving orders	$21,455	15%
Processing orders	21,811	16%
Scheduling shipments	31,292	22%
Invoicing customers	15,409	11%
Maintaining customer files	3,144	2%
Maintaining inventory files	4,905	4%
Processing returns	9,744	7%
Preparing reports	12,825	9%
Administering	12,825	9%
Filing	6,190	4%
Total	**$139,600**	**100%**

Figure 13-2. *Activities in a customer service department.* Note that some activities are similar, such as receiving and processing orders. They can be combined to create a single macro activity. Other activities carry an insignificant cost, such as maintaining customer files. The cost of such activities can be assigned to other activities in the department.

The rule is to match the level of detail to the purpose of the model. Suppose the model's primary purpose is to determine the cost of servicing customers. For this, the single activity—processing customer orders—is sufficient. This activity allows you to compute the cost of a customer order and assign it to customers based on the number of times each customer places an order.

But suppose the model's primary purpose is to provide information for performance improvement. Now the four activities involved in processing a customer order become important. Each of these activities represents a separate unit of work in the customer service department. Each has its own problems and opportunities for improvement. So each should be individually considered in the ABC model.

Rule #2:   Use macro activities if you have conflicting objectives.

What do you do if your system has both process improvement *and* strategic objectives?

Process improvement requires detailed information about activities. Supplying this amount of detail in the system, however, may confuse strategic users.

The solution is to use *macro activities.*[1] Macro activities are aggregations of related activities, and have their own additional set of rules:

Macro Rule #1:   The activities are the same level.
Macro Rule #2:   The activities use the same activity driver.
Macro Rule #3:   The activities have a common purpose.

In the example of the customer service department, the four activities associated with processing a customer order can be assigned to a single macro activity. They are all customer service activities (the same level). All use *the number of customer orders* as the activity driver. And all are part of the customer order process. This satisfies all three Macro Rules.

Using macro activities creates two tiers of activity, with each tier meeting a different need. At the lower tier, information about the four activities supports improvement of the process. At the higher tier, strategic users can ignore the detail and focus on the single macro activity.

Rule #3:   Combine insignificant items.

Activities that are too small to be worth recognizing individually should be combined. This helps reduce system clutter.

The activities listed in *Figure 13-2*, for example, include *maintaining customer files* and *maintaining inventory files*. These two activities could be combined in the ABC system.

This combination is possible—and usually desirable—because their cost is insignificant. The cost assigned to each of these activities is about 2% and 4% of the customer service department. Also the cost of both activities can be traced to customers using the same activity driver (*the number of customers*).

Rule #4:   Describe activities clearly and consistently.

How you describe activities determines the effectiveness of the system and the information it provides. A *clear description* enhances the ability to communicate the work that each activity represents. A *consistent definition* of activities makes it easy to find activities of the same type or process.

The key to describing activities clearly is to use short, understandable, and descriptive labels. In one company, for example, an activity involved loading finished goods onto truck trailers. This was described in the ABC system as "M/H-load f.g.-semi." Such a description has meaning only for the people working in the material handling department. In contrast, *loading finished goods* is short, understandable, and fully descriptive of the work done.

Labels chosen for activities should end in "ing" to denote action. This has the advantage of avoiding confusion.

For example, is *setup* the activity or the activity driver? Actually, *setting up* is the activity, and *the number of setups* is the activity driver.

Activity labels should also be consistent across the entire company. Like activities should be described in a like manner no matter where they are performed.

At National Semiconductor, for example, a *patterning* activity was performed in the manufacture of integrated circuits (ICs). In this activity, an image was exposed onto photosensitive material. This image allowed creation of electrical circuits on the ICs.

National Semiconductor Corporation

National Semiconductor Corporation designs, manufactures and markets high-performance semiconductor products. Headquartered in Santa Clara, California, the company is a global leader in mixed analog and digital technologies.

The description of the *patterning* activity was inconsistent from one department to another. It was variously called *stepping*, *aligning*, and *exposing*.

Despite these inconsistencies, the activities were essentially the same. They differed only in the resources used and the age and type of technology.

This lack of consistency in description would have inhibited prioritization of improvement efforts. Each separate activity would have appeared less significant in a Pareto analysis than the overall activity.

A set of common definitions and descriptions of activities is called a *chart of activities*. This chart of activities sets a standard for ABC within functions and across plants and companies. Its use improves system design and has helped large, diverse companies such as National Semiconductor coordinate ABC across multiple sites in the same company.

Reconstructing the General Ledger

After identifying activities, the next step is to establish activity costs. This begins with the general ledger, which is the starting point for establishing the flow of costs in ABC.

The general ledger is where you find the financial information about company resources. For example, how much was paid in salaries so far this year? How much depreciation did we have? How much did we accrue in taxes? How does it all compare with the budget (what we should have spent)?

In short, the general ledger is a useful data source for ABC system designers. It provides, in one place, a summary of all important (and unimportant) financial data about the company.

Unfortunately, when looking for activity cost information, the general ledger is also a source of frustration and difficulty. This is because:

- General ledgers are usually organized around the type of expenditure, such as rent or interest (the *line items*), rather than the activity.
- General ledgers are often full of excruciating detail of the wrong kind. The chart of accounts for a medium size company or division may run to hundreds of different items. There may be dozens of different accounts, for example, detailing the many elements of employee benefits. In addition to pensions, there may be vacations, health care, dental care, and insurance of various types.
- Despite the many detailed accounts, general ledgers are sometimes aggregated at too high of an organizational level. For example, line items of expenditure, such as salaries or building depreciation, may be available only at the division level.
- Costs are collected in the general ledger for time periods that may not be consistent with economic life cycles. The general ledger follows the accounting period, with account totals accumulated by month, quarter, and year. Resources, however, such as those in engineering, may benefit several years of product and process life.
- Costs in the general ledger may comply with generally accepted accounting principles, but lack economic sense. Depreciation, for example, is often computed using lives that are shorter than the true economic lives. As a result, depreciation fails to parallel actual consumption of the asset.

The basic problem is that most general ledgers are not designed around activities. Instead, they are well designed for one specific purpose—preparing financial statements. To be useful in determining activity costs for an ABC system, the general ledger must be reconstructed. This reconstruction is governed by the following three rules.

Rules for Reconstructing the General Ledger

1. Combine related accounts.
2. Decompose to the department level.
3. Adjust uneconomic items.

Rule #1: Combine related accounts.

A fact of life for most companies is that the general ledger is not activity-based. This is not surprising since most general ledgers are designed for financial reporting and control and not for ABC.

It's common to find hundreds of accounts in a general ledger, even in relatively small companies. This amount of detail may satisfy an accountant's need to pinpoint the type of expenditure. But it also creates a burden of excruciating detail for ABC.

Numerous accounts create clutter in the ABC system. They also create additional work because each account's cost must be assigned to activities.

The solution is to combine accounts that are related. Related accounts share a common purpose and are assigned to activities in the same way.

For example, salaries, health insurance, and pension costs can be combined into an account called, let's say, *personnel costs*. This title is descriptive of all its constituent accounts, and it's assigned to activities using a single resource driver (typically an estimate of effort expended on each activity).

Combining accounts in this way reduces clutter in the model. It also reduces system design effort since there are fewer paths for assigning costs. If it is done within the ABC model, it is still possible to verify the sources of each cost element.

Rule #2: Decompose to the department level.

Once you've combined related accounts, subdivide (decompose) them to obtain department costs. For example, if costs are maintained at the division level, decompose (assign) costs to the plant level first, then to departments within the plants. If the general ledger already maintains cost data at the department level, no decomposition (assignment) is required.

The department is a convenient level for cost assignment to activities. This is because most activity data is obtained directly from the departments. For example, the percent of department effort expended on each activity can be applied as a resource driver to the department's personnel cost.

Rule #3:   Adjust uneconomic items.

There's no need to follow generally accepted accounting principles in ABC. This is because ABC's primary purpose is business improvement, not financial reporting.

Thus, it makes sense to adjust general ledger items that aren't economically realistic. For example, depreciation can be recomputed on a *consumed* basis. Development costs can also be collected in a special holding account and assigned to production over the product's life.

There could just as well be a Rule #4 here, too. Tell your accountants to build an activity-based general ledger. This would be one where costs are already assigned to activities. Such a ledger would certainly make ABC system modeling much easier. It would also ensure that most data collection gets done on an on-going basis.

Creating Activity Centers

Activity centers are clusters of activities. They give structure to activity information in the system and facilitate reports about related activities.

Rule #1:   Put activities into departmental activity centers first.

The simplest way to organize activities is by department. This is familiar since departmental activity centers parallel the organization chart. It also fits naturally into the process of functional decomposition. The receiving activities in *Figure 13-1*, for example, constitute a receiving department activity center.

Rules for Creating Activity Centers

1. Put activities into departmental activity centers first.
2. Use attributes to create activity centers *on demand*.
3. Use nested activity centers to create hierarchies of activity information.

Rule #2:   Use attributes to create activity centers *on demand*.

Activity centers can be formulated *on demand* for users who want information about various groups of activities. A user may be interested in a process that cuts across department lines. This could be the engineering change process for example. Or the user may be interested in a specific type of activity, such as one associated with detecting poor quality. In both cases, it's possible to prepare an *on demand activity center report* that provides the desired information.

Attributes make it possible to create activity centers on demand. Attributes are labels describing the type of activity. Their virtue is that they allow you to easily locate activities with identical characteristics.

Dayton Extruded Plastics used this approach by labeling each activity associated with preventing, detecting, and correcting poor quality *(Figure 13-3)*. This facilitated activity center reports that highlighted information about the three types of activity.

Preventing	Detecting	Correcting
Training	Inspecting	Inspecting
Preparing	Checking line work	returns
quality	Trying out	Grinding
reports	Evaluating	Trouble-
	shrinkage	shooting

Figure 13-3. *Using attributes to create reports.* Dayton Extruded Plastics labeled activities associated with preventing, detecting, and correcting defects. This allowed them to prepare reports about *poor quality*.

Rule #3:   Use nested activity centers to create hierarchies of activity information.

Nested activity centers are centers contained in other centers. This is illustrated by *Figure 13-4*, which shows a single activity center for a company's procurement process.

Within the procurement activity center, there's another activity center for each department in the procurement process. In turn, each of these lower-level activity centers contains various activities and may even contain other activity centers. For example, the *Testing* activity center would contain various testing activities. It could also contain a *Calibration* activity center covering activities associated with calibrating the test equipment used by the Testing activity center.

The value of nesting is that it creates hierarchies of activity information. This allow users to easily focus on different levels and breadths of information. A process level activity center, for example, provides a high-level view. From this, each nested activity center and its constituent activities take you progressively deeper into the bowels of the organization.

Defining Resource Drivers

The fourth step in designing an ABC model is defining the resource drivers. Resource drivers, in turn, define the consumption of resources by activities. For example, the activity *tapping parts* uses power to run the tapping machines. The driver for this resource consumption might be the *number of machine hours*.

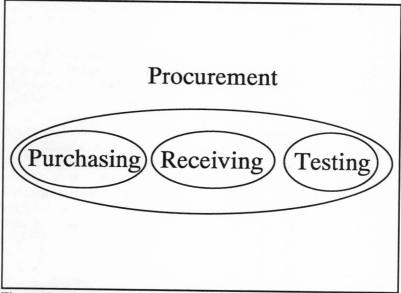

Figure 13-4. *Nested activity centers.* The individual support departments are *nested* in the procurement process. They're part of an activity-information hierarchy that can be accessed at different levels for different purposes.

The Rules for Defining Resource Drivers

1. Assign the cost of sustaining activities to primary activities.
2. Use tracing wherever possible.
3. Use common sense to determine how you allocate.
4. Separate effort and noneffort costs.

Attaching cost to activities often requires multiple steps, with a resource driver for each step. The process of cost assignment starts in the accounts in the general ledger. Cost is then moved progressively downward or sideways until it reaches the activities.

Rule #1:   Assign the cost of sustaining activities to primary activities.

One of the activities in the order processing department in *Figure 13-5* is *Administering*. This activity includes tasks such as evaluating employee performance and supervising employees. It also supports other activities in the department, such as *receiving customer orders*.

Administering is a *sustaining* activity, one that benefits other activities. It does not, however, directly benefit cost objects.

In contrast, *receiving customer orders* is a primary activity. It directly benefits cost objects (the customers in this case).

The cost of sustaining activities is assigned to the primary activities they benefit. This is preferable to trying to find an activity driver for an activity that has no direct link to cost objects. (What is an appropriate activity driver for *administering*?)

Rule #2:   Use tracing wherever possible.

Cost should be traced wherever possible and allocated only in the last resort. The cost of *administering*, for example, can be traced to the primary activities based on estimates of time spent by the administrator on each primary activity.

Tracing is the assignment of costs based on specific data. For example, supplies consumed in machine maintenance can be traced directly to this activity (assuming that records have been kept). This creates an unambiguous assignment of cost.

Allocation is the indirect assignment of cost. For example, the cost of administering can be allocated to the benefitting activities. A common allocation method is to use the relative effort devoted by nonadministrative employees to the primary activities.

Keep in mind, however, that allocation is a "dirty word" in cost systems—something to avoid if possible. It connotes arbitrariness of measurement and a limit to the meaning of the resulting information.

Knowing whether a cost is allocated or traced is important to users. For example, allocated costs, such as the cost of space, are unlikely to "go away" if the activity is eliminated. In contrast, traced costs, such as the costs of supplies, often disappear if the activity is no longer performed.

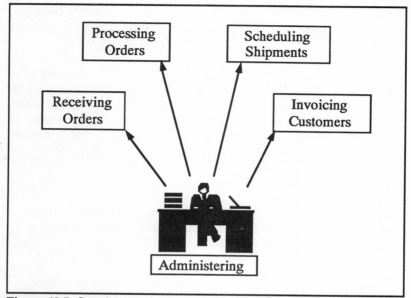

Figure 13-5. *Sustaining activities.* Sustaining activities are those that support other activities. Their costs should be assigned to the activities they benefit. In this case, *administering* the order processing department benefits several customer-related activities, and its cost is assigned based on the proportion of time spent on each activity.

You should use allocation only when direct tracing is impossible or doesn't make sense. This will generally be the case in the following three situations:

1. *Resources are shared by activities.* A building may be shared by many activities for example, but its cost is incurred for the entire facility. It's impossible to attach a portion of a jointly incurred cost directly to an activity. As a result, the cost must be allocated using a resource driver such as the percent of floor space occupied.

2. *Measurement is impractical or costly.* It may be possible to measure the use of a resource directly. But the data for the driver may be unavailable, costly, or intrusive. You can ask the janitors to record how much time they spend cleaning the areas occupied by each activity, for example, but they may balk at filling out the time-cards.

Tracing may not be possible simply because records have not been maintained. The cost of supplies, for example, can be traced if records of usage have been kept by the activities.

3. Lack of materiality. It's possible to measure the use of a resource directly, but the additional information is not justified by the amount of cost involved. For example, you could measure the amount of waste generated by each activity. However, the cost of waste disposal may be too low to justify the additional measurement cost. Thus, it's more economical to allocate than trace.

The Allocation Conundrum

The problem with allocation is that you cannot prove that one method is better than another. You also need to be very careful how you interpret allocated costs.

Here's an example using two alternative allocation methods:

Cost of facilities (e.g., building depreciation and property taxes) = $100,000.

Alternative 1 (Resource driver = % of space occupied)		Alternative 2 (Resource driver = same per activity)	
Activity 1	Activity 2	Activity 1	Activity 2
10,000 sq.ft.	5,000 sq.ft.	50%	50%
$67,000	$33,000	$50,000	$50,000

A building may be shared by many activities, for example, but its cost is incurred for the entire facility. Should we allocate using floor space? This commonly used approach assumes each square foot costs the same. This may be a reasonable assumption in some cases, but it's still an assumption. In other cases the assumption is clearly wrong. A plant with clean and nonclean rooms, for example, will not comply with this assumption (a weighted cost per square foot makes more sense in this case).

The solution is to use common sense when you allocate—and use the results with care.

Sometimes, however, allocations can be converted to tracing with justifiable additional measurement cost. For example, the cost of power is often allocated to machines based on machine hours. This may not be accurate when a variety of machines are used. But, if meters are installed on the machines, power cost can be traced directly to each machine.

Rule #3: Use common sense to determine how you allocate.

Look at the resource, look at how it's shared by the activities, and do what makes the most sense. You may not be able to prove you are right, and you will still need to use the results with care.

For example, many companies use *percent of occupied floor space* to allocate facility costs. Does this make sense? It does if you believe that the cost of space is equal per square foot.

But what if the plant was built to eliminate vibrations in certain key processes? Does an equal cost per square foot make sense here? Should the purchasing activity, for example, bear part of the additional structural cost that really only benefits some other process?

In this case, the cost per square foot is not equal across the facility. A different resource driver—such as a *weighted cost per square foot* that assigns more cost to the key processes—makes more sense.

Rule #4: Separate effort and noneffort costs.

Assignment of cost differs for effort costs and noneffort costs. Effort costs are those associated with people doing work. Primarily, these are the salaries and benefits that people receive. Noneffort costs are resources other than salaries and related costs.

The resource driver for effort costs is an estimate of effort expended on each activity. This estimate is derived from information gathered from interviews, time cards, or questionnaires. It's summarized on an *effort analysis worksheet* such as shown in *Figure 13-6*.

Figure 13-6 shows how each person in the department spent his or her time. Karen Lu, for example, spent 90% of her time implementing changes to bills of materials and 10% of her time testing products.

Activity Dept: Production Int date 8-17	Setting up	Scheduling	BOM Chg*	Testing	Running Machines	Moving Material	Must Equal 100%
Name							
Henry Carter		30	70				100
Karen Lu			90	10			100
Bob Gray	10			5	5	80	100
Jack Zimmer	25					75	100
Khalid Kahn	10	75	15				100
TOTAL	45	105	175	15	80	80	500
Activity Drivers	Setup Hours	# Batches	# ECNs*	# Tests	# Machine Hours	# Movements	

BOM Chg* = Changing Bill of Materials
#ECNs* = Engineering Change Notices

Figure 13-6. *Effort analysis worksheet.* This worksheet summarizes information about who does what and the time spent on each activity. The percentages are used to trace effort-related costs to activities.

The simplest resource driver for this effort is to take the sum of each column (or activity), divide this by total department effort, and multiply this ratio by the department's total salaries and benefits. Scheduling, for example, would receive 105/500 of this total cost.

Implicit in this resource driver is the assumption that each person in the department receives the same salary. If Karen Lu is paid less than the department average, the above driver will assign too much cost to the activities she works on.

A more refined method is to adjust the estimates of time to reflect the relative salaries. This can be done using approximate weights or by tracing the cost of each person directly to the activities performed. For example, you can assign Karen Lu's salaries and benefits to the two activities she performs. Implementing changes to bills of materials receives 90% of this total, and testing receives the other 10%.

The additional cost of adjustment may not be worthwhile or even possible. This is because the differences in salaries may be minimal, or the design team may not have access to information on individual salaries.

As for noneffort costs, they should be traced to activities wherever possible. Costs such as travel, entertainment, training, and utilities are susceptible to tracing.

The overall problem is finding records of cost consumption. General ledger systems, for example, typically do not record cost consumption by activity. It is common, however, for departments to keep such records. At TriQuint, for example, department managers maintained detailed records of the use of supplies by each activity.

Remember, your primary goal is to chose resource drivers that accurately measure the consumption of resources by the activities. But be careful of the cost of doing this. Don't spend valuable time and money to achieve marginal gains in accuracy.

Determining Attributes

Rules for Determining Attributes

1. Let the objective of the model govern the choice of attributes.
2. Let the user assign sensitive or judgmental attributes.

Determining attributes is the fifth step in designing an ABC system. Attributes are labels that enhance the meaning of the information in the ABC model. For example, you could attach the attribute *customer* to an activity to signify that the activity supports customers and not products.

Rule #1: Let the objective of the model govern the choice of attributes.

ABC models vary in the objectives they support. At the same time, different objectives require different attributes.

To expand on this, consider an ABC model that supports process improvement. The model uses attributes to identify cost elements as fixed or variable for example. This enhances the ability to estimate the cost impact of improvement decisions. Other attributes, such as cost drivers and performance measures, facilitate judgements about the way the work is carried out and how it may be improved.

Strategic models also benefit from attributes. For example, customers in a particular distribution channel can be identified using a channel-specific attribute. This allows preparation of reports based on the cost of products sold through this distribution channel.

Rule #2: Let the user assign sensitive or judgmental attributes.

Some attributes are best left for the user to create. Examples are attributes that are too user sensitive to be defined by the designer or those that cannot be specified in advance.

Designating an activity as *value-added* or *non-value-added*, for example, can be a sensitive issue. The ABC designer may be an "outsider" and should be cautious in making judgements about the work done by someone else. Would you feel good being told that your work is non-value-added?

By all means, help people arrive at a conclusion about value-added or non-value-added. And support their efforts to eliminate waste. But it may be counter-productive to impose any judgement on them.

Also, some attributes cannot be specified in advance or are unique to the user. For example, does the cost of salaries and benefits assigned to a receiving activity vary with the number of receipts?

The cost is variable if the change in the number of receipts is large enough and the time frame is long enough for the resources to be redeployed or increased. The designer cannot make this determination in advance, however, because these factors are unknown at the time of design.

Selecting Activity Drivers

Activity drivers capture demands placed on activities by cost objects. It's important to pick activity drivers carefully so that products, customers, and other cost objects are costed accurately.[2]

Rules for Selecting Activity Drivers

1. Pick activity drivers that match the type of activity.
2. Pick activity drivers that correlate well with the actual consumption of the activity.
3. Minimize the number of unique drivers.
4. Pick activity drivers that encourage improved performance.
5. Pick activity drivers having a modest cost of measurement.
6. Don't pick activity drivers that require new measurements.

Rule #1: Activity drivers should match the type of activity.

Pick activity drivers that match the type of activity. For example, scheduling production of a batch of parts is a batch activity. It's best suited to a batch activity driver such as the number of production runs. (You schedule the batch each time it's run.)

For the above case, it's not acceptable to use a unit activity driver such as direct labor hours. This is because the number of units (and direct labor hours) varies from one product to another with little regard to the number of batches produced.

Rule #2: Activity drivers should correlate well with the actual consumption of the activity.

Simply matching the level of activity driver and activity does not always assure accuracy. The activity *setting up*, for example, requires a choice between the number of setups and the number of setup hours. The question is, which correlates best with the performance of the activity?

The correct choice actually depends on the circumstances. Using *number of setups* is adequate if the effort per setup does not vary from one type of part to another. But if the time required differs from part to part, then the *number of setups* doesn't correlate well with the variation in effort from one part to another. This variation in effort is better measured by using the *number of setup hours* as the activity driver.

Rule #3:   Minimize the number of unique drivers.

The cost of measurement is affected by the number of activity drivers you choose. You need just enough drivers to assign cost to the cost objects accurately. Additional drivers beyond this point increase the cost of measurement but not the value of the model.

The number of activity drivers in ABC models varies from two to hundreds—depending on the complexity of the situation. In most cases, however, ten to thirty drivers is sufficient.

Rule #4:   Pick activity drivers that encourage improved performance.

Activity drivers are often used as performance indicators. Because of this, designers should try to choose activity drivers that encourage performance improvement.

The Oscilloscope Group of Tektronix, for example, used the *number of part numbers* as an activity driver to communicate the cost of component proliferation to product design engineers. The engineers responded to this activity driver by dramatically reducing the number of different parts used in products.[3]

Also, activity drivers that are detail-specific are more likely to encourage improved performance. For example, the driver *time spent in first-piece inspection* focuses attention on the time and cost required by the inspection activity. In contrast, *number of production runs* as a driver may yield accurate product costs, but it doesn't focus attention on the inspection activity.

Rule #5:   Pick activity drivers having a modest cost of measurement.

Different activity drivers incur different measurement costs. Measuring the *number of setup hours* is usually more difficult and costly than just simply counting the *number of setups*. Moreover, the *number of setups* may already be counted for you by the existing information system. By contrast, measuring setup hours may require establishing a new timkeeping system.

Rule #6: Don't pick activity drivers that require new measurements.

Try to avoid picking activity drivers that will require new measurements. Numerous useful drivers often already exist in the company's current information systems. Using these existing drivers avoids the cost of making new measurements.

Always take a careful look around. Even if the data are not in the information system, you may find what you need in someone's desk drawer or personal computer.

If not, you can still come up with a "wish list" for next year. This should identify areas where new measurements will improve the quality of the system. If ABC is an important tool in your company, then it deserves its share of information systems support.

Summary

Designing an ABC system is a typical managerial task. You apply some basic rules, and you use a lot of judgement to achieve your objective. As discussed in this chapter, the following six major steps will help you complete a successful design:

1. Identify activities. In this step you decide how much detail you need about the activities and how you are to describe and define the activities.

2. Reconstruct the general ledger. The second step is to reconstruct the general ledger. This reduces the amount of detail as well as the work required. It also adjusts the financial data to fit ABC needs, such as assigning development costs over the life cycle of products.

3. Create activity centers. This third step groups (and reports) activities in ways that are more meaningful to the user. This includes departmental and cross-functional reports of activities.

4. Define resource drivers. The fourth step is to attach cost to activities. This uses resource drivers that define the costs consumed by activities. The goal is to use resource drivers that accurately measure consumption of cost without incurring excessive time and cost.

5. Determine attributes. The fifth step is to attach attributes to the data in the system. Attributes are labels that enhance the meaning of the activity-based information.

6. Select activity drivers. The sixth step is selection of activity drivers to capture the demand placed on activities by cost objects. The goal is to pick activity drivers that cost products and customers accurately, but also at a reasonable cost themselves.

Key Terms in Chapter 13

Allocation–Indirect assignment of costs, usually in a manner that spreads costs arbitrarily across multiple benefiting activities.
Chart of activities–A common set of definitions and descriptions of activities. It's used to set standards of consistency for ABC system design.
Functional decomposition–The breaking down of departments into their constituent activities. A structured approach to identifying activities.
Macro activity–An aggregation of related activities. This helps manage detail in an ABC system without reducing the useful information available.
Nested activity center–An activity center contained within another activity center. Part of a hierarchy of information within an ABC system that allows users a choice in the level of detail and organization of information they prefer.
Sustaining activity–An activity that supports other activities rather than cost objects.
Tracing–Assignment of costs based on specific activity-related data.

References:

1. Macro activities were described in Chapter 6.

2. Rule 1 was first described in "TriQuint Semiconductor," Anne Riley and Peter B.B. Turney, (Portland: Cost Technology), 1990. Rules 2, 4, and 5 were discussed by Robin Cooper in "The Rise of Activity-Based Costing–Part Three: How Many Cost Drivers Do You Need, and How Do You Select Them?," *Journal of Cost Management*, (Winter 1989), pp. 34-46. Rule 3 is discussed in "The Impact of Continuous Improvement on the Design of Activity-Based Cost Systems," Peter B.B. Turney and James M. Reeve, *Journal of Cost Management*, (Summer 1990), pp. 43-50. Rule 6 is discussed in "Ten Myths About Implementing an Activity-Based Cost System," Peter B.B. Turney, *Journal of Cost Management*, (Spring 1990), pp 24-32.

3. Robin Cooper and Peter B.B. Turney, "Tektronix: The Portable Instrument Division," 188-142/3/4, (Boston: Harvard Business School), 1988.

Chapter 14

ENSURING SUCCESSFUL USE

Completing the ABC model is just the first stage. It may have taken several months from start to finish, so a big sigh of relief is certainly appropriate here. But that sigh should be followed with immediate recommitment to the ABC system and what its use can do for your company.

In the last four chapters, you learned how careful planning and attention to detail are necessary for successful completion of an ABC project. The ultimate goal, however, is not just completion of the project. It's to use ABC extensively and continuously for business improvement.

You have to stick with it after initial implementation. You have to make sure that ABC gets used for positive change. The obvious, common-sense benefits derived from positive change will simplify and accelerate acceptance of and conversion to ABC methods.

But for any of this to happen, high-quality ABC information must be provided to those in the organization that can best use it for positive change. Moreover, these people must be encouraged to actually use this information. This requires putting in place a plan for ABC use and then managing the process of change.

The Plan for Use

To make sure ABC information is widely used, a plan of action must be put into place. *Figure 14-1* lists the key steps in such a plan. These steps are so crucial to successful ABC use that it's certainly worth examining each of them in greater detail.

Step 1	Create useful reports.
Step 2	Update the ABC model.
Step 3	Improve support systems.
Step 4	Distribute the ABC information.
Step 5	Train the users.

Figure 14-1. *The plan for using ABC information.* Getting a good start on your ABC project does not guarantee that you will stay the course. You also need to take steps to ensure that the ABC system remains current, cost effective, and widely used.

Creating Useful Reports

Useful reports are powerful communication tools. Such reports are:

- Understandable,
- Relevant,
- Accurate,
- Timely, and
- Up-to-Date.

Reports that follow the above criteria provide ABC users with the information they need when they need it. And, when properly designed, the report's information literally leaps off the computer screen or printed page.

Understandable reports. ABC information is always provided in reports of some form or another. For the information to be useful, it must be understandable. The report has to clearly communicate its content. Moreover, the report must be designed specifically with the user in mind. In fact, the user is the whole reason for the report.

Unfortunately, clarity is not the hallmark of many reports. But any report can be made much clearer if you use the following guidelines:

Don't prepare reports that look like a computer printout. Typical system-level computer printouts have tiny type, too much data, and cryptic headings. Such printouts are useful for "hard-copy backup," but not for reporting ABC information to users.

> ### What Is a Report?
>
> We usually think of a report as a printout from the computer, a memo from the boss, a summary of a consultant's recommendation, or some other written document. These are all reports, but the concept of reporting goes well beyond the written word.
>
> Paper is not essential to the communication of information. The era of computing has given us many choices. A report can be stored on magnetic media such as a floppy disk. Alternatively it can be viewed on a computer screen.
>
> A report may only be a *potential* report. Modern report generators and data bases allow you to create custom reports upon demand.
>
> Finally, we don't usually think of oral communication as a report. But it can be the most effective communication medium of all.

Don't prepare reports that can only be digested by system designers. ABC designers can handle complex reports, but the user probably cannot. Make it easy for the user.

Avoid technical terms wherever possible. Prepare reports with the users' own terminology. You will communicate more if you speak their language.

Don't just prepare reports for executives. Prepare reports that can be understand by workers on the shop floor—not just executives. The broader your audience the greater the potential impact of ABC on improvement.

Don't use just words and numbers. Use graphs wherever possible. Remember, a picture is worth a thousand words (or a thousand numbers in this case).

Figure 14-2 is an example of a powerful report. It's simple and graphical. And it immediately communicates its startling message.

The graph in *Figure 14-2* was prepared by Cellular One. Cellular One is the nation's largest cellular communications company. It provides cellular telephone service in many of the major cities in the United States.

Cellular One implemented ABC because its conventional financial systems did not provide the performance indicators necessary for managing growth and initiating change. Its rapid growth—and need for increasing profitability in a highly competitive environment—made ABC an attractive alternative.

The graph shows the relative cost per new subscriber of three distribution channels used by Cellular One. Each channel represents a group of subscribers obtained in a certain way. Subscribers in the direct channel were acquired by Cellular One's own sales department. Subscribers in the retail channel were acquired by discount stores such as Silo. Subscribers in the third-party channel were acquired by independent distributors.

The cost shown in *Figure 14-2* is for credit department activities for each new subscriber. This includes checking credit and collecting receivables.

Each distribution channel consumes these activities in different ways. For example, the resources required to check credit in the direct channel are higher than for the other two channels. This is because a higher proportion of the customers in the direct channel are business customers. Business credit checks require more effort than do those for individuals.

The impact of this channel diversity is portrayed vividly by the graph. The relative height of the bars shows that the direct channel is much more costly than the other two channels. It also suggests that a review of distribution channel, credit policies, and other strategic issues is in order.

Relevant reports. Relevant reports contain information that fits your needs. What is relevant depends on the answers to two questions.

First, what is your intended purpose for the ABC information? If it's to find waste in activities and make improvements, you need detailed information about activities. If you want to assess the relative profitability of your company's main product lines, you need product line cost and profit data.

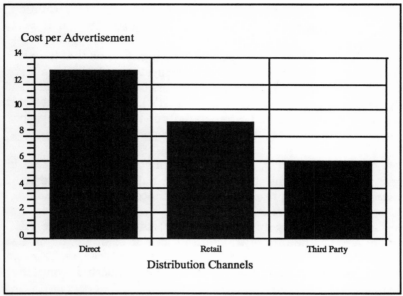

Figure 14-2. *The power of graphs for ABC reports.* This bar chart was prepared by Cellular One to highlight differences between groups of customers. One glance is sufficient to get the picture about customer differences.

Second, what's your specific need for ABC information at the present time? Let's say your overall need is for detailed information on activities to guide improvement efforts. Your specific task at hand, however, is to investigate the scope of activities having to do with poor quality. A relevant report is one that summarizes and highlights key data about poor quality. For example, it may list all activities that detect and correct defects. Alternatively it may provide information about the root causes—the cost drivers—of poor quality.

Reporting relevant information is easy if you apply the techniques you have learned in *Common Cents*. For example, Chapter 6 showed you how to build intelligence into the ABC system. You learned how to highlight pertinent information using attributes. You also learned how to organize information in meaningful ways using activity centers and macro activities. Chapter 13 showed you how to build these features into your system.

All of these things are important for organizing information. But the system must also be designed for reporting. If it isn't, useful reports will be difficult to create.

In particular, you need to avoid creating systems that have the characteristics of a *black box*. These are systems where lots of data are poured into the computer and reams of paper spew out. But the model is hidden in the black box. It's difficult to understand what's in the model and what its output means. The black box generates information, but not useful reports.

Accurate reports. Reported information should be free of errors and distortions. Inaccurate information can mislead ABC users. Not only that, user perception of inaccuracy can be the "kiss of death" for any system.

Accuracy is largely determined by the design of the ABC model and the quality of the data used. For example, if you use too few activity drivers, product costs will be inaccurate. This can also happen if there are errors in the data imported from other company information systems.

If you suspect the input data or system design is faulty, reapply the rules of data collection and design. Look for ways to improve accuracy. Try to catch any errors before the ABC system loses credibility with its users.

Timely reports. Information should be available at the time it's needed. It must be timely, but what is timely is totally dependent on the user's need for information.

For example, a strategic review of customer profitability by market segment can be met with information that is weeks or months old. You're looking for patterns that are established over time, rather than yesterday's sales.

On the other hand, if you're measuring the performance of a key activity in your plant, you probably need real-time information. The printed circuit board plant discussed in Chapter 9, for example, prepared reports on the *cost of poor quality* for each key process and for each product. These reports were prepared for each shift. The plant then used the reported information to take daily action for quality improvement.

The value of real-time information can be seen from the following example. A production activity receives a daily quality report. It shows that the entire previous day's production of 200 is defective and must be scrapped. At $1,000 cost-to-date for each unit, that's a total loss of $200,000. A real-time report would have focused immediate attention on the high cost of the problem, and most of the $200,000 could have been saved.

Up-to-date reports. Out-of-date information is of no value. In fact, it may be dangerous if it misleads ABC users.

Data generally goes out of date when it's captured periodically and circumstances have changed since the last capture period. While periodic data capture can be useful as an ABC snapshot, the snapshot may quickly go out of focus for any of the following reasons:

Spending on resources may change. Restrictions on air travel, for example, reduces travel and entertainment costs.

New activities may be introduced. An electronics assembly plant, for example, attached parts to circuit boards using new surface mount equipment. (Previously the plant just inserted parts into holes in the circuit boards using various insertion activities.)

Activities may be discontinued. For example, parts are no longer inspected when received from the vendor because of improved parts quality.

Performance of activities improves or deteriorates. An equipment setup activity is improved via a program to reduce setup time.

The mix of products produced or sold changes. New products being introduced and other products being discontinued is a typical case.

Product volumes change. The volume of standard products goes up during a recession, for example, while the volume of specialty products goes down.

Changes in number and type of customers. This can happen when orders are won from customers who require a different level of service than existing customers.

Products are redesigned. New products may use fewer production activities than the products they replace.

Let's look at how distortions can occur when circumstances change. For example, a maintenance department performs three activities—setting up machines, routine repairs, and unscheduled repairs. Initially, the department spent one third of its time on each of these activities. ABC reflected this by assigning one third of department resources to each activity. The design of this ABC model is shown in *Figure 14-3*.

However, some changes occurred subsequent to the completion of the ABC model. The number of setups went down because of increased production of high-volume products. The number of scheduled repairs went up because of a new *total preventive maintenance* policy. The number of unscheduled repairs went down because of the increase in routine maintenance.

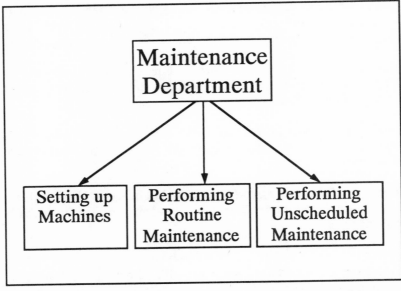

Figure 14-3. *Activities in a maintenance department.* ABC provides a snapshot of the activities and resource consumption in this department. If this snapshot goes out of focus, it's necessary to take a new picture.

These changes decreased the setup and unscheduled repair activities while increasing routine repair activity. The ABC system, however, still shows that the department expends one third of its effort on each activity and assigns one third of the cost to each.

The result is inaccurate information about current activity and product costs. The cost of resources assigned to each activity is wrong. The rates per driver unit for the setup and unscheduled repair activities are too high, and the rate for routine repair is too low. The cost of products using these activities is, therefore, distorted.

Updating the ABC Model

How often you update ABC information depends on the pace of change, the type of information, and the cost and feasibility of updating. The more rapid the pace of change in your company, the more often you'll need to seek new information. New product introductions, new process technology, continuous improvement—all create changes that make ABC information obsolete.

Different types of information can be updated on different schedules. For example, some companies update general ledger, cost object, and activity driver data monthly. Information about efforts expended on activities, however, is updated less frequently (such as every six months).

Up-to-date information does have a cost. This cost should be factored into the schedule. For example, it takes time and effort to conduct interviews and update the ABC design to reflect the new information gained. Is the additional accuracy worth the extra cost?

The feasibility of frequent updates of ABC information depends on system support and the size and complexity of the system. At one extreme, updating was easy in the case of the Printed Circuit Board (PCB) plant because ABC was integrated into the computer integrated manufacturing (CIM) system. This allowed low-cost, daily preparation of ABC performance reports.

At the other extreme, a defense contractor employed an ABC design team of five people full time for four months just to interview all the managers in the plant. Also, the bill of materials was so complex it took several hours to download to the ABC system. Frequent updating simply wasn't feasible for this company without changes in its methods and systems.

In any case, a feasible update schedule must be determined. Then the ABC system update responsibility needs to be formally assigned. Someone has to see that system procedures are in place and that feedback is obtained about changes in activities. Making all of this a formal assignment ensures that the ABC system is kept up-to-date.

Responsibility for system procedures differ depending on the type of system. A stand-alone system, for example, requires periodic updating and procedures for downloading new information. An integrated system is updated according to the rhythm of the main system.

Responsibility for obtaining feedback about changes in activities (and consequently the design of the system) should be placed in the hands of department managers. Each manager is responsible for providing up-to-date activity information monthly. This has three advantages.

First, it ensures that the users of ABC information become involved in the design. They are more likely to use the information if they have ownership of the design. The design is also more likely to reflect the users' needs.

Second, it allows the ABC design team to go out of business. Finding a group of bright and capable managers who can devote several weeks of their time to designing an ABC system is difficult the first time. It may be impossible the second time. It is also infeasible when there are hundreds of managers to reinterview. In short, it's far better to keep the system updated on a continuing basis.

Third, it ensures that information about activities, including resource drivers, cost drivers and performance measures, are kept up-to-date. Distortions from obsolete data, such as those in the maintenance department example cited *Figure 14-3*, become a thing of the past.

Improving Support Systems

To a certain degree, cost and feasibility are controllable. It's possible to introduce improvements in data collection techniques and systems to both reduce updating costs and to make updating easier.

For example, timekeeping on a sample basis can replace interviewing. The general ledger can be maintained on an activity basis by accounting (this eliminates the need to restructure the general ledger). And finally a stand-alone ABC system can be replaced by one that's fully integrated into the company's information systems.

Making ABC Information Widely Available

The best information in the world will not stimulate improvements in your company if that information just sits in a computer or in the accounting department. For it to work, you must put the information in the hands of those doing the improvement.

The key to *information empowerment* is distributed ABC. Distributed ABC is the placement of ABC information on the desk or work bench of every key person in your organization.

Marketers, engineers, production supervisors, accountants, and executives alike should all have their own personal ABC model. This may include a copy of a central company ABC model as well as custom tailored models to support specific local applications.

Here's how National Semiconductor is empowering its people with ABC. Every National Semiconductor location in the world has a copy of the *master* ABC model. This is the *official* ABC model that follows standard terminology and definitions.

Each location also has its own *local* ABC versions to support their own improvement needs. These are developed locally using PC-based software.

Accounting does not dictate what these local models should look like. Rather it helps facilitate the development and use of these models by providing training and assistance.

Distributed ABC can have significant benefits. Users are more likely to keep data up-to-date, and to use the information creatively. ABC can be tailored to individual needs and respond rapidly to problem solving requirements.

Training ABC Users

Good training is the key to getting users on-line fast with ABC. Experience has shown that the speed of business improvement is essentially limited only by the availability of ABC information and how well people are prepared to use that information.

But Will the Auditors Approve?

Distributing ABC to the users may supercharge your improvement project. But will it give your auditors cold feet? Auditors may be concerned about the ability of users to make unauthorized modifications to data in the system. ABC contains a lot of operational and financial data that affect the accounting systems. This is particularly true if ABC replaces the existing cost accounting system.

These fears can be put to rest quite easily. One approach is to make it impossible for unauthorized users to modify key files such as the bill of materials and inventory control. This can be done by use of passwords. Another possibility is to maintain a master ABC model. This master model is the only source of information for financial reporting purposes. All other ABC models are *unofficial* and used for internal decision making purposes only.

Well-trained users are able to quickly assimilate ABC information and put it to use in successfully improving their departments. It's a key element of information empowerment— the further down the organization you go with training, the more impact ABC will have.

Manage the Process of Change

It's also important to manage ABC's role in the change process. The purpose is to create positive expectations for improvement, link ABC to company improvement goals, define areas where improvement will occur, provide users with technical support, and communicate what's learned to other parts of the organization.

A plan for managing the process of change includes the five steps listed in *Figure 14-4*. These steps are implemented as follows:

Step 1 Brief management.
Step 2 Identify improvement goals.
Step 3 Assign responsibility for change.
Step 4 Provide user support.
Step 5 Give feedback.

Figure 14-4. *The plan for change.* The five steps listed here constitute a deliberate attempt to foster positive use of ABC information. If successful, ABC will become a vital part of company improvement efforts.

1. Brief management.

Tell management what has been accomplished. Make sure they understand the opportunities. Give them a list of areas where benefits will be achieved. And get them excited about ABC's potential for fostering improvement.

2. Identify improvement goals.

Build ABC into the company's overall improvement program. Show how activity-based management integrates total quality control (TQC), waste elimination, lead-time reduction, and other aspects of improvement. Set goals for activity-based improvement efforts that tie in to the company's mission.

A good place to start is by drawing an activity road map for each key area. This map shows the activities, resource drivers, activity drivers, cost drivers, and performance measures for the process. With this reference point, you can proceed to:

- Identify non-value-added activities and other improvement opportunities,
- Rank improvement opportunities in order of cost savings or profit potential, and
- Pick the targets for action.

Once you have done this a few times, everyone will begin to think of their own job in terms of activities and the value they add. Activity-based management will quickly become a new way of thinking about your business.

3. Assign responsibility for change.

Develop specific assignments for each user. Help each user plan improvement projects that use activity-based information.

4. Provide user support.

Work with each user group. Train users how to use the ABC system and how to put ABC information to work. Help them do "what if?" simulations. And help them prepare reports that highlight the key issues. (There's an important opportunity here for the accounting department, *if they chose to accept it.*)

5. Give feedback.

Collect assignment results from the users. Evaluate the usefulness of activity-based costing. Communicate the lessons to the rest of the company. Develop recommendations for future design and use.

When properly implemented, the above plan for change creates momentum for improvement. Once use of ABC information for improvement is ingrained, the momentum becomes self sustaining.

The Zytec Case

Let's turn to the case of Zytec, a Minnesota-based manufacturer of power suppliers.[1] Zytec's experience with ABC provides some important lessons on creating useful information.

Zytec adopted ABC to reinforce their continuous improvement program. They had experienced significant reductions in cost, cycle time, and defects as result of this program.

Zytec Corporation

Zytec produces power supplies for a variety of electronics products such as medical equipment, telephone switching equipment, and hard disk drives. Zytec concentrates on selling high-volume, complex power supplies to large electronics companies. From their base in Redwood Falls, Minnesota, they supply about 1% of the overall market.

Their purpose for ABC was to focus improvement efforts on the company's mission. This was done by picking four activity drivers to measure improvements in the key elements of the mission *(Figure 14-5)*. Unfortunately, these drivers didn't work very well. Let's see why.

Linearity measured deviation of actual production from plan. It was thought that a more stable production environment (greater linearity) improved quality and reduced cost.

Cycle time measured the elapsed time for a product to move through the plant. Experience had shown that lower cycle times were accompanied by lower costs and increased flexibility.

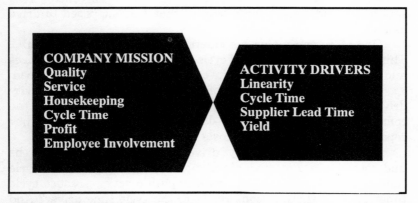

COMPANY MISSION
Quality
Service
Housekeeping
Cycle Time
Profit
Employee Involvement

ACTIVITY DRIVERS
Linearity
Cycle Time
Supplier Lead Time
Yield

Figure 14-5. *Drivers that didn't work.* Zytec picked activity drivers to focus improvement efforts on accomplishing the corporate mission. However, the activity drivers were difficult to understand and reported inaccurate product costs. This caused confusion and ABC was rejected by management and customers alike.

Supplier lead time measured elapsed time from placing an order for a component to its arrival in the warehouse. A shorter lead time was believed to be accompanied by lower procurement costs and improved flexibility.

Yield measured the proportion of production needing rework. Not only was this a direct measure of quality, it was thought to correlate well with overall cost.

Lynn Richter, the Controller, explained their intent as follows:

"We wanted to pick a set of drivers that was meaningful to the people on the floor. We wanted these drivers to capture the essence of our drive for continuous improvement. In particular, we were convinced that the cost system could become a potent tool for behavior modification."

Unfortunately, the ABC model did not fulfill the intent. ABC cost reports were greeted with confusion and rejection.

Part of the difficulty was the desire of users to compare ABC costs with those reported by the conventional system. But no one could explain the differences.

The purchasing manager complained that supplier lead time—one of the key activity drivers—was beyond his control. This was a real indictment for a system that was supposed to drive behavior.

One of Zytec's major customers also complained about ABC. This customer rejected use of cycle time to develop contract prices and demanded that Zytec use its conventional cost system instead.

What was the source of confusion and rejection? The activity drivers were relevant. They tied closely to the mission of the company. But they were also difficult to understand, and they reported inaccurate product costs.

Specifically, the activity drivers were too abstract to be understandable. For example, it's one thing to agree that cycle time should be reduced. But which specific actions reduce cycle time? How do those actions relate to the cycle time driver? And how do they affect product costs?

It was also likely that reported product costs were inaccurate. A complex product with a short cycle time, for example, could require a lot of engineering time and resources. But it would be assigned relatively less cost by ABC, according to the lower cycle time.

The lesson of Zytec is to do it right. ABC is not superior to the systems it replaces if it reports inaccurate and incomprehensible information. It's only superior if it's done right.

Zytec is pondering the lessons of its first foray into ABC. The next step is to build an ABC model that reports accurate costs and information—such as cost drivers—that is actionable at the activity level.

Making understandable, relevant, accurate, timely, and up-to-date information available to the user is important to the successful use of ABC. This, in turn, increases the power of ABC to foster positive change.

Summary

The end of the implementation phase is the opportunity to roll out ABC to all the people who can *make a difference*. This involves communicating good quality ABC information. Good quality means that the information is understandable, relevant, accurate, timely, and up-to-date.

Rolling out ABC also involves taking steps to make ABC information easy to use. These steps keep the information up-to-date, put the information in the hands of those who can improve the business, and train those people to use the information productively.

Finally, the plan for change creates momentum for improvement. It creates positive expectations about what ABC can do, it provides users with technical support, and it communicates the knowledge associated with improvement to other parts of the organization.

Key Terms in Chapter 14

Distributed ABC–Giving each person a copy of the ABC model and its information. A way of ensuring that useful information gets into the hands of the people who can apply it to foster improvement.

Plan for change–A statement of what will be done to encourage use of ABC information and focus on the ultimate goal of ABC–to foster positive improvement in the organization.

Plan for use–A statement of the steps that will keep ABC up-to-date and provide users with ABC information and the ability to use it.

References:

1. Robin Cooper and Peter B.B. Turney, "Zytec Corporation (B) and (C),"9-190-117 (Boston: Harvard Business School), 1989.

Part VI

HOW TO APPLY THE LESSONS

This is the story of the ABC performance breakthrough. It's *Common Cents* to provide people with the information they need to meet today's competitive challenges.

Early in this book you learned why your cost system needs changing. You saw how flawed cost information can sabotage your competitive position. You also learned why you need to scrap the outmoded cost systems that so mislead you.

You discovered that the solution to cost system ills is *activity-based costing* (ABC). ABC is not a "band-aid" fix to your existing cost system. It's a breakthrough that reveals the problems you need to correct and the opportunities you should take advantage of. It fits like a glove with *world-class* business improvement programs.

ABC looks a lot different from your old cost system. It provides cost information about the work going on in an organization, as well as about the products and customers benefitting from the work. ABC also provides information about why work is performed and how well it's carried out.

You've seen how ABC information is used in a program of *activity-based management* to improve profitable delivery of value to your customers. You've learned how to use ABC information to improve performance and reduce cost. You've looked at improvement tools, such as *value analysis* and *target costing*, that follow the activity-management approach. And you've seen how activity-based management can be applied to achieve world-class standards of business performance.

However, none of this improvement can be accomplished without a concerted—and successful—effort to implement ABC in your organization. *Getting started* with the implementation involves convincing management of the value of ABC. *Following through* requires careful planning and design of an ABC model that meets your organization's needs. *Staying with it* involves communicating quality ABC information to the people who can improve your organization.

All that's left to do now is to "land on your feet running." To help you do this, Chapter 15 reviews the three major steps to achieving your goals with ABC. These steps are:

- Complete the implementation steps to success,
- Design an ABC model that meets your needs, and
- Apply ABC in an activity-based management program of improvement.

Chapter 15

LANDING ON YOUR FEET

Landing on your feet comes down to three things. *First*, you must plan and execute a successful ABC implementation project. *Second*, you must design an ABC model that meets your specific needs. *Third*, you should apply ABC in an improvement program of activity-based management.

The Steps to Success

There are 28 steps to success. These steps start with convincing management to change and end with executing a plan to ensure that positive change occurs *(Figure 15-1)*.

Convincing management to change. It's difficult to change course in midstream. But it can be done. You just need to take the right steps to generate interest, remove any barriers to adopting ABC, and obtain a firm commitment from management to support ABC implementation and use.

Planning the implementation. You'll move faster and closer to the desired course if the implementation is planned carefully. Implementation steps include defining the deliverables (what you expect to get out of the project), organizing and staffing the project, and training the implementation team.

Gathering the information. ABC requires a lot of financial and operational data. This data can be found in the accounting department, the operating departments, and your company's information systems. It's obtained via interviews, storyboards, and other tools of data collection.

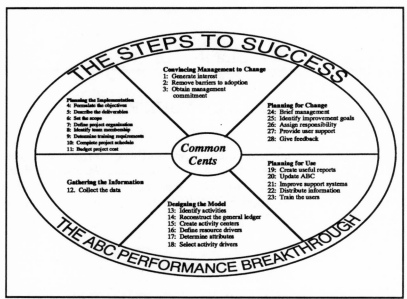

Figure 15-1. *The 28 steps to success for an ABC implementation project.*

Designing the model. During ABC model design is when information is structured and system intelligence is created. The goal is to create a model that provides whatever information is needed to support ABC's strategic and process improvement goals. The design should also be completed with reasonable cost and effort.

Planning for updating. Getting a good start with your implementation project isn't enough. You must stay with it. This means keeping information up-to-date and training the users to take responsibility for keeping the model current.

Planning for change. Don't wait for change to happen. Take steps to hurry the process along. Follow a plan to create positive expectations of change. Define areas for improvement. Provide support for improvement effort. And, lastly, communicate what is learned.

Designing the Right Model

It's important that you design a model that fits your needs. For example, if you intend to use ABC to improve operating performance, your design should capture the detailed information needed for that task. It's also important to "do it right" to ensure high-quality information.

There are 22 steps to designing it right. These begin with identifying activities and end with selecting activity drivers *(Figure 15-2)*.

Identifying activities. Defining and describing activities are at the heart of designing an ABC model. This is where you learn about the work that goes on in the company and build that knowledge into the ABC model.

Reconstructing the general ledger. Most general ledgers were designed prior to ABC and need to be reconstructed. This reconstruction eliminates unnecessary detail, builds departmental cost data, and puts the accounts on an economic rather than accounting basis.

Creating activity centers. Activity centers provide structure to the activities within the model. They also facilitate preparation of reports about related activities.

Defining resource drivers. Resources are consumed by the work going on in the company. Resource drivers measure this consumption. They should accurately assign the cost of resources to activities.

Determining attributes. This is the step that adds intelligence to the model. Attributes are labels that enhance the meaning of ABC information. They should support the purposes of the model and the needs of users.

Selecting activity drivers. Activity drivers determined the accuracy with which products, customers, and other cost objects are costed. Activity drivers should be selected carefully to achieve acceptable accuracy at reasonable cost.

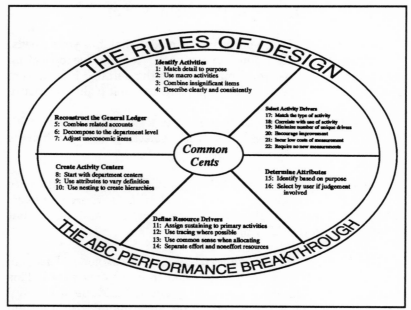

Figure 15-2. *The 22 steps to successfully designing an ABC model.*

Achieving the Performance Breakthrough

The performance breakthrough comes from using ABC information in a program of activity-based management. If successful, this leads to continuous improvement in profitable delivery of value to your customers and to achieving world-class performance *(Figure 15-3)*.

Activity-based management should be applied in every corner of the company. It helps set strategic priorities and implement the chosen strategy. It's used to improve the profitability of performance. And it's the basis for managing supplier relationships and directing investments to the areas with the greatest improvement potential.

Activity-based management uses various "tools of the trade" to improve performance. These tools include *cost analysis* and *customer value analysis.*

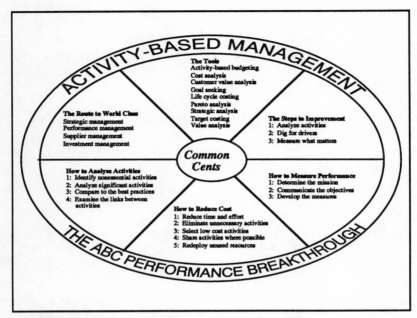

Figure 15-3. *Achieving the ABC performance breakthrough.*

Activity-based management is quite different from "business as usual" approaches to improvement. It involves analyzing activities in the search for waste. It includes looking for *and eliminating* the negative effects of cost drivers. And it involves measuring what matters to the customer in order to focus improvement efforts.

Activity-based management integrates all these improvement efforts into one package. It ensures that the benefits apply to the overall company and that the results go straight to the bottom line.

Part VII

GLOSSARY & INDEX

GLOSSARY

ABC–Acronym for activity-based cost or activity-based costing.

ABM–Acronym for activity-based management.

Activity–A unit of work performed within an organization. A description of the work that goes on in the organization and consumes resources. Testing materials is an example of an activity.

Activity analysis–The evaluation of activity performance in the search for improvement opportunities.

Activity-based budgeting–Preparation of cost budgets using ABC to help estimate work load and resource requirements.

Activity-based costing (ABC)–A method of measuring the cost and performance of activities and cost objects. Assigns cost to activities based on their use of resources, and assigns cost to cost objects based on their use of activities. ABC recognizes the causal relationship of cost drivers to activities.

Activity-based management(ABM) A discipline that focuses on the management of activities as the route to continuously improving the value received by customers and the profit achieved by providing this value. This discipline includes cost driver analysis, activity analysis, and performance analysis. Activity-based management draws on activity-based costing as a major source of information.

Activity center–A report of pertinent information about the activities in a function or process.

Activity cost pool–Total cost assigned to an activity. The sum of all the cost elements assigned to an activity.

Activity driver–A factor used to assign cost from an activity to a cost object. A measure of the frequency and intensity of use of an activity by a cost object. If drilling holes is an activity performed on a board, the number of holes drilled could be an activity driver.

Allocation–Indirect assignment of costs, usually in a manner that spreads costs arbitrarily across multiple benefiting activities.

Attribute–Labels attached to data in an activity-based cost system to signify the meaning of the data.

Batch activity–An activity that is performed on a batch of a product. Inspecting the first piece of each batch is a batch activity.

Benchmark–An activity that is *best practice* and by which a similar activity will be judged. Benchmarks are used to help identify opportunities for improving the performance of comparable activities. The source of a benchmark may be internal (such as another department in the same company) or external (such as a competitor).

Bill of activities–A list of the activities and costs associated with a cost object. The bill may include additional information such as which activities are non-value-added.

Chart of activities—A common set of definitions and descriptions of activities. It's used to set standards of consistency for ABC system design.

Continuous improvement—The relentless and on-going search for ways to improve business performance.

Conventional cost system—Any of the older, traditional cost systems that use direct material and labor consumed as the primary means of apportioning overhead.

Cost analysis—Simulation of cost-reduction opportunities. Cost analysis helps you select opportunities that yield the greatest improvement. It also helps build commitment for improvement actions and helps communicate the knowledge gained through the improvement.

Cost assignment view—The part of ABC where cost is assigned to activities and the cost of activities is assigned to cost objects.

Cost driver—A factor that causes a change in the performance of an activity and, in doing so, affects the resources required by the activity. For example, the quality of parts received by an activity is a determining factor in the effort required by that activity. An activity may have multiple cost drivers associated with it.

Cost element—The amount paid for a resource and assigned to an activity. Part of an activity cost pool.

Cost object—The reason for performing an activity. Products and customers are reasons for performing activities. *Cost objects include products, services, customers, projects, and contracts.*

Cost object activity—An activity that benefits products or customers.

Customer value—The difference between customer realization and sacrifice. Realization is what is received by the customer. It includes product features, quality, and service as well

as the cost to use, maintain, and dispose of the product. Sacrifice is what is given up by the customer. It includes the amount paid for the product plus the time spent acquiring the product and learning how to use it. To maximize customer value, maximize the difference between realization and sacrifice.

Customer value analysis—Study of customer activities directed at finding ways to improve customer value and reduce the cost of delivering that value.

Death spiral—The sequential outsourcing or dropping of products in response to inaccurate cost information.

Deliverable—A tangible benefit of activity-based costing.

Distributed ABC—Giving each person a copy of the ABC model and its information. A way of ensuring that useful information gets into the hands of the people who can apply it to foster improvement.

Flexibility—The ability to respond to changing customer needs quickly.

Focused factory—The organization of production around a narrow range of products to provide low cost and high throughput.

Full absorption—A requirement that all overhead costs, even those associated with unused capacity, be assigned to existing products.

Functional decomposition—The breaking down of departments into their constituent activities. A structured approach to identifying activities.

Functional silos—Vertical dimensions of an organizational hierarchy where functional considerations override organizational considerations.

Goal seeking—The search for ways to improve the competitiveness of a product or service. The search starts with identifying high-cost activities in the bill of activities. It then proceeds through the causes of high cost and finishes with actions to reduce or eliminate the effect of these causes.

Interviews—In-person question and answer sessions. This is the method of choice in ABC. It's time consuming, but interviews yield a wealth of reliable information.

Investment management—The use of ABC to manage capacity for maximum profitability and to direct capital spending to the most profitable improvement targets.

Just-in-time (JIT)— 1.) the determination of work load based on the use of output by the next activity; 2.) Continuous improvement.

Life-cycle costing—Costing products over their entire life cycle rather than for a single accounting period. The product life cycle spans development, introduction, growth, maturity, decline, and abandonment. Life-cycle costing helps assess product profitability.

Macro activity—An aggregation of related activities. This helps manage detail in an ABC system without reducing the useful information available.

Myth—A belief about ABC that is a barrier to acceptance. Demolishing these myths increases the chances of a successful ABC implementation.

Nested activity center—An activity center contained within another activity center. Part of a hierarchy of information within an ABC system that allows users a choice in the level of detail and organization of information they prefer.

Non-value-added activity—An activity that is judged *not to* contribute to customer value. Also, an activity that can be eliminated without reducing the quantity or quality of output. An example is the activity of moving parts back and forth.

Pareto analysis—Arrangement of activities or activity drivers in descending order of cost. The activities or drivers accounting for the majority of cost are targeted for cost reduction.

Performance management—The use of ABC to improve profitability. It includes searching for low-cost product designs, identifying cost reduction opportunities, guiding efforts to improve quality, and measuring performance.

Performance measure—An indicator of the work performed and the results achieved in an activity. A measure of how well an activity meets the needs of its customers. Performance measures may be financial or nonfinancial.

Pilot project—A test of the applicability and utility of activity-based costing.

Plan for change—A statement of what will be done to encourage use of ABC information and focus on the ultimate goal of ABC—to foster positive improvement in the organization.

Plan for use—A statement of the steps that will keep ABC up-to-date and provide users with ABC information and the ability to use it.

Process—A series of activities that are linked to perform a specific objective.

Process view—The part of ABC that provides operational information about activities.

Product activity—An activity that benefits all units of a type of product. Changing engineering specifications on a product is a product activity.

Project team—The individuals who plan, design, and implement the ABC system.

Quality function deployment (QFD-)—The design of products and processes based on customer requirements.

Questionnaire—Compilations of questions about the work that goes on in the company. Questionnaires don't have the *personal* touch of interviewing, but they can be an efficient way to collect data.

Real-time—Rapid reporting of data from an activity or process. Provides the ability to change the performance of the activity while the work continues.

Resource drivers—The links between resources and activities. They take a cost from the general ledger and assign it to the activities.

Resources—Economic elements applied or used in the performance of activities.

Steering committee—An upper management group that oversees planning and implementation of the ABC system.

Storyboards—A group problem-solving technique that creates a picture of each department's activities and related information. An efficient data gathering technique, it extends the reach of ABC to everyone in the organization.

Strategic analysis—Analysis of products, services, and customers for strategic opportunities. Strategic analysis may point out opportunities for repricing, redirecting resources to more profitable opportunities, and changing product strategy.

Strategic management—The use of activity-based analysis to set and implement strategic priorities.

Supplier management—The use of ABC to identify waste in supplier relationships and to develop supplier partnerships that help eliminate this waste.

Sustaining activity—An activity that benefits the organization (such as another activity or the department), but not a cost object. Landscaping the plant is an example.

Symptom—A visible sign of a broken cost system. Symptoms provide ammunition to advocates of ABC.

Target costing—Setting cost targets for new products based on market price. The analysis starts with an estimate of the selling price and subtracts profits and distribution costs to arrive at the target cost. Engineers then use ABC to help design a product for this cost.

Timekeeping system—A record of the time devoted to activities or cost objects. Not commonly used outside of tracking direct labor, may be costly and intrusive, but can still be a useful data gathering device.

Tracing—Assignment of costs based on specific activity-related data.

Unit activity—An activity that is performed on a unit of a product. Inserting a resistor into a printed circuit board is an example of a unit activity.

Value analysis—Intense study of a business process with the intent of improving the process and reducing cost. Its goal is to ensure that you perform the right activities in the right way.

World class—An organization that has achieved high standards of business performance and is continuously improving its ability to meet its customers' needs.

INDEX

Cost Technology offers numerous training programs that give managers the skills to put the *ABC Performance Breakthrough* to work. Cost Technology also provides exposure programs and presentations that show how *Common Cents* can be an integral part of your organization. For more information about these products and services, call:

The Common Cents Hotline
1-800-368-COST.
(In Portland, Oregon, call (503) 321-5795.)

Now that you've read *Common Cents* we encourage you to share your thoughts on the book and its application to your organization. Write to us at:

Cost Technology
P.O. Box 25124
Portland, OR 97225-0124

Attn: *Common Cents*